sex and temperament

sex and temperament

in three primitive societies

margaret mead

HARPER ⦿ PERENNIAL

NEW YORK • LONDON • TORONTO • SYDNEY • NEW DELHI • AUCKLAND

HARPER ● PERENNIAL

A hardcover edition of this book was originally published in 1935 by
William Morrow and Company.

SEX AND TEMPERAMENT. Copyright © 1935, 1950, 1963 by Margaret
Mead. Words for a New Century copyright © 2001 by Mary Cather-
ine Bateson. Introduction copyright © 2001 by Helen Fisher. All
rights reserved. Printed in the United States of America. No part of this
book may be used or reproduced in any manner whatsoever without
written permission except in the case of brief quotations embodied in
critical articles and reviews. For information, address HarperCollins
Publishers, 195 Broadway, New York, NY 10007.

HarperCollins books may be purchased for educational, business, or
sales promotional use. For information, please e-mail the Special
Markets Department at SPsales@harpercollins.com.

First Quill edition published 1963.
First Perennial edition published 2001.

Library of Congress Cataloging-in-Publication Data is available.
ISBN 0-06-093495-6

HB 10.07.2019

to franz boas

contents

acknowledgements

The results recorded in the following chapters are part of the material accumulated by Dr. Fortune and myself during our two years' expedition to New Guinea, in 1931–33. My part of the investigation was undertaken in regular pursuit of my duties in the anthropological department of the American Museum of Natural History, and my expedition was financed by the Voss Research Fund. I owe, therefore, very special thanks to the Museum, and particularly to Dr. Clark Wissler, Curator-in-Chief of the Department of Anthropology of that institution, for the opportunity to pursue these researches. Dr. Fortune's work was conducted under a grant from the Social Science Research Council of Columbia University. Working together throughout the expedition made it possible for us to share and thus reduce many of our expenses; my thanks are therefore due to both the bodies that supported our respective researches.

For assistance in the field my major thanks are due to Dr. Fortune, for the partnership that made it possible for me to work with peoples more savage and more inaccessibly located than I would have been able to reach alone; for cooperation in the collection of the linguistic and ethnological material upon which these studies are based; and for much concrete material concerning the men's cults and all those aspects of the men's lives which a woman ethnologist is practically debarred from studying. I am particularly indebted for his analysis of the very difficult Arapesh language, and for accounts of ceremonies that took place outside of Alitoa, to which the precipitous nature of the country confined me—more especially for material bearing upon the Plains. The division of labour between us varied from one tribe to another. Among the Mundugumor and the Tchambuli a large share of the ethnographical work fell to him; for this reason I have treated the Arapesh most extensively and in treating of the other two tribes I have given only the minimum of ethnological material that is necessary to an understanding of the special problems discussed.

For preliminary orientation in the selection of a field, which finally resulted in the choice of the Arapesh region, I am indebted to Dr. Briggs of Sydney University, who had made a survey trip through this region some years previously. For the background of the work in Tchambuli, I am indebted to Mr. Bateson's published and unpublished work, and to his assistance in obtaining some knowledge of the culture of the Middle Sepik, which made it possible to conduct research in Tchambuli as an intensive study of a variant of a known cultural form.

For administrative endorsement I have to thank the Department of Home and Territories of the Commonwealth of Australia. For assistance, encouragement, and hospitality on the part of members of the Government, I am indebted to His Honour the Acting Administrator, Judge Wanless; to His Honour Judge Phillips; to Mr. Chinnery, Government Anthropologist; to District Officers T. E. McAdam and E. D. Robinson; to Patrol Officers MacDonald, Thomas, and Bloxam. I am specially indebted to Mr. and Mrs. M. V. Cobb of Karawop Plantation, who offered me the most extensive hospitality and permitted me the use of their plantation as a base during the Arapesh work. For many courtesies, especially in the matter of transportation of supplies, I have to thank Mr. and Mrs. Thomas Ifould of Boram, Mr. and Mrs. MacKenzie of the *Lady Betty*, and Messrs. Mason, Overall, Gibson, and Eichorn.

This manuscript was prepared while the impressions derived from the Seminar on Human Relations, held at Hanover in the summer of 1934, were still fresh in my mind, and I wish to acknowledge my special indebtedness to Mr. Laurence K. Frank and Dr. Earle T. Engle for insights developed during the seminar. I am further most particularly indebted for criticisms of the theoretical approach and for detailed assistance in the organisation of the manuscript to Dr. Ruth F. Benedict and Dr. John Dollard. For assistance in the preparation of the manuscript I have to thank my mother, Emily Fogg Mead, Miss Marie Eichelberger, Miss Isabel Ely Lord, and Mrs. Violet Whittington.

Margaret Mead

The American Museum of Natural History
New York
January, 1935

words for a new century

by Mary Catherine Bateson

When my mother, Margaret Mead, was ready to seek a publisher for her first book, *Coming of Age in Samoa,* she found her way to William Morrow, the head of a new publishing company, and he gave her a key suggestion for the rest of her career, that she add "more about what all this means to Americans." This set a course she followed throughout her life, establishing not only the appeal of anthropology as a depiction of the exotic but as a source of self-knowledge for Western civilization. The last chapter of *Coming of Age* laid out a theme for the years ahead: "Education for Choice."

Even before World War II, still using the terminology of her time that now seems so outmoded and speaking of "primitives" or even of "savages," she believed that Americans should learn not only about the peoples of the Pacific, but from them. And after almost every field trip she went back to William Morrow, now HarperCollins, where many of her books have remained in print ever since, offering new meanings to new generations of Americans. A century after her birth, they are offered once again, now for a new millennium, and today they still have much to offer on how individuals mature in their social settings and how human communities can adapt to change.

Several of Mead's field trips focused on childhood. Writers have been telling parents how to raise their children for centuries; however, the systematic observation of child development was then just beginning, and she was among the first to study it cross-culturally. She was one of those feminists who have combined an assertion of the need to make women full and equal participants in society with a continuing fascination with children and a concern for meeting their needs. A culture that repudiated children "could not be a good culture," she believed. [*Blackberry Winter: My Earlier Years*, New York: William Morrow and Company, Inc., 1972, p. 206.]

After studying adolescents in Samoa, she studied earlier childhood in Manus (*Growing Up in New Guinea*) and the care of infants and toddlers in Bali; everywhere she went, she included women and children, who had been largely invisible to earlier researchers. Her work continues to affect the way parents, teachers, and policy makers look at children. I, for one, am grateful that what she learned from the sophisticated and sensitive patterns of childcare she observed in other cultures resonated in my own childhood. Similarly, I have been liberated by the way her interest in women as mothers expanded into her work on gender (*Sex and Temperament* and *Male and Female*).

In addition to this growing understanding of the choices in gender roles and childrearing, the other theme that emerged from her fieldwork was change. The first postwar account of fieldwork that she brought to her longtime publisher described her 1953 return to the Manus people of New Guinea, *New Lives for Old*. This was not a book about how traditional cultures are eroded and damaged by change but about the possibility of a society choosing change and giving a direction to their own futures. Mead is sometimes labeled a "cultural determinist" (so obsessed are we with reducing every thinker to a single label). The term does reflect her belief that the differences in expected behavior and character between societies (for instance, between the Samoans and the Manus) are largely learned in childhood, shaped by cultural patterns passed on through the generations that channel the biological potentials of every child, rather than by genetics. Because culture is a human artifact that can be reshaped, rather than an inborn destiny, she was not simple determinist, and her convictions about social policy always included a faith in the human capacity to learn. After the 1950s, Mead wrote constantly about change, how it occurs, and how human communities can maintain the necessary threads of connection across the generations and still make choices. In that sense, hers was an anthropology of human freedom.

Eventually, Mead wrote for Morrow the story of her own earlier years, *Blackberry Winter*, out of the conviction that her upbringing by highly progressive and intellectual parents had made her "ahead of her time," so that looking at her experience would serve those born generations later. She never wrote in full of her later years, but she did publish a series of letters, written to friends, family, and colleagues over the course of fifty years of fieldwork, that bring the encounter with unfamiliar cultures closer to our own musings. Although *Letters from the Field* was published elsewhere, by Harper & Row, corporate metamorphoses have for once been serendipitous and made it possible to include *Letters from the Field* in this HarperCollins series, where it belongs. Mead often wrote for other publishers, but this particular set of books was linked by that early desire to spell out what her personal and professional experience could and should mean to Americans. That desire led her to write for *Redbook* and to appear repeatedly on television, speaking optimistically and urgently about our ability to make the right choices. Unlike many intellectuals, she was convinced of the intelligence of general readers, just as she was convinced of the essential goodness of democratic institutions. Addressing the public with respect and affection, she became a household name.

Margaret Mead's work has gone through many editions, and

the details of her observations and interpretations have been repeatedly critiqued and amended, as all pioneering scientific work must be. In spite of occasional opportunistic attacks, her colleagues continue to value her visionary and groundbreaking work. But in preparing this series, we felt it was important to seek introductions outside of ethnography that would focus on the themes of the books as seen from the point of view of Americans today who are concerned about how we educate our children, how we provide for the full participation of all members of society, and how we plan for the future. Times change, but comparison is always illuminating and always suggests the possibility of choice. Teenage girls in Samoa in the 1920s provided an illuminating comparison with American teenagers of that era, who were still living in the shadow of the Victorian age, and they provide an equally illuminating comparison with girls today, who are under early pressure from demands on their sexuality and their gender. Preteen boys in Manus allow us to examine alternative emphases on physical skills and on imagination in childhood—and do so across fifty years of debate about how to offer our children both. Gender roles that were being challenged when Mead was growing up reverted during the postwar resurgence of domesticity and have once again opened up—but the most important fact to remember about gender is that it is culturally constructed and that human beings can play with the biology of sex in many different ways. So we read these books with their echoes not only of distant climes but also of different moments in American history, in order to learn from the many ways of being human how to make better choices for the future.

Introduction to the Perennial Edition

a way of seeing

In the 1930s Margaret Mead ushered into American intellectual circles a powerful "way of seeing," as she called it, the cross-cultural perspective. She recorded life in societies around the world; then she compared the conduct and beliefs of these traditional peoples with those of us in the United States. With this anthropological view, she provided fresh insights into many American social problems, from the *Sturm und Drang* of teenage years, to the rising divorce rate, to the strained relations between women and men. This cross-cultural perspective pervades books such as *Sex and Temperament: In Three Primitive Societies* and *Male and Female.*

In both books, Mead also addresses a complex issue: How malleable is human nature? And in both books she champions the view that culture, not biology, is the primary force in shaping individual personality.

She came to this conclusion as a child. As she wrote in her autobiography, *Blackberry Winter,* "When our neighbors in the many places we lived during my childhood behaved in ways that were different from ours and from one another, I learned that this was because of their life experiences . . . not because of differences in the color of our skin or the shape of our heads" (3). And soon after she arrived in New Guinea in 1931, at the age of thirty, she found firsthand evidence of this human flexibility. As she wrote in *Sex and Temperament*, Arapesh men and women were both "womanly" and "unmasculine" (165); Mundugumor men and women were both "masculine," "virile," and "aggressive" (165; 279); and Tchambuli women were the "dominant, impersonal, managing partner," while Tchambuli men were "less responsible" and more "emotionally dependent."(279).

Sex roles in these cultures, Mead reported, were different from one another and from those in the United States. So she concluded that "human nature is almost unbelievably malleable" (280). In one of her most well known and vivid summations, she wrote, "we may say that many, if not all, of the personality traits which we have called masculine or feminine are as lightly linked to sex as are the clothing, the manners, and the form of head-dress that a society at a given period assigns to either sex" (280).

Mead's data suited the times. Armed with vicious racial theories, Hitler was rising to power. Racism and sexism were rampant across America and Europe. Countering this, Mead provided evidence that men and women of all ethnic and social groups were inherently equal; it was culture—not biology—that made us the varied individuals that we are. The distinguished anthropologist Marvin Harris would write of her, "The artful presentation of cultural differences to a wide professional and lay public by Mead . . . must be reckoned among the important events in the history of American intellectual thought" (Harris, 1968: 409).

Indeed, Mead entered the intellectual fray at a pivotal moment not only in world affairs, but in the bitter nature/nurture debate. This controversy had existed at least since 1690 when John Locke argued that at birth the human mind was an empty tablet, a *tabula rasa*, on which the environment inscribed personality.

Locke's view came under forceful attack in the mid-nineteenth century when the British political philosopher and social scientist

Herbert Spencer began to publish essays arguing that human social order was the result of evolution, specifically the "survival of the fittest." This was a term that he, not Charles Darwin, introduced. And Spencer used this intellectual platform to defend unregulated capitalism and to oppose any state-sponsored aid to the poor. Certain classes, nations, and ethnic groups dominated others, Spencer maintained, because they were more "fit."

Darwin's *On the Origin of Species,* published in 1859, delivered the *coup de grâce.* Humankind had evolved from simpler forms by means of natural selection—creating genetic variations between individuals and populations. Darwin was not interested in political applications of his theories. Moreover, the concept of natural selection does not support racism or sexism. But, unfortunately, Spencer's views soon became known as "Social Darwinism."

This pernicious dogma then spread into social policy. Prosperous, male-dominated Europe was in the grips of the industrial revolution and many wished to justify laissez-faire capitalism, colonialism, expansionism, and sexism. In the 1870s Sir Francis Galton began to advocate specific social programs to improve the human race, spawning the eugenics movement. As a result, in the 1920s some thirty states in the U.S. enacted involuntary sterilization programs to curb breeding among confirmed criminals and the feebleminded. Strict immigration laws also emerged to curtail the influx of immigrants who might bear genetic flaws. And many argued that women, long regarded as inferior to men, were biologically the lesser sex.

It was in this intellectual climate that Mead entered Columbia University in the 1920s. Her mentor, Franz Boas, often called the "father of anthropology," was an immigrant and a vehement opponent of the eugenics movement. He unquestionably recognized that biology and evolution created aspects of human nature. But he staunchly defended the idea that one's cultural environment had an overriding impact on one's personality and behavior.

Boas shared this view with such disparate thinkers as

Bertrand Russell and H. L. Mencken, as well as with a growing number of fellow social scientists. Psychologist John Watson argued that children were almost infinitely malleable and Freudians were showing how childhood traumas molded adult personality. Moreover, African Americans were migrating north to join the industrial labor force; women were entering the business world; and both groups were displaying their intelligence and adaptability. And with Hitler's ascent to power, almost every thinking Western scientist began to endorse the view that ethnic and gender differences were sculpted largely by one's upbringing. Mead was a leader of this school of thought and both *Sex and Temperament* and *Male and Female* reflect this point of view.

However, like Boas, Mead did acknowledge that there were biological differences between the sexes. Indeed, in *Sex and Temperament*, she devoted a chapter to cultural "deviants"—those men and women in New Guinean societies who, because of their inherent nature, could not conform to their culture's ideal sex roles. And in *Male and Female* she discussed a few biological differences between women and men. In fact, in the 1962 introduction to the latter, she wrote, "I would, if I were writing it today, lay more emphasis on man's specific biological inheritance from earlier human forms and also on parallels between *Homo sapiens* and other than mammalian species" (xix).

So although Mead was primarily concerned with the ways in which culture builds personality, she did endorse what would become the predominant view regarding the nature/nurture debate: Currently most informed scientists believe that biology and culture are inextricably entwined, that neither determines human behavior; that *both* play an essential role in shaping human thought and action. But I wonder what she would think of the new research on the brain, which yields data suggesting that a third force contributes to human behavior: a force that has variously been called the self, the ego, the psyche, and/or the mind. Here's my thinking.

Scientists now maintain that the human brain is composed of

"modules," "circuits," or "systems" that perform specific tasks—such as counting backward; rhyming words; remembering faces; or feeling sexual desire, anger, or romantic love. A primary brain region that integrates one's feelings, thoughts, and actions is the prefrontal cortex, an area that lies directly behind the forehead. Neuroscientists call this region the "central executive" or the "crossroads of the mind" because it has connections to many sections of the brain and body and is devoted to processing information. With this region of the brain we register myriad bits of data, order and weigh them as they accumulate, and find patterns in them. We also reason hypothetically, analyze contingencies, consider options, plan for the future, and make decisions.

As philosopher John Dewey said, "Mind is a verb." I agree; the mind does something. So I have come to believe that with the development of the prefrontal cortex during human evolution, our ancestors acquired a brain mechanism—what I will call the mind—that enabled them to make decisions and behave in unique ways, ways that could modify, even override, the potent forces of biology *and* culture.

In short, biology predisposes us to perceive the world and behave in general ways. Cultural experiences shape these perceptions and behavioral predispositions, pruning and building synaptic connections in the brain. Then, with our minds, each of us assimilates the forces of biology and culture in his or her own unique fashion, further modifying brain circuits and cultural perceptions. And all three forces affect our courtship and mating habits—selecting for a new generation of individuals who carry some different genes, adopt some new cultural traditions, and integrate the world around them in some original ways. Genes, mind, and culture are interdependent. Each force constantly remodels the other two; none *ever* acts alone; and all evolve together. I believe that as scientists learn more about how human biology, the mind, and the environment interact, the nature/nurture dichotomy that Mead sought to understand will finally be laid to rest.

The intellectual—and economic—climate is changing in

other ways that would interest Mead. In *Male and Female* she voiced the prescient view that we should "make as full use of woman's special gifts as we have of men's" (6). Mead would be pleased to see that this is happening. The burgeoning communications industries, health care fields, service professions, nonprofit organizations, and other segments of the twenty-first-century economy are especially suited to women's natural talents—and these economic forces are pulling record numbers of women into the job market in cultures around the world.

Margaret Mead has had many critics. One legitimate criticism, I think, concerns a practice easily seen in both *Sex and Temperament* and *Male and Female*. Mead often generalized; she made sweeping statements about the societies she recorded. But her proclivity to generalize stems, it seems to me, from her graduate-school training.

Under the direction of "Papa Franz," she and her notable colleague Ruth Benedict developed a new anthropological subfield, the school of "culture and personality." Central to its philosophy was Mead's belief that a culture was like a language. It had a grammar, an underlying structure, a personality based on a few major psychological traits. As Benedict put it, "Cultures from this point of view are individual psychology thrown large upon a screen" (Benedict, 1932: 24; quoted in Harris, 1968: 398). So just as Benedict portrayed the national character of the Japanese with a few adjectives in *The Chrysanthemum and the Sword*, Mead would use a few adjectives to summarize the various peoples of New Guinea in her writings.

Today few agree with all of Margaret Mead's conclusions. I, for example, do not think that human fatherhood is a social invention, something she maintains in *Male and Female*. I would argue, instead, that millennia ago humanity evolved specific circuits in the brain for romantic attraction and attachment to a partner. Others have voiced different objections.

Some say that Mead's largest contribution was her pioneering use of film to record tribal life. Indeed, with her field partner and

marital partner, Gregory Bateson, Mead took some 25,000 Leica
stills and some 22,000 feet of 16 mm film to study traditional
societies in a new way. But I am convinced that Margaret Mead's
contribution has been far wider and much more important. Her
cross-cultural perspective offered a valuable means of understanding several vital American social issues. Her emphasis on the role
of culture in producing character and social rank gave hope to
ethnic minorities and to women. And I am convinced that Mead
also influenced society in many other, less perceptible ways—as
an event on a rainy night in 1976 made clear to me.

I was at the annual business meeting of the American
Anthropological Association in Washington, D.C. It was almost
midnight, and a motion had been put forth to ban the new book,
Sociobiology: The New Synthesis, by Harvard biologist Edward O.
Wilson. The book discussed the role of biology in understanding
such complex behaviors as altruism and deceit, and many anthro-
pologists feared that it augured the return of Social Darwinism to
academic thought. In fact, many were lined up at the microphone, denouncing Wilson and vehemently urging that *Sociobiology* be officially rejected by the anthropological community.

At that point, Mead swept up to the microphone, staff in
hand. She was no proponent of sociobiology. But she leaned into
the mike and declared, "Book-burning—we are talking about
book-burning." She then delivered a stunning speech on freedom
of speech. Shortly we voted. I stood up for freedom. So did 177
others. And the "book-burning" resolution was defeated by 53
votes. How many other controversial people and ideas did Mead
support? We will never know. But she must have galvanized
many scholars and laymen to pursue their interests—individuals
who subsequently improved society.

There is an apocryphal story about Mead's last hours. A nurse
came to her bedside in a hospital in New York, held her hand to
soothe her, and whispered, "Dr. Mead, everyone has to die."
Mead reportedly replied, "I know, but this is different." I suspect
that Margaret Mead's "way of seeing," her tremendous energy,

her torrent of original ideas, and her staunch support of many people and many causes, has seeped deep into the fabric of modern life. Indeed, her achievements were different. Even now, one hundred years after her birth, with the republication of her books, she continues to change the world.

—*Helen Fisher*

References

Harris, Marvin. *The Rise of Anthropological Theory.* New York: Thomas Y. Crowell Company, 1968.

Mead, Margaret. *Blackberry Winter: My Earlier Years.* New York: Morrow, 1972.

———. *Male and Female: The Classic Study of the Sexes.* New York: Morrow, 1975.

———. *Sex and Temperament: In Three Primitive Societies.* New York: Quill, 1963.

preface to the 1950 edition

This is my most misunderstood book, and I have devoted some attention to trying to understand why. These are the difficulties as I see them.

I went into the field, in 1931, to study one problem, the "conditioning of the social personalities of the two sexes." I hoped that such an investigation would throw light on *sex* difference. I found, after two years' work, that the material which I had gathered threw more light on *temperamental* differences, i.e. differences among *innate* individual endowments, irrespective of sex. I concluded that, until we could understand very thoroughly the way in which a society could mold all the men and women born within it to approximate an ideal of behaviour which was congenial to only a few of them, or could limit to one sex an ideal of behaviour which another culture succeeded in limiting to the opposite sex, we wouldn't be able to talk very intelligently about sex differences. But when this book came out and often since, oftenest perhaps since I published *Male and Female* (in which I did discuss sex differences), I have been accused of having believed when I wrote *Sex and Temperament* that there are no sex differences.

In the second place, according to some readers, my results make "too beautiful" a pattern. Here, admittedly looking for light on the subject of sex differences, I found three tribes all conveniently within a hundred mile area. In one, both men and women act as we expect women to act—in a mild parental responsive way; in the second, both act as we expect men to act—in a fierce initiating fashion; and in the third, the men act according to our stereotype for women—are catty, wear curls and go shopping, while the women are energetic, managerial, unadorned partners. This, many readers felt, was too much. It was too pretty. I must have found what I was looking for. But this misconception comes from a lack of understanding of what anthropology means, of the open-mindedness with which one must look and listen, record in astonishment and wonder, that which one would not have been able to guess. It is true that if by some trick of fate (and it would have taken only a very slight one—a different bit of advice from some local district officer, an attack of malaria on some different date), any one of these three tribes had not been chosen and some other chosen in its stead, this book would not have been written in this form. Yet the seemingly "too good to be true" pattern is actually a reflection of the form which lay in these three cultures themselves, following as cultures do the intricate and systematic potentialities of our common human nature. These three cultures were illuminating in *this* particular way, and gave me a wealth of material on how completely a culture may impose, on one sex or both sexes, a pattern which is appropriate to only a segment of the human race.

Third, it is difficult to talk about two things at once—sex in the sense of biologically-given sex differences, and temperament in the sense of innate individual endowment. I wanted to talk about the way each of us belongs to a sex and has a temperament, a temperament shared with others of our own sex *and* others of the opposite sex. In our present-day culture, bedeviled by a series of *either-or* problems, there is a tendency to say: "She can't have it both ways, if she shows that different cultures can mold men and women in ways which are opposite to our ideas of innate sex differences, then she can't also claim that there *are* sex differences."

Fortunately for mankind, we not only can have it both ways, but many more than both ways. Mankind can draw on the contrasts which lie in our different temperamental potentialities, on the infinite and varied ways in which human culture can impart either congenial or uncongenial patterns of behaviour. The biological bases of development as human beings, although providing limitations which must be honestly reckoned with, can be seen as potentialities by no means fully tapped by our human imagination.

Margaret Mead

New York—July, 1950

preface to the 1963 edition

In the twenty-seven years since this book was first published women in the United States have come to rely more on the definition of themselves in terms of sex, and to lay less emphasis upon finding themselves as individuals. One important aspect of individuality is temperament. I would hope that this exploration of the way in which simple primitive cultures have been able to rely upon temperamental clues may be useful in shifting the present extreme emphasis upon sex roles to a new emphasis on human beings as distinct personalities, who, men and women, share many of the same contrasting and differing temperamental approaches to life.

Since this book was written we have come seriously to consider ourselves as possibly one kind of living creatures in a universe that may contain many other kinds of living creatures, possibly more intelligent than we. This possibility adds new zest to the exploration of our own potentialities—as members of one species, entrusted with the preservation of an endangered world. Each difference is precious and to be cherished.

Margaret Mead

New York—November 26, 1962

introduction

When we study the simpler societies, we cannot but be impressed
with the many ways in which man has taken a few hints and
woven them into the beautiful imaginative social fabrics that we
call civilisations. His natural environment provided him with a
few striking periodicities and contrasts—day and night, the
change of seasons, the untiring waxing and waning of the moon,
the spawning of fish and the migration-times of animals and
birds. His own physical nature provided other striking points—
age and sex, the rhythm of birth, maturation, and senescence, the
structure of blood-relationship. Differences between one animal
and another, between one individual and another, differences in
fierceness or in tenderness, in bravery or in cunning, in richness
of imagination or plodding dulness of wit—these provided hints
out of which the ideas of rank and caste, of special priesthoods, of
the artist and the oracle, could be developed. Working with clues
as universal and as simple as these, man made for himself a fabric
of culture within which each human life was dignified by form
and meaning. Man became not merely one of the beasts that
mated, fought for its food, and died, but a human being, with a

name, a position, and a god. Each people makes this fabric differently, selects some clues and ignores others, emphasises a different sector of the whole arc of human potentialities. Where one culture uses as a main thread the vulnerable ego, quick to take insult or perish of shame, another selects uncompromising bravery and even, so that there may be no admitted cowards, may like the Cheyenne Indians invent a specially complicated social position for the overfearful. Each simple, homogeneous culture can give scope to only a few of the varied human endowments, disallowing or penalising others too antithetical or too unrelated to its major emphases to find room within its walls. Having originally taken its values from the values dear to some human temperaments and alien to others, a culture embodies these values more and more firmly in its structure, in its political and religious systems, in its art and its literature; and each new generation is shaped, firmly and definitely, to the dominant trends.

Now as each culture creates distinctively the social fabric in which the human spirit can wrap itself safely and intelligibly, sorting, reweaving, and discarding threads in the historical tradition that it shares with many neighbouring peoples, it may bend every individual born within it to one type of behaviour, recognising neither age, sex, nor special disposition as points for differential elaboration. Or a culture may seize upon the very obvious facts of difference in age, in sex, in strength, in beauty, or the unusual variations, such as a native propensity to see visions or dream dreams, and make these dominant cultural themes. So societies such as those of the Masai and the Zulus make a grading of all individuals by age a basic point of organisation, and the Akikiyu of East Africa make a major drama out of the ceremonial ousting of the older generation by the younger. The aborigines of Siberia dignified the nervously unstable individual into the shaman, whose utterances were believed to be supernaturally inspired and were a law to his more nervously stable fellow-tribesmen. Such an extreme case as this, where a whole people bows down before the word of an individual whom we would classify as insane, seems clear enough to us. The Siberians have imaginatively and from the point of view of our society unjustifiably, elevated an abnormal person into a socially important one. They have built upon a human deviation that we would disallow, or if it became troublesome, imprison.

If we hear that among the Mundugumor people of New Guinea children born with the umbilical cord wound around their necks are singled out as of native and indisputable right artists, we feel that here is a culture which has not merely institutionalised a kind of temperament that we regard as abnormal—as in the case of the Siberian shaman—but also a culture that has arbitrarily associated, in an artificial and imaginative way, two completely unrelated points: manner of birth and an ability to paint intricate designs upon pieces of bark. When we learn further that so firmly is this association insisted upon that only those who are so born can paint good pictures, while the man born without a strangulating cord labours humble and unarrogant, and never attains any virtuosity, we see the strength that lies in such irrelevant associations once they are firmly embedded in the culture.

Even when we encounter less glaring cases of cultural elaboration, when we read of a people in which the first-born son is regarded as different in kind from his later-born brethren, we realise that here again the human imagination has been at work, re-evaluating a simple biological fact. Although our own historical tradition hints to us that the first-born is "naturally" a little more important than the others, still when we hear that among the Maori the first-born son of a chief was so sacred that only special persons could cut his infant locks without risking death from the contact, we recognise that man has taken the accident of order of birth and raised a superstructure of rank upon it. Our critical detachment, our ability to smile over these imaginative flights of fancy—which see in the first-born or the last-born, the seventh child of the seventh child, the twin, or the infant born in a caul a being specially endowed with precious or maleficent powers—remains undisturbed. But if we turn from these "self-evident" primitive constructs to points of elaboration that we share with primitive peoples, to points concerning which we are no longer spectators, but instead are deeply involved, our detachment vanishes. It is no doubt purely imaginative to attribute ability to paint to birth with the cord about the neck, or the power to write poetry to one born a twin. To choose leaders or oracles from aberrant and unusual temperaments that we brand as insane is not wholly imaginative, but at least is based on a very different premise, which selects a natural potentiality of the human race that we neither use nor honour. But the insistence upon a thousand and one innate differences between men and women, differences many of which show no more immediate relationship to the biological facts of sex than does ability to paint to manner of birth, other differences which show a congruence with sex that is neither universal nor necessary—as is the case in the association of epileptic seizure and religious gift—this indeed we do not regard as an imaginative creation of the human mind busy patterning a bare existence with meaning.

This study is not concerned with whether there are or are not actual and universal differences between the sexes, either quantitative or qualitative. It is not concerned with whether women are more variable than men, which was claimed before the doctrine of evolution exalted variability, or less variable, which was claimed afterwards. It is not a treatise on the rights of women, nor an inquiry into the basis of femininism. It is, very simply, an account of how three primitive societies have grouped their social attitudes towards temperament about the very obvious facts of sex-difference. I studied this problem in simple societies because here we have the drama of civilisation writ small, a social microcosm alike in kind, but different in size and magnitude, from the complex social structures of peoples who, like our own, depend upon a written tradition and upon the integration of a great number of conflicting historical traditions. Among the gentle mountain-dwelling Arapesh, the fierce cannibalistic Mundugumor, and the graceful head-hunters of Tchambuli, I studied this question. Each of these tribes had, as has every human society, the point of sex-difference to use as one theme in the plot of social life, and each of these three peoples has developed that theme differently. In comparing the way in which they have dramatised sex-difference, it is possible to gain a greater insight into what elements are social constructs, originally irrelevant to the biological facts of sex-gender.

Our own society makes great use of this plot. It assigns different rôles to the two sexes, surrounds them from birth with an expectation of different behaviour, plays out the whole drama of courtship, marriage, and parenthood in terms of types of behaviour believed to be innate and therefore appropriate for one sex or for the other. We know dimly that these rôles have changed even within our history. Studies like Mrs. Putnam's *The Lady** depict woman as an infinitely malleable lay figure upon which mankind has draped ever varying period-costumes, in keeping with which she wilted or waxed imperious, flirted or fled. But all discussions have emphasised not the relative social personalities assigned to the two sexes, but rather the superficial behaviour-patterns assigned to women, often not even to all women, but only to women of the upper class. A sophisticated recognition that upper-class women were puppets of a changing tradition blurred rather than clarified the issue. It left untouched the rôles assigned to men, who were conceived as proceeding along a special masculine road, shaping women to their fads and whims in womanliness. All discussion of the position of women, of the character and temperament of women, the enslavement or the emancipation of women, obscures the basic issue—the recognition that the cultural plot behind human relations is the way in which the rôles of the two sexes are conceived, and that the growing boy is shaped to a local and special emphasis as inexorably as is the growing girl.

------

*E. J. S. Putnam, *The Lady*, Sturgis & Walton, 1910.

The Vaërtings attacked the problem in their book *The Dominant Sex*[*] with their critical imagination handicapped by European cultural tradition. They knew that in some parts of the world there had been and still were matriarchal institutions which gave to women a freedom of action, endowed women with an independence of choice that historical European culture granted only to men. By simple sleight-of-hand they reversed the European situation, and built up an interpretation of matriarchal societies that saw women as cold, proud, and dominant, men as weak and submissive. The attributes of women in Europe were foisted upon men in matriarchal communities—that was all. It was a simple picture, which really added nothing to our understanding of the problem, based as it was upon the limiting concept that if one sex is dominating in personality, the other sex must be *ipso facto* submissive. The root of the Vaërtings' mistake lies in our traditional insistence upon contrasts between the personality of the two sexes, in our ability to see only one variation upon the theme of the dominant male, and that the hen-pecked husband. They did conceive, however, of the possibility of a different arrangement of dominance from our traditional one, mainly because to thinking based upon patriarchal institutions the very existence of a matriarchal form of society carries with it an implication of an imaginary reversal of the temperamental position of the two sexes.

But recent studies of primitive peoples have made us more sophisticated.[†] We know that human cultures do not all fall into one side or the other of a single scale and that it is possible for one society to ignore completely an issue which two other societies have solved in contrasting ways. Because a people honour the old may mean that they hold children in slight esteem, but a people

---

[*]Mathilde and Mathis Vaërting, *The Dominant Sex*, Doran, 1923.
[†]See especially Ruth Benedict, *Patterns of Culture*, Houghton Mifflin, 1934.

may also, like the Ba Thonga of South Africa, honour neither old people nor children; or, like the Plains Indians, dignify the little child and the grandfather; or, again, like the Manus and parts of modern America, regard children as the most important group in society. In expecting simple reversals—that if an aspect of social life is not specifically sacred, it must be specifically secular; that if men are strong, women must be weak—we ignore the fact that cultures exercise far greater licence than this in selecting the possible aspects of human life which they will minimise, overemphasise, or ignore. And while every culture has in some way institutionalised the rôles of men and women, it has not necessarily been in terms of contrast between the prescribed personalities of the two sexes, nor in terms of dominance or submission. With the paucity of material for elaboration, no culture has failed to seize upon the conspicuous facts of age and sex in some way, whether it be the convention of one Philippine tribe that no man can keep a secret, the Manus assumption that only men enjoy playing with babies, the Toda prescription of almost all domestic work as too sacred for women, or the Arapesh insistence that women's heads are stronger than men's. In the division of labour, in dress, in manners, in social and religious functioning—sometimes in only a few of these respects, sometimes in all—men and women are socially differentiated, and each sex, as a sex, forced to conform to the rôle assigned to it. In some societies, these socially defined rôles are mainly expressed in dress or occupation, with no insistence upon innate temperamental differences. Women wear long hair and men wear short hair, or men wear curls and women shave their heads; women wear skirts and men wear trousers, or women wear trousers and men wear skirts. Women weave and men do not, or men weave and women do not. Such simple tie-ups as these between dress or occupation and sex are easily taught to every child and make no assumptions to which a given child cannot easily conform.

It is otherwise in societies that sharply differentiate the

behaviour of men and of women in terms which assume a genuine difference in temperament. Among the Dakota Indians of the Plains, the importance of an ability to stand any degree of danger or hardship was frantically insisted upon as a masculine characteristic. From the time that a boy was five or six, all the conscious educational effort of the household was bent towards shaping him into an indubitable male. Every tear, every timidity, every clinging to a protective hand or desire to continue to play with younger children or with girls, was obsessively interpreted as proof that he was not going to develop into a real man. In such a society it is not surprising to find the *berdache*, the man who had voluntarily given up the struggle to conform to the masculine rôle and who wore female attire and followed the occupations of a woman. The institution of the *berdache* in turn served as a warning to every father; the fear that the son might become a *berdache* informed the parental efforts with an extra desperation, and the very pressure which helped to drive a boy to that choice was redoubled. The invert who lacks any discernible physical basis for his inversion has long puzzled students of sex, who when they can find no observable glandular abnormality turn to theories of early conditioning or identification with a parent of opposite sex. In the course of this investigation, we shall have occasion to examine the "masculine" woman and the "feminine" man as they occur in these different tribes, to inquire whether it is always a woman of dominating nature who is conceived as masculine, or a man who is gentle, submissive, or fond of children or embroidery who is conceived as feminine.

In the following chapters we shall be concerned with the patterning of sex-behaviour from the standpoint of temperament, with the cultural assumptions that certain temperamental attitudes are "naturally" masculine and others "naturally" feminine. In this matter, primitive people seem to be, on the surface, more sophisticated than we are. Just as they know that the gods, the food habits, and the marriage customs of the next tribe differ from those of their own people, and do not insist that one form is true or natural while the other is false or unnatural, so they often know that the temperamental proclivities which they regard as natural for men or for women differ from the natural temperaments of the men and women among their neighbours. Nevertheless, within a narrower range and with less of a claim for the biological or divine validity of their social forms than we often advance, each tribe has certain definite attitudes towards temperament, a theory of what human beings, either men or women or both, are naturally like, a norm in terms of which to judge and condemn those individuals who deviate from it.

Two of these tribes have no idea that men and women are different in temperament. They allow them different economic and religious rôles, different skills, different vulnerabilities to evil magic and supernatural influences. The Arapesh believe that painting in colour is appropriate only to men, and the Mundugumor consider fishing an essentially feminine task. But any idea that temperamental traits of the order of dominance, bravery, aggressiveness, objectivity, malleability, are inalienably associated with one sex (as opposed to the other) is entirely lacking. This may seem strange to a civilisation which in its sociology, its medicine, its slang, its poetry, and its obscenity accepts the socially defined differences between the sexes as having an innate basis in temperament and explains any deviation from the socially determined rôle as abnormality of native endowment or early maturation. It came as a surprise to me because I too had been accustomed to use in my thinking such concepts as "mixed type," to think of some men as having "feminine" temperaments, of some women as having "masculine" minds. I set as my problem a study of the conditioning of the social personalities of the two sexes, in the hope that such an investigation would throw some light upon sex-differences. I shared the general belief of our society that there was a natural sex-temperament which could at the most only be distorted or diverted from normal expression. I was innocent of any suspicion that the temperaments which we regard as native to one sex might instead be mere variations of human temperament, to which the members of either or both sexes may, with more or less success in the case of different individuals, be educated to approximate.

part one

the mountain-dwelling Arapesh

1

mountain life

The Arapesh-speaking people occupy a wedge-shaped territory that stretches from the sea-coast across a triple range of steep mountains, and down on the grass plains of the Sepik watershed to the west. The people on the beach remain in spirit a bush people. They have borrowed the custom of canoe-building from the neighbouring islands, but they feel much happier fishing not in the sea, but in the ponds that lie sheltered among the sago-swamps. They hate the sea-sand and build little palm-leaf shelters against its invasion. Forked sticks are set up on which carrying-bags can be hung and so kept out of the sand, and many palm-leaf mats are woven so that the people will not have to sit upon the sand, which is regarded as filthy. No such precautions are taken by the mountain people, who sit habitually in the mud without any feeling that it is dirt to be avoided. The beach-dwelling Arapesh live in large houses, fifty to sixty feet in length, built upon piles, with specially enclosed verandahs and decorated gable-ends. They cluster together in large villages, and the people go daily to their gardens and sago-patches, which are situated at no great distance from the village. These beach people are plump and well fed. The rhythm of their lives is slow and peaceful; there is plenty of food; pots and baskets, shell ornaments, and new dance-forms can be purchased from the passing canoes of the coastal trading peoples.

But as one begins to climb up the narrow slippery trails that extend to definite networks over the precipitous mountains, the whole tone of life changes. There are no more large villages, but only tiny settlements in which three or four families live, clusters of ten to twelve houses, some built on piles, the others built on the ground and so slightly constructed as to be hardly worth the name of house. The land is barren and infertile, the sago rare and planted instead of growing uncultivated in great natural swamps. The streams yield little except a few prawns, which are only occasionally worth fishing for. There are great areas of bushland in which there are no gardens, areas that are set aside for hunting tree-kangaroo, wallaby, opossum, and cassowary. But in these same regions the ancestors of the Arapesh have hunted for many generations, and game is rare and not to be counted upon. The gardens perch precariously on the sides of hills, presenting an almost insoluble problem in fencing, a problem with which the natives hardly attempt to deal. They merely resign themselves to the ravages of the pigs that have run wild in the bush.

The village pigs are not plump like the pigs in the beach villages, but skinny and more razor-backed, and so ill fed that they often die. When a pig dies the woman who was raising it is blamed for her greediness in eating not only all the taro but all of the taro-skin also, and sharing none of it with her pig. Gardens, sago-patches, hunting-grounds, are farther afield than on the beach, and the people accentuate the difficulties by electing always to work in small co-operative groups, now in one man's garden, now in another's. This necessitates an endless amount of walking about on the slippery precipitous paths and a great amount of shouting from mountain peak to mountain peak to send messages from one member of a family to another.

Level land is so scarce that there is seldom space to build even a small village. The biggest village in the mountain region was

Alitoa,* the village in which we lived for many months. It had twenty-four houses, in which eighty-seven people had residence claims; but these claims were only sporadically exercised and there were only three families who made Alitoa their main residence. Even with so few houses, some of them were built jutting out over the steep declivity that sloped away from the village upon all sides. When a feast is held, the visitors overflow the capacity of the village, dogs and children spill over the edges, and people must sleep on the wet ground underneath the houses because there is not room enough within the houses. When an Arapesh refers oratorically to a feast, he says: "We were burned by the sun and washed by the rain. We were cold, we were hungry, but we came to see you."

Collecting enough food and firewood to maintain any number of people in one place is also difficult. The hills surrounding a village have been combed for firewood for generations; the gardens are far away, and the women must toil for days to carry in supplies for a single day's feasting. Men carry nothing on these occasions except pigs and other heavy loads of meat and the large logs that are used for cigarette-lighting fires in the centre of the village. When they carry pigs, many relays of men combine, because the carrying-pole chafes their unaccustomed shoulders. But the women plod up and down the mountain paths with loads of sixty and seventy pounds suspended from their foreheads, sometimes also with a suckling baby in a bark sling at the breast. Their jaws are shut like rat-traps beneath the pressure of the headbands, giving their faces a grim forbidding expression that is seen at no other time and which contrasts with the gay, festive pig-carrying of the men, who go

---

*I have used the present tense for all customary acts; the past tense when I am describing an event that occurred in the past or a condition that obtained in the past of the continuance of which I have no evidence; and the perfect tense for customary behaviour that government control or European contact has modified or eliminated.

whooping and singing through the bush. But then it is appropriate that women should carry heavier loads than the men do, because women's heads, they say, are so much harder and stronger.

The manners of the mountain people proclaim at once that this is no country accustomed to the raids of head-hunters. Women go about unattended; pairs of tiny children stray along the paths, hunting lizards with their miniature bows and arrows; young girls sleep alone in deserted villages. A party of visitors from another locality asks first for fire, which their hosts immediately give them; then a low-voiced excited conversation begins. Then men cluster about an open fire; the women cook near by, often in the open, supporting their tall black cooking-pots on huge stones; the children sit about in sleepy contentment, playing with their lips, sucking their fingers, or sticking their sharp little knees into their mouths. Someone relates a slight incident and everyone laughs uproariously and happily, with a laughter that stirs easily at the slightest touch of humour. As the night falls and the chill of the damp mountain evening drives them all closer to the fire, they sit around the embers and sing songs imported from far and wide, which reflect the musical canons of many different peoples. A slit gong may sound far away and the people speculate happily and irresponsibly upon its message: someone has killed a pig or a cassowary; visitors have come and an absent host is being summoned; someone is dying, is dead, has been buried. All the explanations are offered as equally valid and there is no attempt made to sift their relative probabilities. Soon after sunset hosts and guests retire to sleep in small houses in which the fortunate sleep next to the fire and the unfortunate "sleep nothing." It is so cold the people often push too close to the burning logs on the earthen fire-place, only to awaken with a burned grass skirt or a shower of spark-burns on the baby's skin. In the morning, the visitors are always pressed to stay, even though this means that the host family will go hungry on the morrow, as the supply of food is running low and the nearest garden is a half-day's walk away. If the visitors refuse the invitation, the hosts accompany them to the edge of the village and with laughing shouts promise an early return visit.

In this steep, ravine-riddled country, where two points within easy shouting distance of each other may be separated by a descent and an ascent of some fifteen hundred feet, all level land is spoken of as a "good place," and all rough, steep, precipitous spots are "bad places." Around each village the ground falls away into these bad places, which are used for pigs and for latrines, and on which are built the huts used by menstruating women and women in childbirth, whose dangerous blood would endanger the village, which is level and good and associated with food. In the centre of the village, or sometimes in two centres if the village straggles a little, is the *agehu*, the feasting and ceremonial place of the village. Around the *agehu* stand a few stones that are vaguely associated with ancestors and whose names share the masculine gender with all the words for men.* When the divinatory oven is made to discover the location of the sorcery that is wasting some-one away, one of these stones from the village *agehu* is placed in the fire. But the *agehu* is a good rather than a sacred place; here children tumble and play, here a baby may take its first steps, and a man or a woman sit threading opossum-teeth or plaiting an arm-band. Sometimes the men build small palm-leaf shelters on the *agehu*, under which they can sit during a shower. Here people with headaches, their sad state proclaimed by a tight band about the forehead, come to parade up and down and console them-selves with the sympathy that they receive. Here yams are piled for feasts, or rows of the great black feast-plates and the smaller brightly painted clay bowls are set out filled with the beautiful

---

*The Arapesh speak a language that contains thirteen noun classes or gen-ders, each one of which is distinguished by a separate set of pronominal and adjectival suffixes and prefixes. There is a masculine gender, a feminine gender, a gender that contains objects of indeterminate or mixed gender, and ten other classes whose content cannot be so accurately described.

white coconut croquettes, the preparation of which is a recently imported art of which the mountain people are very proud.

All such luxuries and refinements of life, songs and dance-steps, new-made dishes, a different style of doing the hair and a new cut of grass skirt, are imported by slow stages from the beach villages, which have previously purchased them from the maritime trading peoples. The beach stands, in the minds of the mountain people, for fashion and for light-heartedness. From the beach came the idea of wearing clothes, an idea that had not yet penetrated the most inland of the mountain villages, and which still sits lightly upon the mountain men, who fasten their bark-cloth G-strings with a carelessness and disregard of their purpose that shocks the more sophisticated beach people. The women have imported their fashions piecemeal and in a haphazard manner; their grass aprons hang slackly from a cord that encircles the stoutest part of their thighs, and tight, unrelated belts, with nothing to support, girdle their waists. The men have imported the beach style of head-dress, a long psyche knot, drawn sharply back from the forehead and passed through a deep basketry ring. This way of doing the hair accords very badly with hunting in the thick bush and is periodically abandoned and resumed by individuals as their enthusiasm for hunting rises or wanes. Hunting is an occupation that a man may follow or not, at will; those who make it their main pursuit wear their hair cut close.

All of these importations from the beach are grouped into dance-complexes, which are sold from village to village. Each village, or cluster of small villages, organises through a long preliminary period to collect the necessary pigs, tobacco, feathers, and shell rings (which constitute the Arapesh currency) with which to purchase one of these dances from a more seaward village that has wearied of it. With the dance they purchase new styles of clothing, new bits of magic, new songs, and new divining tricks. Like the songs that the people sing, songs which are remnants of long-forgotten dances, these importations have very little relationship to each other; every few years a new sort of diving trick, a new style of head-dress or arm-band, is imported, enjoyed enthusiastically for a few months and then forgotten—except as some material object, lying neglected on a dusty house-shelf, may recall it to mind. Behind these importations lies the belief that all that comes from the beach is superior, more sophisticated, more beautiful, and that some day the people of the mountains, in spite of their poor land and miserable pigs, will catch up, will acquire a ceremonial life as gay and intricate as that of the coastal peoples. But always they remain far behind the beach people, who shrug their shoulders when they import a new dance, and remark that parts of the complex—this handsome tortoise-shell forehead-plate, for instance—will never leave the beach because the miserable mountain people will never have enough to pay for it. And still, generation after generation, the mountain people save to import these lovely things, not as individuals but as villages, so that every member of the village may sing the new songs and wear the new styles.

Thus the Arapesh regard the country towards the sea as a source of happiness. There are, it is true, traditions of hostile encounters with more warlike beach people in former days when the mountain people went down to obtain sea-water for salt. But more often the emphasis is upon the dances, and the beach villages are referred to as "mother villages" and the lines of mountain villages that stretch directly back of them are called their "daughters." Mother villages and daughter villages are connected by intertwining paths that constitute three main systems of roads, called the "road of the dugong," the "road of the viper," and the "road of the setting sun." Along these roads the dance-complexes are imported, and along the paths that make up the roads individual travellers walk in safety from the house of one hereditary trade-friend to another. Between these friends there is an informal gift-exchange that supplies the mountain people with stone axes, bows and arrows, baskets and shell ornaments, and the beach people with tobacco, bird-feathers, pots, and net bags. All of this exchange, even though it involves the supply of tools and utensils that are absolutely essential to the life of the people, is phrased as voluntary gift-giving. No exact accounting is kept, no one is ever dunned or reproached, and in the whole period that we spent among the Arapesh I never heard, or heard of, an argument over these exchange gifts. Because the mountain people have no surplus tobacco or manufactures of their own, beyond a few wooden plates, unornamented net bags, crude coconut-shell spoons, and wooden pillows that are inadequate even for their own use, a return for the objects that they receive from the beach has to be made in tobacco and manufactured objects which they receive from the Plainsmen* beyond the mountains. The profit of the transaction, out of which the mountain man obtained his own stock of necessities, lies theoretically in the carriage; a mountain man will walk one day inland to receive a net bag from a Plainsman friend, and two days back towards the sea to present the bag, which now possesses a scarcity value, to a beach friend. This the Arapesh call "walking about to find rings," an occupation in which men show varying degrees of interest. But so casual, informal, and friendly is the system that as often as not a man walks in the wrong direction for profit, as when a beach man goes up into the mountains to receive a net bag rather than waiting for his mountain friend to bring it to him.

As the beach stands for gaiety and new and colourful things, so the plains country beyond the last mountain range has a very definite meaning to the mountain people. Here live a people of their own speech but possessed of a very different character and physical appearance. While the mountain people are slight, small-headed, and only sparsely hairy, the Plains people are squatter, heavier, with huge heads and definite beards, which they wear in a fringe below grim clean-shaven chins. They fight with spears, and do not use the bow and arrow that the mountain people share with the beach. Their men are naked and their women, whom they guard jealously, are naked until marriage, and then wear only the most diminutive

---

*To distinguish the Plains branch of the Arapesh from other plains tribes, I have capitalised the word "Plains" and used it as an adjective definitely referring to them.

aprons. As the mountain people look to the beach for all their new inspirations, the Plains Arapesh look to the neighbouring Abelam tribe, a gay artistic head-hunting people, who occupy the great tree-less grass plains of the Sepik basin. From the Abelam the Plains Arapesh have borrowed the style of their tall triangular temples, which rise seventy or eighty feet above the square plaza of the big villages, temples with sharply sloping ridge-poles and brilliantly painted facades. And with the Abelam and other plains people, the Plains Arapesh share the practice of sorcery, through which they terrorise their mountain and beach neighbours.

The Plains Arapesh are entirely cut off from the sea, hemmed in by enemies and dependent upon their tobacco-crop and the manufacture of shell rings from giant clam-shell for all their trad-ing with the Abelam, from whom they import net bags, etched cas-sowary daggers, spears, masks, and dance paraphernalia. The giant clam-shells come from the coast, and it is important to the Plains-men that they should be able to walk safely through the mountain country to obtain them. They walk through haughtily, arro-gantly, without fear, because of sorcery. With a bit of a victim's exuviae, a piece of half-eaten food, a strip of worn bark-cloth, or best of all a little sexual secretion, the Plains sorcerer is believed to be able to cause his victim to sicken and die. Once a mountain man or a beach man has lost his temper with a neighbour, stolen a piece of his "dirt,"* and delivered it into the hands of a sorcerer,

---

*The word "dirt" is used in pidgin English throughout the Mandated Ter-ritory to mean "exuviae used in sorcery practises." The Arapesh classify these exuviae into two groups; to one group, which includes parts of food, half-smoked cigarettes, butts of sugar-cane, and so on, they apply the adjec-tive that means "external" or "outside"; to the other, which includes ema-nations from the body that are felt to retain a close connection with the body—perspiration, saliva, scabs, semen, vaginal secretion, are included here, but except in the case of very young infants, excreta of all sorts are excluded—they apply a different specialised term. The Arapesh regard

the victim is for ever after in the sorcerer's power. The quarrel that caused the theft of the dirt may be healed, but the dirt remains in the hands of the sorcerer. On the strength of holding the lives of many mountain peoples in his hands, the sorcerer walks unafraid among them, and so do his brothers and his cousins and his sons. From time to time he levies a little black-mail, which the victim has to pay for fear of the sorcerer's putting the carefully preserved dirt back on the charmed fire. Years after the original misunderstanding, when the mountain victim dies the death is attributed to the Plainsman who was not satisfied with the blackmail, or to the malice of some new and unknown enemy who has subsidised the sorcerer anew. So the mountain Arapesh live in fear of this enemy outside their gates, and manage to forget that it was a relative or a neighbour who has delivered each one into the sorcerers' power. Because of the possibility of sorcery, because it is so easy to pick up a half-gnawed opossum-bone and hide it in a ditty-bag, because one's relatives and neighbours occa-sionally do things that arouse fear and anger, dirt passes into the hands of the sorcerers. But if there were no sorcerers, if they did not constantly pass back and forth, drumming up trade, fanning slight quarrels, hinting how easily a revenge might be encom-passed, then, say the Arapesh, there would be no death by black magic. How could there be, they ask, when the people of the mountains and the beach know no death-dealing charms?

Not only illness and death, but misfortune, an accident while hunting, a burned house, the defection of one's wife—all of these are due also to the Plains sorcerers. To bring about these minor disasters, the sorcerer need not possess the dirt of the actual vic-tim; he need only smoke the dirt of someone else from the same locality while he mutters over it his malevolent wishes.

If it were not for the beach people, there would be no new

---

these emanations from the body with a well-defined disgust, and it there-fore seems congruent with their attitudes to retain the pidgin-English term.

delights, no fresh excitements, no drain upon the slender resources of the mountain people to purchase the baubles of a few days' gaiety; if it were not for the Plainsmen, there would be no fear, people would live to grow old, and die, toothless and doddering, after a gentle and respected life. But for the influences that come from the plains and the beach, there would remain only the quiet adventure of living in their mountains, mountains so infertile that no neighbour envies them their possession, so inhospitable that no army could invade them and find food enough to survive, so precipitous that life among them can never be anything except difficult and exacting.

While the Arapesh feel their major joys and chief trials as coming to them from others, they nevertheless do not feel themselves as trapped and persecuted, victims of a bad position and a poor environment. Instead, they see all life as an adventure in growing things, growing children, growing pigs, growing yams and taros and coconuts and sago, faithfully, carefully, observing all of the rules that make things grow. They retire happily in middle age after years well spent in bringing up children and planting enough palm-trees to equip those children for life. The rules that govern growth are very simple. There are two incompatible goods in the world: those associated with sex and the reproductive functions of women; and those associated with food, growth, and the hunting and gardening activities of men, which owe their efficacy to supernatural aids, and to the purity and growth-giving aspects of male blood. These two goods must be kept from coming into too close contact. The duty of every child is to grow, the duty of every man and woman is to observe the rules so that the children and the food upon which the children depend will grow. Men are as wholly committed to this cherishing adventure as are women. It may be said that the rôle of men, like the rôle of women, is maternal.

2

a co-operative society

Arapesh life is organised about this central plot of the way men and women, physiologically different and possessed of differing potencies, unite in a common adventure that is primarily maternal, cherishing, and oriented away from the self towards the needs of the next generation. It is a culture in which men and women do different things for the same reasons, in which men are not expected to respond to one set of motivations and women to another, in which if men are given more authority it is because authority is a necessary evil that someone, and that one the freer partner, must carry. It is a culture in which if women are excluded from ceremonies, it is for the sake of the women themselves, not as a device to bolster up the pride of the men, who work desperately hard to keep the dangerous secrets that would make their wives ill and deform their unborn children. It is a society where a man conceives responsibility, leadership, public appearance, and the assumption of arrogance as onerous duties that are forced upon him, and from which he is only too glad to escape in middle years, as soon as his eldest child attains puberty. In order to understand a social order that substitutes responsiveness to the concerns of others, and attentiveness to the needs of others, for aggressiveness, initiative, competitiveness, and possessiveness—the familiar motivations upon which our culture depends—it is necessary to discuss in some detail the way in which Arapesh society is organised.

There are no political units. Clusters of villages are grouped into localities, and each locality and its inhabitants have names. These names are sometimes used rhetorically at feasts, or to refer to the region, but the localities themselves have no political organisation. Marriages, feasting organisations, and occasional semi-hostile clashes between neighbouring groups take place between hamlets or clusters of hamlets across locality lines. Each hamlet belongs theoretically to one patrilineal family line, which again has a name to distinguish it. The patrilineal families, or small localised clans, also possess hunting and gardening land, and located somewhere on their hunting-land is a water-hole or a quicksand or a steep waterfall that is inhabited by their *marsalai*, a supernatural who appears in the form of a mythical and bizarrely coloured snake or lizard, or occasionally as a larger animal. In the abode of the *marsalai* and along the borders of the ancestral lands live the ghosts of the clan dead, including the wives of the men of the clan, who after death continue to live with their husbands instead of returning to their own clan-lands.

The Arapesh do not conceive of themselves as owning these ancestral lands, but rather as belonging to the lands; in their attitude there is none of the proud possessiveness of the landowner who vigorously defends his rights against all comers. The land itself, the game animals, the timber trees, the sago, and especially the bread-fruit-trees, which are thought of as very old and dear to the ghosts—these all belong to the ghosts. For the feelings and attitudes of the ghosts the *marsalai* is a focusing-point. This being is not exactly an ancestor and not exactly not an ancestor—Arapesh casualness does not attempt to answer the question. The *marsalai* has a special touchiness about a few ritual points; he dislikes menstruating women, pregnant women, and men who come directly from intercourse with their wives. Such trespass he punishes with illness and death to the women or unborn children, unless he is specially placated by a mimic offering of a pig's tusk, an empty betel-sheath, a sago-container, and a taro-leaf, on which one of the ancestor souls will alight as a bird or a butterfly and absorb the spirit of the offering. The ghosts themselves are the residents of the lands, and a man going upon his own inherited land will announce himself, his name and relationship to them, remarking: "It is I, your grandson, of Kanehoibis. I have come to cut some posts for my house. Do not object to my presence, nor to my timber-cutting. As I return pluck back the brambles from my path, and bend back the branches so that I walk easily." This he must do even if he goes alone on the land that he has inherited from his forefathers. More often he has with him someone less directly connected, a relative or a brother-in-law, who is hunting with him or plans to make a garden on his land. Then introductions are in order. "See, my grandfathers, this is my brother-in-law, the husband of my sister. He comes to garden here with me. Treat him as your grandson, do not object to his being here. He is good." If these precautions are neglected, a hurricane will knock down the careless man's house or a landslip destroy his garden. Wind and rain and landslips are sent by the *marsalais*, who employ these means to discipline those who are careless about expressing the proper attitudes towards the land. In all of this there is none of the sense of ownership with which a man bids a stranger welcome to his land or proudly chops down a tree because it is his.

On a neighbouring hill-top, the village of Alipinagle was sadly depleted. In the next generation there would not be enough people to occupy the land. The people of Alitoa sighed: "Alas, poor Alipinagle, after the present people are gone, who will care for the land, who will there be beneath the trees? We must give them some children to adopt, that the land and the trees may have people when we are gone." Such generosity had, of course, the practical consequences of placing a child or so in a more advantageous position, but it was never phrased in this way, nor did the people recognise any formulations based upon possessive-ness about land. There was just one family in the locality that was possessive, and its attitude was incomprehensible to everyone else. Gerud, a popular young diviner and the eldest son of this family, once in a *séance* suggested as a motive for an alleged theft of dirt that the accused grudged to the children of a new-comer in the village a future share in the hunting-grounds. The rest of the community regarded his reasoning as little short of mad. Surely, people belonged to the land, not land to the people. As a correlate of this point of view, no one is at all particular as to where he lives, and as often as not members of a clan live not in their ances-tral hamlets, but in the hamlets of cousins or brothers-in-law. Without political organisation, without any fixed and arbitrary social rules, it is easy enough for people to do this.

As with residence sites, so with gardens. The Arapesh gar-dening is of two types: taro-gardens and banana-gardens, in which the men do the initial clearing, tree-lopping, and fencing, and the women do the planting, weeding, and harvesting; and yam-gardens, which with the exception of a little help rendered by women in weeding and in carrying the harvest are entirely men's work. Among many New Guinea tribes each married pair clears and fences a patch of land in their own inherited gardening-bush, and cultivates it more or less alone, with the help of their imma-ture children, perhaps calling in other relatives at the harvest. In this way a New Guinea garden becomes a private place, almost as private as a house, and is frequently used for copulation; it is their own place. A man or his wife can go to the garden every day, repair any gaps in the fencing, and so protect the garden from the inroads of bush animals. All the external circumstances of the Arapesh environment would suggest such a gardening method as exceedingly practical. The distances are long and the roads diffi-cult. People often have to sleep in their gardens because they are too far from other shelter, so they build small, badly thatched, uncomfortable huts on the ground, as it is not worth while to build a house on piles for one year's use. The steep slopes make fencing unsatisfactory and the pigs are always breaking in. Food is scarce and poor and it would seem likely that under these conditions of hardship and poverty people would be very possessive of and attentive to their own gardens. Instead the Arapesh have evolved a different and most extraordinary system, expensive in time and human effort, but conducive to the warm co-operation and sociability that they consider to be much more important.

Each man plants not one garden, but several, each one in co-operation with a different group of his relatives. In one of these gardens he is host, in the others he is guest. In each of these gardens three to six men, with one or two wives each, and sometimes a grown daughter or so, work together, fence together, clear together, weed together, harvest together, and while engaged in any large piece of work, sleep together, crowded up in the little inadequate shelter, with the rain dripping down the necks of more than half of the sleepers. These gardening groups are unstable—some individuals are unable to stand the strain of a bad crop; they tend to blame their gardening partners for it, and to seek new alliances the following year. Choice, now of one piece of long-fallow ground, now of another, sometimes makes next year's gardening-plot too far away for some of those who planted together last year. But each year a man's food-stakes lie not in one plot directly under his control, but scattered about, beneath the ghosts and on the land of his relatives, three miles in one direction, five miles in another.

This arrangement of work has several results. No two gardens are planted at the same time and therefore the Arapesh lack the "time hungry" so characteristic of yam-raising peoples where all of the yam-gardens are planted simultaneously. Where several men work together to clear and fence one plot before scattering to co-operate in clearing and fencing other plots, the harvests succeed each other. This method of gardening is not based upon the slightest physical need for co-operative labour. Tall trees are simply ringed, not felled, and the branches are cut off to let in light, so that a garden looks like an army of ghosts, white against the surrounding deep-green of the bush. The fencing is done with saplings that an adolescent boy could cut. But the preference is strong for working in small happy groups in which one man is host and may feast his guest workers with a little meat—if he finds it. And so the people go up and down the mountain sides, from one plot to another, weeding here, staking vines there, harvesting in another spot, called hither and thither by the demands of gardens in different states of maturity.

This same lack of individualism obtains in the planting of coconut-trees. A man plants such trees for his young sons, but not upon his own land. Instead, he will walk four or five miles carrying a sprouting coconut in order to plant it by the doorstep of his uncle, or of his brother-in-law. A census of the palm-trees in any village reveals a bewildering number of distantly residing owners and bears no relation to the actual residents. In the same way, men who are friends will plant new sago-palms together, and in the next generation their sons become a working unit.

In hunting, too, a man does not hunt alone, but with a companion, sometimes a brother, as often a cousin or a brother-in-law; the bush, the ghosts, and the *marsalai* belong to one of the pair or trio. The man, be he host or guest, who sees the game first claims it, and the only tact that is necessary here is the tact of not seeing game very much more often than other people do. Men who make a practice of always claiming first sight are left to hunt by themselves, and may develop into far better hunters, with increasingly unsocial characters. Such a man was Sumali, my self-nominated father, who in spite of his skill was little esteemed in co-operative enterprises. It was his son who divined stinginess about hunting-lands as a motive for imputed sorcery; and when Sumali's house burned accidentally to the ground, Sumali attributed the accident to jealousy over land. His traps yielded more than the traps of anyone else in the region, his tracking skill was greatest and his aim most accurate, but he hunted alone, or with his young sons, and presented his game to his relatives almost as formally as he might have presented it to strangers.

It is the same also with house-building. The houses are so small that they actually require very little communal labour. Materials from one house or several dilapidated houses are reassembled into another house; people take their houses down and rebuild them in another orientation; there is no attempt made to cut the rafters the same length or to saw off the ridge-pole if it is too long for the projected house—if it does not fit this house it will undoubtedly fit the next one. But no man, except one who has failed to help with the house-building of others, builds alone. A man announces his intention of building a house, and perhaps makes a small feast for raising the ridge-pole. Then his brothers and his cousins and his uncles, as they go about the bush upon their several errands, bear his partly completed house in mind, and stop to gather a bundle of creeper to bind the roof, or a bunch of sago-leaves for the thatching. These contributions they bring to the new house when they pass that way, and gradu-ally, casually, a little at a time, the house is built, out of the uncounted labour of many.

But this loosely co-operative fashion in which all work, even the routine of everyday gardening and hunting, is organised means that no man is master of his own plans for many hours together. If anything, he is less able to plan and carry through any consecutive activities than are the women, who at least know that meals and firewood and water must be provided each day. The men spend over nine-tenths of their time responding to other people's plans, digging in other people's gardens, going on hunt-ing-parties initiated by others. The whole emphasis of their eco-nomic lives is that of participation in activities others have initiated, and only rarely and shyly does anyone tentatively sug-gest a plan of his own.

This emphasis is one factor in the lack of political organisa-tion. Where all are trained to a quick responsiveness to any plan, and mild ostracism is sufficient to prod the laggard into co-operation, leadership presents a different problem from that in a society where each man pits his own aggressiveness against that of another. If there is a weighty matter to be decided, one that may involve the hamlet or a cluster of hamlets in a brawl or accusations of sorcery, then the decision is arrived at in a quiet, roundabout, and wholly characteristic fashion. Suppose for instance that a young man finds that a pig belonging to a distant village has strayed into his garden. The pig is a trespasser, meat is scarce, he would like to kill it. But would it be wise to do so? Judgment must be made in terms of all kinds of relationships with the pig's owners. Is a feast pending? Or is a betrothal still unsettled? Does some member of his own group depend upon the pig's owner for assistance in some ceremonial plan? All these things the young man has not the judgment to decide. He goes to his elder brother. If his elder brother sees no objection to killing the pig, the two will take counsel with other elder male relatives, until finally one of the oldest and most respected men of the community is consulted. Of such men every locality with a population of one hundred and fifty to two hundred has one or two. If the big man gives his approval, the pig is killed and eaten and no censure will fall upon the young man from his elders; everyone will stand together to defend their bit of legal piracy.

Warfare is practically unknown among the Arapesh. There is no head-hunting tradition, no feeling that to be brave or manly one must kill. Indeed, those who have killed men are looked upon with a certain amount of discomfort, as men slightly apart. It is they who must perform the purificatory ceremonies over a new killer. The feeling towards a murderer and that towards a man who kills in battle are not essentially different. There are no insignia of any sort for the brave. There is only a modicum of protective magic which can be used by those who are going into a fight: they may scrape a little dust from their fathers' bones and eat it with areca-nut and magic herbs. But although actual warfare—organised expeditions to plunder, conquer, kill, or attain glory—is absent, brawls and clashes between villages do occur, mainly over women. The marriage system is such that even the most barefaced elopement of a betrothed or married woman must be phrased as an abduction and, since an abduction is an unfriendly act on the part of another group, must be avenged. This feeling for righting the balance, for paying back evil for evil, not in greater measure, but in exact measure, is very strong among the Arapesh. The beginning of hostilities they regard as an unfortunate accident; abductions of women are really the result of marital disagreements and the formation of new personal attachments, and are not unfriendly acts on the part of the next community. So also with pigs, since people attempt to keep their pigs at home. If the pigs stray, it is a bad accident, but if a pig is killed, it should be avenged.

All such clashes between hamlets start in angry conversation, the aggrieved party coming, armed but not committed to fighting, into the village of the offenders. An altercation follows; the offenders may justify or excuse their conduct, disclaim any knowledge of the elopement, or deny having known the owner-ship of the pig—it had not had its tail cut yet, how could they know it was not a bush pig? and so on. If the aggrieved party is protesting more as a matter of form than from real anger, the meeting may end in a few harsh words. Alternatively, it may progress from reproach to insult, until the most volatile and eas-ily angered person hurls a spear. This is not a signal for a general fracas; instead everyone notes carefully where the spear—which is never thrown to kill—hits, and the next most volatile person of the opposite party throws a spear back at the man who hurled the first one. This in turn is recorded during a moment of attention, and a return spear thrown. Each reprisal is phrased as a matter of definite choice: "Then Yabinigi threw a spear. He hit my cross-cousin in the wrist. I was angry because my cross-cousin was hit and I threw a spear back and hit Yabinigi in the ankle. Then the mother's brother of Yabinigi, enraged that his sister's son had been wounded, drew back his arm and hurled a spear at me which missed," and so on. This serial and carefully recorded exchange of spears in which the aim is to wound lightly, not to kill, goes on until someone is rather badly wounded, when the members of the attacking party immediately take to their heels. Later, peace is made by an interchange of rings, each man giving a ring to the man whom he has wounded.

If, as occasionally happens, someone is killed in one of these clashes, every attempt is made to disavow any intention to kill: the killer's hand slipped; it was because of the sorcery of the Plainsmen. Almost always those on the other side are called by kinship terms, and surely no man would willingly have killed a relative. If the relative killed is a near one, an uncle or a first cousin, the assumption that it was unintentional and due to sorcery is regarded as established, and the killer is commiserated with and permitted to mourn whole-heartedly with the rest. If the relative is more distant, and the possibility of genuine intent more open, the killer may flee to another community. No blood feud will follow, although there may be an attempt to subsidise the sorcery of the Plainsmen against him. But in general sorcery deaths are avenged with sorcery deaths, and all killings within the locality or within avenging distance are regarded as too aberrant, too unexpected and inexplicable, for the community to deal with them. And each man who is wounded in a fight has a further penalty to pay, for he must reimburse his mother's brothers, and his mother's brothers' sons, for his own shed blood. All blood comes to the child from its mother; it is therefore the property of the mother's group. The mother's brother has the right to shed a sister's son's blood; it is he who must open a boil, he who scarifies the adolescent girl. So the man who is injured in any way suffers not only in his person but in his supply of valuables: he must pay for having been in any scene in which he is injured. This sanction is extended to cover injuries in hunting, and involvement in a shameful situation.

The general policy of Arapesh society is to punish those who are indiscreet enough to get involved in any kind of violent or disreputable scene, those who are careless enough to get hurt in hunting, or stupid enough to let themselves become the butt of public vituperation from their wives. In this society unaccustomed to violence, which assumes that all men are mild and cooperative and is always surprised by the individuals who fail to be so, there are no sanctions to deal with the violent man. But it is felt that those who stupidly and carelessly provoke violence can be kept in order. In mild cases of offence, as when a man has been one member of a fighting group, his individual mother's brother calls out for payment. After all, the poor sister's son has already suffered a wound and loss of blood. But if instead he has got himself involved in an undignified public disputation with a wife, or with a young relative who has been overheard by others to insult him, then the whole men's group of the hamlet or cluster of hamlets may act, still instigated by the mother's brothers, who are the official executors of the punishment. The men's group will take the sacred flutes, the voice of the *tamberan*—the supernatural monster who is the patron of the men's cult—and going by night to the house of the offender, play his wife and himself off the premises, break into his house, litter his house-floor with leaves and rubbish, cut down an areca-palm or so, and depart. If the man has been steadily falling in the esteem of the community, if he has been unco-operative, given to sorcery, bad-tempered, they may take up his fire-place and dump it out, which is practically equivalent to saying that they can dispense with his presence—for a month at least. The victim, deeply shamed by this procedure, flees to distant relatives and does not return until he has obtained a pig with which to feast the community, and so wipe out his offence.

But against the really violent man the community has no redress. Such men fill their fellows with a kind of amazed awe; if crossed they threaten to burn down their houses, break all their pots and rings, and leave that part of the country for ever. Their relatives and neighbours, aghast at the prospect of being deserted in this way, beseech the violent man not to leave them, not to desert them, not to destroy his own property, and placate him by giving him what he wishes. It is only because the whole education of the Arapesh tends to minimise violence and confuse the motivations of the violent that the society is able to operate by disciplining those who provoke and suffer from violence rather than those who actually perpetrate it.

With work a matter of amiable co-operation, and the slight warfare so slenderly organised, the only other need that the community has for leadership is for carrying out large-scale ceremonial operations. Without any leadership whatsoever, with no rewards beyond the daily pleasure of eating a little food and singing a few songs with one's fellows, the society could get along very comfortably, but there would be no ceremonial occasions. And the problem of social engineering is conceived by the Arapesh not as the need to limit aggression and curb acquisitiveness, but as the need to force a few of the more capable and gifted men into taking, against their will, enough responsibility and leadership so that occasionally, every three or four years or at even rarer intervals, a really exciting ceremonial may be organised. No one, it is assumed, really wants to be a leader, a "big man." "Big men" have to plan, have to initiate exchanges, have to strut and swagger and talk in loud voices, have to boast of what they have done in the past and are going to do in the future. All of this the Arapesh regard as most uncongenial, difficult behaviour, the kind of behaviour in which no normal man would indulge if he could possibly avoid it. It is a rôle that the society forces upon a few men in certain recognised ways.

While boys are in their early teens, their elders tend to classify their potentialities to become "big men." Native capacity is roughly divided into three categories: "those whose ears are open and whose throats are open," who are the most gifted, the men who understand the culture and are able to make their understanding articulate; "those whose ears are open and whose throats are shut," useful quiet men who are wise but shy and inarticulate; and a group of the two least useful kinds of people, "those whose ears are closed but whose throats are open" and "those whose ears and throats are both shut." A boy of the first class is specially trained by being assigned in early adolescence a *buanyin*, or exchange partner, from among the young males of a clan in which one of his elder male relatives has a *buanyin*. This *buanyin* relationship is a reciprocal feast-giving relationship between pairs of males, members of different clans, and preferably of opposite dual organisation membership—which is loosely hereditary. It is a social institution that develops aggressiveness and encourages the rare competitive spirit. It is the duty of *buanyins* to insult each other whenever they meet, to inquire sneeringly whether the other *buanyin* ever means to make anything of his life—has he no pigs, no yams, has he no luck in hunting, has he no trade-friends and no relatives, that he never gives feasts or organises a ceremony? Was he born head first like a normal human being, or perhaps he came feet first from his mother's womb? The *buanyin* relationship is also a training-ground in the kind of hardness that a big man must have, which in an ordinary Arapesh is regarded as undesirable.

The functioning of this *buanyin* relationship must be understood against Arapesh attitudes about the exchange of food. To a people who disguise all their trading as voluntary and casual gift-giving, any rigid accounting is uncongenial. As with trading from village to village, so it is in all exchange between relatives. The ideal distribution of food is for each person to eat food grown by another, eat game killed by another, eat pork from pigs that not only are not his own but have been fed by people at such a distance that their very names are unknown. Under the guidance of this ideal, an Arapesh man hunts only to send most of his kill to his mother's brother, his cousin, or his father-in-law. The lowest man in the community, the man who is believed to be so far outside the moral pale that there is no use reasoning with him, is the man who eats his own kill—even though that kill be a tiny bird, hardly a mouthful in all.

There is no encouragement given to any individual to build up a surplus of yams, the strong reliable crop that can be stored and the increase of which depends upon the conservation of seed. Anyone whose yam crop is conspicuously larger than his neighbor's is graciously permitted to give an *abūllū*, a special feast at which, having painted his yams in bright colours and having laid them out on a ratan measuring-tape, which he may keep as a trophy, all of his yams are given away for seed. His relatives and neighbours come bringing a return gift of their own selection, and carry away a bag of seed. Of this seed he may never eat; even when it has multiplied in the fourth or fifth generation, a careful record is kept. In this way, the good luck or the better gardening of one man does not redound to his personal gain, but is socialised, and the store of seed-yams of the entire community is increased.

From all of this socialised treatment of food and property, this non-competitive, unaccounted, easy give and take, the *buanyin* partnership pattern stands out. Within it are definitely encouraged all the virtues of a competitive, cost-accounting system. A *buanyin* does not wait for the stimulus of an insult given in anger; he insults his *buanyin* as a matter of course. He does not merely share with him of his abundance, but he definitely raises pigs or hunts game in order to give it publicly and ostentatiously to his *buanyin*, accompanied by a few well-chosen insults as to his *buanyin's* inability to repay the gift. Careful accounting is kept of every piece of pig or haunch of kangaroo, and a bundle of coconut-leaf rib is used to denote these in the public altercation during which *buanyins* dun each other. Most astonishing of all is the definite convention of stinginess between *buanyins*. A generous *buanyin* will set aside a special basket of choice entrails and his wife will give it secretly to his *buanyin's* wife, after a feast. For this there need be no return. But while good behaviour is expected everywhere else in social life, people are reconciled to their *buanyins'* neglecting to make this generous gesture.

Thus in a society where the norm for men is to be gentle, unacquisitive, and co-operative, where no man reckons up the debts that another owes him, and each man hunts that others may eat, there is definite training for the special contrasting behaviour that "big men" must display. The young men on the way to become big men suffer continual pressure from their elders, as well as from their *buanyins*. They are urged to assume the responsibility of organising the preliminary feasts that will finally culminate in a big initiation ceremony or the purchase of a new dance-complex from the beach. And a few of them yield to all this pressure, learn to stamp their feet and count their pigs, to plant special gardens and organise hunting-parties, and to maintain the long-time planning over several years that is necessary in order to give a ceremony which lasts no longer than a day or so. But when his eldest child reaches puberty, the big man can retire; he need no longer stamp and shout, he need no longer go about to feasts looking for opportunities to insult his *buanyin;* he can stay quietly at home, guiding and educating his children, gardening, and arranging his children's marriages. He can retire from the active competitive life that his society assumes, usually correctly, to be eminently uncongenial and distasteful to him.

3

the birth of an
Arapesh child

The procreative task of an Arapesh father is not finished with impregnation. The Arapesh have no idea that after the initial act which establishes physiological paternity, the father can go away and return nine months later to find his wife safely delivered of a child. Such a form of parenthood they would consider impossible, and furthermore, repellent. For the child is not the product of a moment's passion, but is made by both father and mother, carefully, over time. The Arapesh distinguish two kinds of sex-activity, play, which is all sex-activity that is not known to have induced the growth of a child, and work, purposive sex-activity directed towards making a particular child, towards feeding it and shaping it during the first weeks in the mother's womb. Here the father's task is equal with the mother's; the child is product of father's semen and mother's blood, combined in equal amounts at the start, to form a new human being. When the mother's breasts show the characteristic swelling and discolouration of pregnancy, then the child is said to be finished—a perfect egg, it will now rest in the mother's womb. From this time on, all intercourse is forbidden, for the child must sleep undisturbed, placidly absorbing food that is good for it. The need of a gentle environment is emphasised throughout. The woman who wishes to conceive must be as passive as possible. Now as the guardian of the growing child, she must observe certain precautions: she must not eat the bandicoot or she will die in hard labour, for the bandicoot burrows too far into the ground, nor the frog, or the child will be born too suddenly, nor the eel, or the child will be born too soon. She must not eat sago that comes from a *marsalai* place, nor coconuts from a tree that has been tabooed by the *tamberan*, the supernatural patron of the men's cult. If the woman wants the child to be male, other women will tell her never to cut anything in half, for this cutting will produce a female.

Morning-sickness during pregnancy is unknown. During all the nine months, the unborn child sleeps. The child is said to grow like the chick in an egg; first there is just blood and semen, then the arms and legs emerge and finally the head. When the head is loosened, the child is born. No one recognises that a child may show signs of life until just before birth, when the child turns over and so produces the first labour-pain.

At the moment of birth the father cannot be present, because of the beliefs that the Arapesh hold concerning the antithetical nature of the physiological functions of women and the magical food-getting functions of men. The blood of birth, like menstrual blood, is dangerous, and the child must be delivered well outside the village. Nevertheless, the verb to "bear a child" is used indiscriminately of either a man or a woman, and child-bearing is believed to be as heavy a drain upon the man as upon the woman, particularly because of the strenuous and exacting sexual activity demanded of the father during the first few weeks after the cessation of menstruation. While the child is being delivered, the father waits within ear-shot until its sex is determined, when the midwives call it out to him. To this information he answers laconically, "Wash it" or "Do not wash it." If the command is "Wash it," the child is to be brought up. In a few cases when the child is a girl and there are already several girl-children in the family, the child will not be saved, but left, unwashed, with the cord uncut, in the bark basin on which the delivery takes place. The Arapesh prefer boys; a boy will stay with his parents and be the joy and comfort of their old age. If after one or two girls have been kept another is also preserved, the chance of having a son is much further postponed, and so, having no contraceptives, the Arapesh sometimes resort to infanticide. Sometimes also when food is scarce, or if there are several children, or if the father is dead, a new-born infant may not be kept, as it is felt that its chances of health and growth are slight.

After the infant is washed, and the afterbirth and cord are disposed of—placed high in a tree because a pig that ate them would become a garden thief—the mother and child are brought up into the village, and sheltered in a small house on the ground. The earth floor of the village is intermediate between the "bad place" and the house-floor of a regular dwelling-house, which cannot be entered by people who are in a special state—the parents of a new-born child, mourners, a man who has shed blood, and so forth. The father now comes to share his wife's task of caring for the new-born child. He brings her a bundle of soft, flannel-like leaves with which she can line the little net bag in which the child is suspended most of its waking hours, in a pre-natal hunched position. He brings her a coconut-shell of water in which to bathe the baby, and special pungent-smelling leaves that will keep evil influences from the hut. He brings his little wooden pillow, which men use to protect their elaborate head-dresses during sleep, and lies down by his wife's side. He is now, in native phrasing, "in bed having a baby." The new life is now as closely joined to his as it is to the mother's. The life-soul that stirs softly beneath the infant's breastbone and which will remain there until old age, unless the machinations of black magic, or the outraged taboo of some *marsalai*, tempts it to rise and with a chocking catch pass out of the body—this life-soul may have come from either father or mother. Later the people will look at the child's face and compare it with its parents, and know

whether the life-soul was given by the father or by the mother.
But it does not really matter, the soul can come as easily from one
parent as from the other; the facial resemblance merely points out
which way it came.

The father lies quietly beside his new-born child, from time
to time giving the mother little bits of advice. He and she fast
together for the first day. They may not smoke or drink water.
From time to time they perform small magical rites that will
ensure the child's welfare and their ability to care for it. The wives
of the father's brother are the official nurses. They bring in the
materials for the magic. Now it is a long peeled rod. The father
calls in some of the children who are loitering about the hut, anxious for a glimpse of the new baby. He rubs the rod over their
strong little backs. Then he rubs the rod against the infant's back,
reciting a charm:

> I give you vertebrae,
>   one from a pig,
>   one from a snake,
>   one from a human being,
>   one from a tree-snake,
>   one from a python,
>   one from a viper,
>   one from a child.

Then he breaks the rod into six small pieces, which are hung up
in the house. This ensures that even should the father's foot break
a twig as he walks about, the infant's back will not suffer. Next he
takes a large yam and cuts it into small pieces. Each piece he
names after a small boy of the hamlet: Dobomugau, Segenamoya,
Midjulamon, Nigimarib. His wife then takes up the tale, and
beginning at the other end she names each piece after a small girl:
Amus, Yabiok, Anyuai, Miduain, Kumati. Then the father
throws the bits of yams away. This charm ensures that the infant

will be hospitable and kindly towards other people; it is for this reason that the names of the neighbour's children are used.

The father of a first child is in an especially delicate position, more delicate than is the mother. For a woman the ceremonies are the same for a first child or for a fifth, for a boy or for a girl; it is the behaviour of the father that is adjusted to these differences. A man who bears a first child is in as precarious a state as a newly initiated boy or a man who has killed for the first time in battle. From this state he can only be purified by a man who has previously borne children, and this man will become his sponsor and perform the necessary ceremony. After a five-day period during which he remains in strict seclusion with his wife, not touching tobacco with his hands, using a stick to scratch his person, and eating all food with a spoon, he is taken to the water-side, where a little leaf house, gaily ornamented with red flowers and the herbs appropriate to yam magic, has been built. This little house is built near a pool, and in the bottom of the pool a large white ring, called ritually an "eel," is placed. The father of the new child and his sponsor go down to the pool, where the father ritually cleans his mouth on a ring that his sponsor hands him. Then the father drinks from the pool, in which a number of aromatic and fragrant herbs have been steeped, and bathes his entire body with the water. He enters the water and successfully captures the eel, which he returns to his sponsor. The eel is closely connected symbolically with the phallus, and is a special taboo of boys during their growth and initiation periods. The ceremony might be said to symbolise the regaining of the father's masculine nature after his important share in feminine functions, but if this is the meaning, it is no longer explicit in the minds of the natives, who regard it merely as a necessary ritual detail in the ceremony. The sponsor then anoints the head of the new father with a special white paint, with which the forehead of an adolescent is also anointed. Now the new father is become one of those who have successfully borne a child.

But his maternal tasks are not yet over. During the next few days, he and his wife perform the ceremonies that free them from all of the taboos except that upon eating meat. Tobacco and areca-nut are distributed to all who come to visit the baby—to the men by the father, to the women by the mother—and all who receive these gifts from the hands of the new parents are pledged to help them in any future undertaking, and thus the new baby's welfare is further assured. The wife performs a special ceremony which will ensure that her cooking will not be injured by the experience through which she has just passed. She makes a mock vegetable-pudding from inedible, coarse wild greens, and this is thrown away so that the pigs will eat it. Finally, the couple go back up into their house, and after a month or so, they make the feast that lifts the taboo on eating meat, and at the same time make a feast for the midwife and the other women who fed them during their confinement. The father and mother may now walk about as freely as they like, but it is not good to carry the baby about until it laughs. When it laughs up into its father's face, it is given a name, the name of some member of the father's clan.

Still the child's life depends upon the constant special attention of the father as well as the mother. The father must sleep each night with the mother and baby, and there is a strict taboo on intercourse, not only with the mother of the child, but also, if he has two wives, with his other wife. Extra-marital intercourse would be dangerous also. For while frequency of intercourse between its parents is believed to be necessary to the child's growth during the first weeks of its pre-natal life, once it is firmly constructed all contact with sex, on the part of either parent, is believed to be harmful to the child until it is about a year old. If a child is puny and ailing or if its bones are weak and it fails to walk quickly, this is the fault of its parents, who have not observed the taboo. But it is seldom believed that parents actually do infringe the taboo; when they elect to keep the child they know what bringing it up involves. There is an instance in a folk-tale of a mother who insisted upon keeping a child although the father wished it destroyed, but the people's comment on this incident was that such behaviour was all very well in the time of the *marsalais*, that is, in the mythical time of long ago, but that nowadays it would be foolish behaviour because the child could not live unless the father actively co-operated in its care, so to what purpose would the mother save a child's life initially only to see it perish for want of its father's solicitude?

The Arapesh keep the taboo upon intercourse until the child takes its first steps, then it is regarded as sufficiently strong to be able to stand the trying contact with its parents' sexuality again. The mother continues to suckle the child until it is three or even four, if she does not become pregnant again. The taboo is lifted after a period of menstrual seclusion. The mother returns from the menstrual hut, and both father and mother spend a day in fasting. After this they may have intercourse and the husband may sleep with his other wife if he wishes; his immediate nightly presence is no longer essential to the child. (Sometimes, of course, the father has had to leave the child and go on expeditions too distant and too dangerous for mother and infant to accompany him; but these absences are not believed to jeopardise the child's health, unless it was sex that kept the father away.) The Arapesh are perfectly self-conscious about the value of these taboos in regulating pregnancy. It is desirable that women should not have children too close together; it is too hard for them, and one child has to be forcibly weaned because another is soon to follow. The ideal is for the child to learn to eat more and more solid food, to seek its mother's breast less often for food and more often merely in affection, insecurity, or pain, until finally only fear and pain will drive it into its mother's arms. But if the mother becomes pregnant, a child may have to be weaned at two. This is done by smearing the nipples with mud, which the child is told, with every strongly pantomimed expression of disgust, is faeces. I had an opportunity to observe closely only two children who had been weaned in this way; both were boys. One of them, a boy of two and a half, had transferred all his dependence to his father, who had assumed the principal care of him; the other, Naguel, was extraordinarily detached from his parents, and at seven wandered about looking for substitute parents in a desolate, miserable fashion that was markedly uncharacteristic of Arapesh children. Two cases are of course not sufficient for any conclusions, but it is worth while remarking that Arapesh parents feel the abrupt weaning to be cruel, and likely to affect the child's growth adversely. They feel guilty over having precipitated a situation unfavorable to the child, and this guilt itself may change the parent-child relationship, making the father, for instance, extra solicitous, as was true of Bischu, the father of the younger child, or particularly overcritical and harsh, which was Kule's attitude to the wretched little Naguel. The parents who have, by their strict self-control, assured the child its full share of its mother's breast, on the other hand, feel virtuous and easy. And this is the typical Arapesh parental attitude. When the child is gradually weaned, the mother feels no guilt in saying to her lusty three-year-old: "You, child, have had enough of milk. See, I am getting all worn out with feeding you. And you are far too heavy to carry about with me everywhere. Here, eat this taro and hush your wailing."

When the Arapesh are questioned as to the division of labour, they answer: Cooking everyday food, bringing firewood and water, weeding and carrying—these are women's work; cooking ceremonial food, carrying pigs and heavy logs, house-building, sewing thatch, clearing and fencing, carving, hunting, and growing yams—these are men's work; making ornaments and the care of children—these are the work of both men and women. If the wife's task is the more urgent—if there are no greens for the evening meal, or a haunch of meat must be carried to a neighbour in the next village—the husband stays at home and takes care of the baby. He is as pleased with and as uncritical of his child as is his wife. One may find at one end of a hamlet a child screaming with rage and a proud father who remarks: "See, my child cries all the time. It is strong, and lusty, just like me," and at the other end a two-year-old stoically suffering a splinter to be painfully extracted from its forehead, while its father remarks, with equal pride: "See, my child never cries. It is strong, just as I am."

Fathers show as little embarrassment as mothers in disposing of the very young child's excreta, and as much patience as their wives in persuading a young child to eat soup from one of the clumsy coconut spoons that are always too large for the child's mouth. The minute day-by-day care of little children, with its routine, its exasperations, its wails of misery that cannot be correctly interpreted, these are as congenial to the Arapesh men as they are to the Arapesh women. And in recognition of this care, as well as in recognition of the father's initial contribution, if one comments upon a middle-aged man as good-looking, the people answer: "Good-looking? Ye-e-s? But you should have seen him before he bore all those children."

4

early influences that mould
the Arapesh personality

How is the Arapesh baby moulded and shaped into the easy, gentle, receptive personality that is the Arapesh adult? What are the determinative factors in the early training of the child which assures that it will be placid and contented, unaggressive and non-initiatory, non-competitive and responsive, warm, docile, and trusting? It is true that in any simple and homogeneous society the children will as adults show the same general personality-traits that their parents have shown before them. But this is not a matter of simple imitation. A more delicate and precise relationship obtains between the way in which the child is fed, put to sleep, disciplined, taught self-control, petted, punished, and encouraged, and the final adult adjustment. Furthermore, the way in which men and women treat their children is one of the most significant things about the adult personality of any people, and one of the points at which contrasts between the sexes come out most sharply. We can only understand the Arapesh, and the warm and maternal temperament of both men and women, if we understand their childhood experience and the experience to which they in turn subject their children.

During its first months the child is never far from someone's arms. When the mother walks about she carries the baby suspended from her forehead in its special small net bag, or suspended under one breast in a bark-cloth sling. This latter method is the beach custom, the net-bag carrier belongs to the Plains, and the mountain women use both, depending in great part upon the health of the child. If the child is fretful and irritable, it is carried in the sling, where it can be given the comforting breast as swiftly as possible. A child's crying is a tragedy to be avoided at any cost, and this attitude is carried over into later life. The most trying period for the mother is when her child of three or so is too old to be comforted by the breast and too young and inarticulate to state clearly the reasons for its weeping. Children are held a great deal, often in a standing position so that they can push with their feet against the arms or legs of the person who holds them. As a result infants can stand, steadied by their two hands, before they can sit alone. Suckled whenever they cry, never left far distant from some woman who can give them the breast if necessary, sleeping usually in close contact with the mother's body, either hung in a thin net bag against her back, crooked in her arm, or curled on her lap as she sits cooking or plaiting, the child has a continuous warm sensation of security. It is only subjected to two shocks, and both of these have their reverberations in later personality development. After the first few weeks, during which it is bathed in a gingerly fashion with warmed water, the child is bathed under a jetting spout of cold water that is catapulted out upon it from a tipped bamboo water-carrier, a harsh, abrupt cold shock. Babies uniformly resent this treatment, and continue to hate the cold and the rain throughout their lives.* Also when an

---

*I do not suggest that the Arapesh dislike of the rain and the cold is entirely or even in major fashion caused by this practice, but it is interesting that the Tchambuli infants, who are bathed in the warm lake-water that hardly

infant urinates or defecates, the person holding it will jerk it quickly to one side to prevent soiling his or her own person. This jerk interrupts the normal course of excretion and angers the child. In later life, the Arapesh have notably low sphincter-control, and regard its loss as the normal concomitant of any highly charged situation.

For the rest the little baby's life is a very warm and happy one. It is never left alone; comforting human skin and comforting human voices are always beside it. Both little boys and little girls are enthusiastic about babies—there is always someone to hold the child. When the mother goes to the garden to work, she takes a small boy or girl along to hold the baby, instead of laying the baby down on a piece of bark or hanging it up for the morning in its little net bag. If the little nurse is a boy, he will hold the child in his arms, if a girl, she will wear the baby-bag on her back.

When the child begins to walk the quiet continuous rhythm of its life changes somewhat. It is now becoming a little heavy for the mother to carry about with her on long trips to the garden, and furthermore it can be expected to live without suckling for an hour or so. The mother leaves the child in the village with the father, or with some other relative, while she goes to the garden or for firewood. She returns often enough to a crying and disgruntled baby. Repentant, desirous of making restitution, she sits down and suckles the child for an hour. This rhythm, which begins as an hour's absence and an hour's compensatory suckling, develops into longer and longer periods, until by the time the child is three or so it is often being given a day's abstinence—supplemented, of course, by other food—followed by a day's nursing, in which the mother sits all day, holding the child on her lap, letting it suckle as it wishes, play about, suckle again, play with her breasts, gradually regain its sense of security. This is an

---

takes on a chill even after sunset, have none of the Arapesh dislike of the rain, and go about quite cheerfully in it all day long.

experience that the mother enjoys as much as the child. From the time the little child is old enough to play with her breasts, the mother takes an active part in the suckling process. She holds her breast in her hand and gently vibrates the nipple inside the child's lips. She blows in the child's ear, or tickles its ears, or playfully slaps its genitals, or tickles its toes. The child in turn plays little tattoos on its mother's body and its own, plays with one breast while suckling the other, teases the breast with its hands, plays with its own genitals, laughs and coos and makes a long, easy game of the suckling. Thus the whole matter of nourishment is made into an occasion of high affectivity and becomes a means by which the child develops and maintains a sensitivity to caresses in every part of its body. It is no question of a completely clothed infant being given a cool hard bottle and firmly persuaded to drink its milk and get to sleep at once so that the mother's aching arms can stop holding the bottle. Instead, nursing is, for mother and child, one long delightful and highly charged game, in which the easy warm affectivity of a lifetime is set up.

Meanwhile, as the child grows older it learns to substitute new delights for its mother's breasts during her ever lengthening absences. It learns to play with its lips. This play it sees all about it among the older children, and the older children also play with the baby's lips and so set the first part of the pattern that fits in so well with the child's temporary loneliness and hunger. Interestingly enough, no Arapesh child ever sucks its thumb or sucks one finger continuously.* But it engages in every other conceivable type of lip-play. It flicks its upper lip with its thumb, with its first finger, with its second finger; it blows out its cheeks and pounds them; it bubbles its lips with the palm of its hand, with the back of its hand; it tickles the inside of its lower lip with its tongue; it

---

*It is probable that thumb-sucking, absent among most primitive people, is a habit built up in the first few months of life, a period during which primitive children are almost always suckled whenever they cry.

licks its arms and its knees. A hundred different stylised ways of playing with the mouth are present in the play of the older children and gradually transmitted to the developing child.

This lip-play is the thread of behaviour which binds together the child's emotional life, which ties the happy security it felt in its yielding mother's arms to placid enjoyment of the long evenings by the fireside among its elders, and finally to a contented, unspecific sexual life. The Arapesh themselves regard playing with the lips as the symbol of childhood. Young boys and girls who tell legends that properly should only be told by grown-up people are warned to bubble their lips afterwards so that their hair will not become prematurely grey. And boys who have been initiated are told by the older men to cease playing with their lips; are they still children that they should do so? At the same time they are permitted to substitute betel-chewing and smoking, so that the lips, so long accustomed to constant stimulation, shall not be lonely. But the girls are permitted to bubble their lips until they have borne children, and we shall see how this fits in with the way in which the women's development is accounted slower than the men's.

While the small child lies on its mother's lap, warm and glowing from her attention, she builds up in it a trust of the world, a receptive and welcoming attitude towards food, towards dogs and pigs, towards persons. She holds a piece of taro in her hand, and as the child suckles the mother remarks in a soft singsong voice, "Good taro, good taro, would you eat, would you eat, would you eat, a little taro, a little taro, a little taro," and when the child releases the breast for a moment, a bit of taro is slipped into its mouth. The dog or the little tame pig that thrusts an inquisitive nose under the mother's arm is held there, the child's skin and the dog's rubbed together, the mother gently rocking them both, and murmuring, "Good dog, good child, good dog, good, good, good." In the same way, all of the child's relatives are commended to its trust and the kinship words themselves are endowed with a happy content. Before the baby can be expected to understand what she says, the mother begins to murmur in its ear, pausing to blow softly between words: "This is your other mother (mother's sister), other mother, other mother. See your other mother. She is good. She brings you food. She smiles. She is good." So complete is this training that the words themselves come to carry so much reassurance that the child acts under their compulsion almost against the evidence of its senses. So when a two-year-old would run screaming from me, a stranger and of a strange colour, the mother could calm its fears by insisting that I was its mother's sister, or its father's sister, or its grandmother. The child who a moment before had been panting with terror would come and sit quietly in my lap, cuddling down in a safe world again.

No gradations of behaviour are forced upon the child except a very mild acknowledgement of difference in age. So a child will be bidden to run more swiftly on an errand for a grandfather than for a father; it will note the extra gentleness and sense of achievement and content with which its grandfather remarks: "I stay at home now and my grandchildren cluster about my house-ladder." The fact that it is second-born or third-born is quite often mentioned. "See, the second-born eats well, and the first-born sits and plays with its food," or, "The second-born goes now to work and the first-born sits quietly at home." Such remarks about its own position in the family and about the relative positions of its elders serve to stress the only point of differentiation to which the Arapesh pay much attention. For the rest, the child learns to trust and love and depend upon everyone whom it encounters. There is no one whom it does not call uncle, or brother, or cousin, or the comparable names for women. And because these terms are used with wide extensions and incomplete disregard of generations, even the gradations of age implied in them are blurred. The child in arms is already accustomed to being chucked under the chin and called playfully "my little grandfather" or "my fat little uncle." Relationships are further blurred by the Arapesh casualness that permits a man to call the eldest of a group of brothers and sister "uncle," the second "grandmother," and the third "son," depending upon the point of view from which he happens to be regarding his relationship at the moment. Or a man may call a woman "sister" and her husband "grandfather." In such a world, and a world where there is no special behaviour dictated between cousins or between brothers-in-law, where no one is shy of anyone else, and all relationships are tinged, with mutual trust and affection, with assurance of gifts of food, co-operation, and a shared life, naturally the young child does not make any clear distinctions.

And although the distinction between the sexes is clear in terminology, it is blurred in behaviour. The child does not learn that only its father and mother may sleep unchaperoned in a house, while an aunt or a cousin would shy away from such close contact with a relative of opposite sex. The Arapesh know nothing about such restrictions. An Arapesh boy is taught by his parents: "When you travel, in any house where there is a mother's sister, or a father's sister, or a female cousin, or a niece, or a sister-in-law, or a daughter-in-law, or a niece-in-law, there you may sleep in safety." The opposite point, that people to whom sex-relations are forbidden had better not be left alone together, is a point so foreign to the Arapesh that it never enters their heads.

Neither little girls nor little boys wear any clothes until they are four or five; they are taught to accept their physiological differences without any shame or embarrassment. Excretion is not a matter about which privacy is insisted upon for small children; indeed the adults merely go casually to the edge of the village— their attitude is characterised by shyness but hardly by shame. Women sleep naked at night, and as has been said before, men at all times wear their G-strings carelessly, pushing them aside to scratch themselves. Little children are taught to observe the rules of cleanliness not through the invocation of shame, but merely through expressions of disgust. This is highly developed in them, so that four- and five-year-olds will shudder away from such new substances as mucilage or green mould on leather. The more usual association of excretion with a vivid consciousness of the genitalia, and consequently of sex-differences, is very slightly developed.

Small children are not required to behave differently to children of their own sex and those of opposite sex. Four-year-olds can roll and tumble on the floor together without anyone's worrying as to how much bodily contact results. Thus there develops in the children an easy, happy-go-lucky familiarity with the bodies of both sexes, a familiarity uncomplicated by shame, coupled with a premium upon warm, all-over physical contact.

As the child grows older, it is no longer confined so closely to the care of its own parents. Children are lent about. An aunt comes to visit and takes home the four-year-old for a week's stay, handing him on to some other relative for eventual return to his parents. This means that a child learns to think of the world as filled with parents, not merely a place in which all of his safety and happiness depend upon the continuance of his relationship to his own particular parents. It widens his circle of trust, without, however, overgeneralising his affection. He does not see half a dozen mothers and half a dozen fathers all of the time, so that his own parents become blurred into a general parental picture. Instead, he sees his own parents most of all, and then other sets of parents, serially, in close intimacy, in the small compact family groups. The quick response of an Arapesh child to demonstrative affection is one of the ways in which this transfer from one household to another is effected. Half an hour's cuddling, and an Arapesh baby will follow one anywhere. Already trained to regard all the world as a safe place in which to wander, it follows happily the last member of the kind world who tickles its stomach, or scratches its always itching little back. Children wriggle about on the ground from one friendly adult to another, settling down beside anyone who pays definite attention to them.

There is no insistence at all upon children's growing up rapidly, or acquiring special skills or proficiencies, and there is a corresponding lack of techniques for training them physically. They are allowed to essay tasks far beyond their powers, to try to climb ladders and lose their nerve halfway up, to play with knives on which they will cut themselves if they are not constantly watched. There is one exception. Little girls are trained to carry; small bulky carrying-bags are placed on their heads while they are still so tiny that they themselves spend most of the time on the trail curled up in larger bags on their mothers' backs. They are permitted as a great favour to carry their parents' possessions, and learn to accept carrying as a proud badge of growing older. But with this one exception, the whole physical training of the children is informal. A baby tries to climb one of the notched logs that serve as house-ladders; overcome with fright, it screams. Someone immediately rushes forward to catch it. A child stumbles; it is picked up and cuddled. The result is that the child grows up with a sense of emotional security in the care of others, not in its own control over the environment. This is a cold, wet world, full of pitfalls, hidden roots in the path, stones over which small feet stumble. But there is always a kind hand, a gentle voice, to rescue one. Trust in those about one is all that is required. What one does one's self matters very little.

This whole attitude towards tools and the control of the body is reflected later in the casual and imperfect technical skills of the adults. The Arapesh have no well-defined techniques; even the knots with which they tie the parts of a house together are varied and made in different styles. When they measure a length, they almost always get it wrong, and far from correcting it, they adjust the rest of the structure to the one mistake. Their houses are carelessly and asymmetrically built. Their few handicrafts, mat-making, basket-making, arm-band and belt plaiting, are crude and imperfect. They constantly import beautifully made models and either degrade the design by crude copying, or give it up all together. No discipline of hand and eye has ever been given them.

Painting is perhaps the art in which they do best. A large impressionistic style of painting on large pieces of bark makes it possible for the specially gifted man to create, almost without a tradition, occasional charming designs. But such a man's skill has little permanent effect upon the people's lack of belief in their own abilities, their continuing dependence upon the artistic work of other peoples because they believe themselves incapable. At best the children are schooled in enthusiasm, in quick happy delight when a bright colour or a new tune is presented to them. This attitude they catch from the adults, whose response to a coloured picture from an American magazine is not "What is it?" but always "Oh, how lovely!"

The continual moving about from one place to another has its reverberation in the children's lives. They are not accustomed to large enough groups to play games; instead each child clings close to an adult or an older brother or sister. The long walks from one garden to another, or from garden-house to village, tire them out, and arrived at the end of the journey, while the mother cooks the supper and the father sits and gossips with the other men, the children sit about, bubbling their lips. Games are hardly ever played. Little children are only allowed to play with each other as long as they do not quarrel. The minute there is the slightest altercation the adult steps in. The aggressor—or both children if the other child resents the attack—is dragged off the scene of battle and held firmly. The angry child is allowed to kick and scream, to roll in the mud, to throw stones or firewood about on the ground, but he is not allowed to touch the other child. This habit of venting one's rage at others upon one's own surroundings persists into adult life. An angry man will spend an hour banging on a slit gong, or hacking with an ax at one of his own palm-trees.

The whole training of the little children is not to teach them to control emotion, but to see that its expression harms no one but themselves. In the case of girls, expression of anger is checked earlier. Their mothers make them pretty grass skirts that will be ruined by a tumble tantrum in the mud, and place on their heads net bags the contents of which it would be a pity to spill. As a result little girls control their fits of rage and crying much earlier than do little boys, who may roll and scream in the mud up to the age of fourteen or fifteen without any sense of shame. The sex-difference here is accentuated by two other points. When small boys are four or five they tend to transfer their major allegiance to their fathers; they follow them about, sleep in their arms at night, and are very dependent upon them. But a man can take a small child everywhere with him even less than a woman. So the small boy is more often deserted, rejected by the one upon whom he chiefly depends, and weeps in agony as his father starts off on a journey. As he grows a little older, his father will sometimes leave him, not to the care of his mother or his mother's cowife whom the child also calls mother, but to older brothers, and here he feels even more deserted. The slightest teasing on the older boy's part, especially a refusal of food, will send him into fits of weeping, followed by a fit of rage. The old traumatic situation when his mother left him alone for hours at a time seems to be reinstated, and he seeks by his childish fit of rage to produce the old sequel, a devoted and repentant parent. And he does in part succeed, for all, including the teasing brothers, are aghast at his misery, and do their best to reassure the child. Little girls, however, join the work of the family earlier; they are more involved with the care of young children, and as they seldom become primarily attached to their fathers, they do not suffer this second weaning. It is notable that the three small girls who did have temper tantrums like the boys were all daughters of fathers who had no sons, and therefore treated the little girls as sons. The inevitable occasions would arrive when the father had to go away hunting or trading, or searching for the sorcerer who was charming a relative to death. Then the small girls tore off their grass skirts and rolled in the mud with as good a will as their brothers. But usually girls are not subjected to a second weaning procedure of this sort unless after they are grown their husbands die, when as widows they go through the traumatic experience of loss of parenthood again, with sometimes violent emotional disturbance. But this experience does not come to every woman, and comes to no girl until much later in life.

Furthermore, as it is considered appropriate for big men to simulate anger and defiance in their public speeches, to wield a spear, stamp their feet, and shout, the little boy has a model of violent expression before him that the little girl lacks, and he is too young to know that the behaviour of the big man is, at least in theory, always merely a theatrical performance.

These temper tantrums are almost always motivated by some insecurity or rejection point. A child is refused a request, is not permitted to accompany someone, is given a push or spoken to roughly by an older child, is rebuked, or, most important of all, is refused food. The tantrums that follow a refusal of food are the most numerous and the most interesting because the child is not to be placated by a subsequent offer of food. The refusal of the longed-for coconut or piece of sugar-cane has set off a whole train of response, far in excess of any power that the mere food has to stop it, and the child may weep for an hour, the helpless victim of a repeat situation in which the parent is equally powerless. These tantrums over rejection serve to channel anger as response to a hostile act on the part of another, and the definite training against aggressiveness towards other children completes this pattern.

The parental disapproval of fighting among children is always reinforced by rebukes couched in terms of relationship: "Would you, the younger brother, hit him who is first-born?" "Would you, his father's sister's son, hit your mother's brother's son?" "It is not right that two cousins should struggle with one another like little dogs." Children get no schooling in accepting harshness, in what we are accustomed to call good sportsmanship, that willingness to take it on the chin which is believed to be more consonant with the masculine temperament in our society. Arapesh small boys are as protected from aggression and struggle, from rude disciplinary measures on the part of older children and irritated parents, as is the most tenderly reared and fragile little daughter among ourselves. As a result, Arapesh boys never develop "good sportsmanship"; their feelings are intolerably wounded by a blow, or even a harsh word. The slightest gibe is taken as an expression of unfriendliness, and grown men will burst into tears at an unfair accusation.

They carry into adult life the fear of any rift between associates. The culture has a few external symbolic ways in which a genuine rift can be expressed, public signs of a disagreement that can be set up to handle the situation without actual personal clash between the individuals concerned. These are seldom used. It sometimes happens, however, that a man finally decides that his wife is incapable of feeding pigs. This is a very serious decision, for feeding pigs is one of woman's crowning glories in social achievement. The situation is further complicated by the fact that it is never, or hardly ever, her own or her husband's pigs that she feeds, but rather a pig belonging to one of her relatives, or to one of her husband's relatives. Its death through sickness, or straying, or capture by a hawk or a python, is a major tragedy, and one for which the husband feels it necessary to discipline her. He does this, in case several such tragic deaths occur and it is apparent to all that she is unfitted to raise pigs, by placing a sign outside her door. Through a piece of bark that has been the pig's feeding-trough he thrusts a spear on which he ties a piece of yam, a piece of taro, and so on. Through the corners of the bark he thrusts arrows. Then everyone will know how he feels about the matter, but he need not discuss the matter with his wife, and if she sulks, she sulks at a situation that has become impersonal and formal. So between relatives who are really angry at each other, the more enraged fastens a mnemonic knot of croton-leaf and hangs it up in his own doorway, which means that he will never eat with his annoying relatives again. To remove this formal sign of breach, a pig must be killed by the person who originally fastened the knot. So also a *buonyin* who finds the *buonyin* relationship intolerable may sever it by placing a carved wooden bowl, with a rim of twigs around it, on the *agehu*, thus declaring the relationship at an end.

But all of these highly stylised methods of breaking off a relationship are rare; a man thinks a long time before taking such a drastic step and establishing a position that will be very uncomfortable to maintain and very expensive to withdraw from.

The fear and discomfort resulting from any expression of anger is further worked into the pattern of sorcery. An angry person may not hit another, he may not resort to any thoroughgoing abuse of another. But one may, in retaliation, take on for a moment the behaviour that is appropriate not to a relative and a member of the same locality, but to a Plainsman, a stranger and an enemy. Arapesh children grow up dividing the world into two great divisions: *relatives*, which division includes some three to four hundred people, all the members of their own locality, and those of villages in other localities which are connected with them or their relatives by marriage, and the long lines of the wives and children of their father's hereditary trade-friends; and *strangers* and *enemies*, usually formalised as *waribim*, Plainsmen, literally, "men from the river-lands." These Plainsmen play in the children's lives the dual rôle of the bogyman to be feared, and the enemy to be hated, mocked, outwitted, upon whom all the hostility that is disallowed in the group is actively displaced. Children hear the mutterings and cursing of their parents when the arrogant Plainsmen pass through; they hear death and misfortune laid to the sorcerers' doors. When they are only five or so they are cautioned: "Never leave any half-eaten food lying about in a place where there are strangers. If you break off a sugar-cane stem, be careful that no stranger sees you do it, or he will return and pick the butt and use it to sorcerise you. If you eat an areca-nut be careful not to throw part of the kernel away in the husk. If you eat the durable tough yam, eat it all; do not leave a piece that a stranger may seize and use against you. When you sleep in a house where there are strangers, lie with your face up, that none of your saliva may drip on the bark, later to be carried away and hidden by the enemy. If anyone gives you an opossum-bone to gnaw, keep the bone until you can hide it somewhere when no one is looking." And a little boy is given a palm-leaf basket, a little girl a tiny net bag in which to carry about these food leavings so that they may not fall into the hands of the stranger. This constant cautioning about "dirt" makes everyone in Arapesh culture obsessive on the subject. By eating, by chewing areca-nut, by smoking, by sex-intercourse, one is constantly having to relinquish some portion of one's person that may fall into the hands of strangers, and falling there cause one to fall ill, or die. Fear of illness, of death, of misfortune, is dramatised in this insistence upon care about one's dirt. The child is led to believe that hostility, itself a feeling that exists only between strangers, normally, regularly expresses itself in the theft and secreting of a bit of dirt. This conception which links fear and anger with a definite behaviour-pattern is compulsive in the adult life of the Arapesh.

Suppose that a brother injures a man, or a cousin uses him hardly, not as a relative would normally act but becoming for the moment the "enemy," the "stranger." The injured man has no sense of gradation to fall back upon; he has not been reared to a small circle of very friendly close relatives and slightly less friendly circle of less close relatives—to differential behaviour towards his brother and his brother-in-law. He knows only two categories of behaviour, that of a member of one's own wide and trusted group, and that of the enemy. The brother with whom he is angry enters for the moment the category of enemy, and he purloins his brother's dirt and gives it to the Plainsmen. Practically all of the dirt of mountain people that finds its way into the little caches of the Plains sorcerers is stolen not by these sorcerers, but by the mountain people themselves, by angry brothers and cousins and wives. This fact the mountain people know well enough. When they wish to locate which sorcerer's village probably holds the dirt of a sick man, they follow the line of hereditary trade-friends of the man to whom the sick man has most recently given cause for anger. But when a man dies, the death is not laid at the door of the man who stole the dirt. He is believed to have forgotten his anger long ago. It is attributed instead to the sorcerer, whose behaviour the angry man originally imitated, compulsively, during his rage at his friend.

So the lack of any intermediate expressions of annoyance and the existence of only two categories, complete friend or complete enemy, force the Arapesh to behave in a way that they themselves disown as invalid and intrusive, as the unexplained madness of a moment. And the lack of any kind of rough-and-tumble sport, any ordinary, lightly charged quarreling among children, makes an Arapesh particularly vulnerable when he meets with the slightest expression of anger. Fear and panic result, and the compulsive theft of dirt is only too likely to follow. When a man relates such an act, he does it without affectation, as he might describe an involuntary movement of his eyes in the presence of a bright light: "He opposed me. He took sides against me. He helped the people who carried off my mother. He said she might remain married to that man. He did not help me. I was staying with him in the house of my mother's brother. He ate a piece of kangaroo-meat. He laid down the bone. He forgot it. He stood up and went outside the house. My eyes saw that no one was looking. My hand reached out and took the bone. I hid it quickly in my basket. The next day I met on the road a man from Dunigi whom I called 'grandfather.' I gave it to him. I just gave it to him. I gave him no ring with it." (If a piece of dirt is given to a sorcerer without a fee, it is understood that he will make no immediate moves, but will wait for a retaining-fee either from the man who originally gave him the dirt or from some more recently angered person; this latter fee is practically non-existent, but is invoked as an alibi.) Such an account as this is given in a low, emotionless voice, without either pride or remorse, without any admission of genuine complicity. The pattern learned in early childhood has simply asserted itself as a whole.

To return again to the play-training of the children: as children grow older and play games, they play none that encourage aggressiveness or competition.* There are no races, no games with two sides. Instead they play at being opossums or at being kangaroos, or one is a sleeping cassowary that the others startle. Many of the games are like the kindergarten games of a very little children, singing games in which some simple pantomime like an imitation of sago-cutting accompanies the traditional words. And even these games are played very seldom. More often the times when children are together in large enough groups to make a game worth while are the occasions of a feast, there is dancing and adult ceremonial, and they find the rôle of spectatorship far more engrossing. This is a rôle to which their lip-bubbling has helped to reconcile them from earliest years. Also, as mere babies they danced on the shoulders of their mothers and aunts, all through the long night dances. In these dances, which celebrate the completion of some piece of work like a yam-harvest or a hunting-trip, the women prefer to dance with children on their shoulders, and so while the women sometimes dance and sometimes sit quietly smoking by the little fires, the little children are handed about from one dancing woman to another, and so dance the whole night through, bobbing up and down half-asleep on the swaying shoulders of the dancing women. Babies learn quite young to sleep astride the neck of an adult, supported by one hand grasped firmly by the adult's hand, adjusting themselves without waking to any movement that the adult makes. All of this early experience accustoms them to be part of the whole picture, to prefer to any active child-life of their own a passive part that is integrated with the life of the community.

In the life of children in groups there is one marked sex-difference that prevails throughout life. Little girls are mainly useful for carrying, weeding, gathering food, and carrying firewood. Whenever there is to be a harvest or a feast, all the small

---

*Football, played with a lime-fruit, is now being introduced by returned work-boys.

feminine relatives are requisitioned, and a whole bevy of little girls meet together to work hard for a day or so. This is practically the only time when they see each other, for on the actual occasions of the feasts they are even busier than on other working-occasions. After a day's carrying, with their small jaws shut tight and their foreheads glistening with sweat under the heavy loads, they are too tired even to gossip, and firm friends, aged eleven or twelve, fall asleep in each other's arms on the same bark bed, humming little tunes together. Crowds and work become closely associated in their minds, while easy conversation and freedom from too exacting labour are associated with the small group of close relatives, gathered about the evening fire in the "small hamlet," the residence village of the clan.

Boys have an exactly opposite experience. Their work lies not in groups but in accompanying a father or an elder brother on a hunting-expedition or into the bush to gather herbs or vines or to cut wood for house-building. One small boy and one or two older men is the pattern group for little boys' work. When there are no such expeditions on foot, then two or three or even more small boys may forgather to make toy bows and arrows and practise shooting at lizards or at targets made of bright orange fruit, to lay traps for rats, or to make rattles or pop-guns. Association with their own age-group is their most casual, happy time, and this may account for the greater restlessness of the men when they are long confined in a "small hamlet," their greater urge to be ever up and visiting their brothers and cousins. The men's greater desire to visit about is a constant cause of jesting reproach of the men by the women, and a man who is too fond of doing so will be nick-named "Walk-about" or "Never-sit-down" by his wives. One of the forms that slight nervous instability takes among the Arapesh is an oversensitivity to social situations; this may express itself either in the individual's becoming a hermit, and living in the heart of the bush, or in his eternally walking about from one festive occasion to another, unable to resist the sound of the most distant drums.

The training that children receive about property is one which encourages a respect for the property of others and a sense of easy security in the property of one's own family group, rather than any stronger sense of possessiveness. Children are rebuked if they injure the property of other people, and a gentle reiterative, "That is Balidu's, be careful of it. That is grandfather's, don't break it," will accompany a child's explorations on the premises of others. But the counter-remark, "That is not yours," which was the constant nagging comment of Manus mothers, is not made. The distinction between "mine" and "thine" is not the point emphasised, but rather the need to be careful of other people's things. The family possessions are treated very differently. The child is given anything it cries for, which often results in its breaking its mother's ear-rings or unstringing her necklace of bandicoot-teeth. The house in which a child lives is not a forbidden world filled with treasures that he is constantly being bidden to let alone, until they come to assume enormous importance in his eyes. If the parents have something that they feel the child will injure, they hide it securely away so that the child will never come to desire it. This whole attitude was vividly illustrated when I showed them a red balloon. It was the clearest and most beautiful piece of colour that the people had ever seen; the children screamed with excitement and even the adults held their breath with joy—for a moment. Then, "Better put it away," they said sadly. "You surely cannot have many such beautiful things and the babies will cry for them."

As the child grows older, he is told that the carved wooden plate that is only used for feasts, or the bird-of-paradise head-dress that his father wears when he dances, is his—the child's. But his parents continue to use these things. His father takes him into the bush and shows him clumps of young sago and, teaching him the names of the clumps, he explains that these also are his. "Own property" comes to mean things that belong to the future, something that is used by others now, or is not yet his own. When he grows up, he will similarly designate all of his belongings as his children's. In such a system no one becomes aggressively possessive about his own, and theft, locked doors, and the primitive equivalent of locks—black magic placed on property—are virtually unknown. The Arapesh possess a few protective garden charms of which they have so far lost the point that when they place them on their garden-fences, they believe that their own wives and children will also suffer from the effects of eating from their own gardens.

5

the growth and initiation of an Arapesh boy

By the time the Arapesh child is seven or eight, its personality is set. Both boys and girls have learned a happy, trustful, confident attitude towards life. They have learned to include in the circle of their affection everyone with whom they are connected in any way whatsoever, and to respond to any relationship term with an active expression of warmth. They have been discouraged from any habits of aggressiveness towards others; they have learned to treat with respect and consideration the property, the sleep, and the feelings of other people. They definitely associate the giving of food with warmth, approval, acceptance, and security, and take any withholding of food as a sign of hostility and rejection. They have learned to be passive participators in the activities of their elders, but they have had very little experience of playing games on their own or organising their own lives. They have become accustomed to respond when others give the signal, to follow where others lead, to be enthusiastic and uncritical about new things that are presented to them. When they are cold, or bored, or lonely, they bubble their lips in a hundred patterned ways.

They have learned to fear the stranger, the Plainsman, the

man who walks among them with eyes alert for a bit of dirt that will be their undoing. And they have been taught to guard every chance piece of unfinished food or old clothing, to keep a sharp watch over these recently separated sections of their personalities when they meet a stranger. They have been permitted no expressions of hostility or aggressiveness towards any one of their hundred relatives, all of whom must be loved and cherished; but they have been allowed to join in their parents' sulky hatred of the sorcerers, and even to hurl a few small spears down a path that a departing group of Plainsmen have taken. So the basic pattern has been laid that in later life will make them identify anyone who hurts them as a stranger, and thus invoke the old sorcery-pattern of purloining the stranger's dirt. Only two sex-differences of importance have been established, the affect surrounding group activities, and the greater expressiveness in anger that is permitted little boys. This latter is blurred by other considerations of order of birth, and sex of siblings; girls who have no brothers show the same tendencies, and boys who are one of many brothers show them less.

When the first signs of puberty appear—the lifting and swelling of a girl's breasts, the appearance of a boy's pubic hair— the adolescent child must observe certain taboos, must avoid eating certain meats and drinking cold water until the yams that are now planted shall be harvested and sprouting in the yam-house, a taboo period of almost a year. It is now the child's duty to observe these taboos, carefully, solemnly "to grow itself," after the rules that everyone knows are correct. For the first time children are now made culturally self-conscious of the physiology of sex. Before this what masturbation there was—and it is slight because of the greater emphasis upon the socially acceptable pleasure of lip-bubbling—was disregarded as children's play. But when a young boy begins to keep the taboos of his pubic hair, he is cautioned against further careless handling of his genitals. And he learns from the older boys what one must do if one has broken any of the rules essential to growth; he learns of the disciplinary and hygienic use of stinging nettles and actual bleeding with a sharpened bamboo instrument. He becomes the responsible custodian of his own growth; and the sanctions are all in terms of that growth. If he breaks the rules, no one will punish him; no one but himself will suffer. He will simply not grow to be a tall strong man, a man worthy to be the father of children. He is now committed to the task of keeping the reproductive function of women and the food-getting function of men apart. The most dramatic representation of this separation of the function of men and women is the *tamberan* cult. The *tamberan* is the supernatural patron of the grown men of the tribe; he,* or they, for sometimes he is conceived severally, must never be seen by the women and uninitiated children, and he is impersonated for their listening benefit by various noise-making devices, flutes, whistles, slit gongs, and so forth. From the time that a child is old enough to pay any attention to its surroundings, the coming of the *tamberan*, his stay in the village, his dramatic departure, are high points of life. But until little boys and girls are six or seven, the coming of the *tamberan* means the same thing to both sexes. There is the bustle and stir that betokens a feast; people gather in one of the larger villages, sleeping packed tight around the fire in the crowded houses. Women and girls bring great loads of firewood on their backs and stack it under the raised houses. The

---

*The word for *tamberan werah* is in the noun class to which also belong such words as "child," words in which the sex is indeterminate. The pairs of flutes are always spoken of as male and female, and the word for *tamberan* in the plural is *warehas*, with the plural ending used for mixed sex-groups, or other mixed groups. Because English lacks a singular pronoun of indeterminate sex-reference, I shall use *he* as representing the nearest equivalent in feeling. In ordinary speech the natives, both men and women, tend to speak of the sound made by the flutes as if it were made by one being, to whom or which they refer in the singular.

men go off for a week's hunting, keeping a sharp look-out for monitor lizards for new drum-heads, while they hunt also for cassowary, kangaroo, and wallaby. There is much talk of a pig, or perhaps two pigs, which are to be contributed by someone in a neighbouring village and brought over for the feast. Yams are brought in by relatives of the man at whose initiation the *tamberan* is to come. These are piled in little mounds on the *agehu*, and the grateful recipients march around them reciting "Wa Wa Wa," which is called to "kill the bush-fowl" and signifies that some day they will return these gifts. Finally there is news that the hunting is finished, a specially large tree-kangaroo has completed the bag. The hunters come in, wearing bird-of-paradise feathers in their hair, proud of their kill, which is brought in in packages tied to poles and festooned with red and green streamers of tracaena-leaves. Speeches of congratulations are made, and tomorrow there will be cooking of the special coconut croquettes that are made only for feasts.

Underneath all of these preparations runs a current of excitement. The *tamberan* will be coming, coming from beyond the hill, coming from seaward. The little children think of him as a huge monster, as tall as a coconut-tree, who lives in the sea except on these rare occasions when he is summoned to sing to the people. When the *tamberan* comes, one runs away, as fast as ever one can, holding on to one's mother's grass skirt, tripping and stumbling, dropping one's mouthful of yam, wailing for fear one will be left behind. The lovely sound of the flutes is getting closer every minute, and something frightful would happen to the little girl or boy caught loitering in the village after the men and the *tamberan* enter it. So they hurry down the slope of the mountain, women and children and puppies, and perhaps a little pig or two that have come squealing after their mistress. One woman carries a new-born baby, with many little bundles of leaves hung from its net bag to protect it against evil, and a banana-leaf over the bag to shelter it from sun and rain. An old woman, her sparse white hair standing up abruptly on her nearly bald head, hobbles along at the tail of the procession, muttering that never again will she try to climb the mountain for a feast, no, after this she will stay in her little place in the valley, she will feed her son's pigs, but when his wife again has a child, she will not climb the mountain to see it. It's too hard, too hard for her old legs, and the tumour is too heavy to carry. The tumour is slowly becoming more pronounced on her abdomen, outlined clearly beneath her sagging skin. That tumour came from giving food to the sorcerers who had killed her brother long ago. As she shuffles along, holding tightly to a stick, the others look at her a little askance. Old women so far past the child-bearing period know a little more than young women. Their feet are not hurried by the same fear that makes a nursing mother clutch her child to her and flee from the sound of the flutes, and later will make her tremble when she hears her husband's step on the house-ladder. What if he has not properly washed his hands in the proper magical herbs? It was for such neglect that Temos lost her baby, and that one child of Nyelahai died. Old women do not fear these things any longer; they go no more to the menstrual hut, men do not lower their voices when they talk near them.

High and clear from the distant hill-side comes the sound of the flutes. "Does not the *tamberan* have a beautiful voice?" whisper the women to each other, and *"Tamberan, tamberan,"* echo the babies. From a knot of small girls comes a sceptical whisper: "If the *tamberan* is so big, how can he get inside his house?" "Be quiet! Hush your talk!" comes sharply from the mother of the new-born child. "If you talk about the *tamberan* like that, we shall all die." Nearer come the flutes, lovely broken sounds played faultily by young unaccustomed musicians. Now surely the *tamberan* is in the hamlet itself, winding among the trees, taking from the palm-trees his sacred mark, which he placed there six months ago, so that now the coconuts may be picked for the feast. The sun, before so hot, goes behind a cloud and a quick shower drenches the waiting women and children. The voice of the *tamberan* does not come so clearly through the rain. A chill settles upon the little company, babies cry and are hastily hushed against their mothers' breasts. Now to the sound of the flutes is added the sound of beaten slit gongs. "The *tamberan* has entered the house," whispers one of the older women. They stir, rearrange the net bags, which they have slackened from their foreheads, call to the children who have wandered farther down the hill-side. A distant halloo is heard from the hill-top; this is the men calling the women and children back to the village, which is once more safe for them now that the *tamberan* is closely housed in the special little house that is more gaily decorated than any of the others, with its painted wall-plates at the four corners and the painted shield set up in the gable. Answering the men's call, they climb laboriously back. There is no feeling that they have been excluded, that they are in any way inferior creatures whom the men have banished from a festive scene. It is only that this is something that would not be safe for them, something that concerns the growth and strength of men and boys, but which would be dangerous for women and children. Their men are careful of them, they protect them diligently.

It is always an exciting moment to re-enter the village where so recently something mysterious has happened. In every house, on the gable or by the door, banners of brightly coloured leaves have been set up. The *tamberan* paused here. At the foot of each palm-tree lies a wreath of red leaves; these are the *tamberan's* anklets, which fell off as he stood beneath the palms. On the rain-softened surface of the *agehu* are large marks. One of the men may remark self-consciously to a woman or a child that these are the marks of the *tamberan's* testicles. It is easy to see how big the *tamberan* is. But although the men have been so careful to arrange this pantomime, the women pay little attention to the details. It is all something that is better let alone, even by the mind. It is something that belongs to the men. They have their *tamberans* also, childbirth, and girl's puberty rites, and the ritual of dyeing grass skirts. These are the *tamberans* of women. And this *tamberan*, he belongs to the men, and does not bear thinking of. From the little *tamberan* house the flutes, accompanied now by slit gongs, sound steadily. In and out from the house pass the men, the initiated boys, and if there are no visitors from the beach, the older uninitiated boys also.

This permission to the uninitiated boys marks another difference between the *tamberan* cult as it is practised by the Arapesh and the emphases among the surrounding tribes. In many parts of New Guinea, the *tamberan* cult is a way of maintaining the authority of the older men over the women and children; it is a system directed against the women and children, designed to keep them in their ignominious places and punish them if they try to emerge. In some tribes, a woman who accidentally sees the *tamberan* is killed. The young boys are threatened with the dire things that will happen to them at their initiation, and initiation becomes a sort of vicious hazing in which the older men revenge themselves upon recalcitrant boys and for the indignities that they themselves once suffered. Such are the primary emphases of the wide-spread *tamberan* cult. Secrecy, age and sex-hostility, fear and hazing, have shaped its formal pattern. But the Arapesh, although they share part of the formal pattern with their neighbours, have changed all the emphases. In a community where there is no hostility between men and women, and where the old men, far from resenting the waxing strength of the young men, find in it their greatest source of happiness, a cult that stresses hate and punishment is out of place. And so the mountain people have revised most of the major points. Where other peoples kill a woman who chances on the secrets, and go to war against a community that does not keep its women sufficiently in the dark, the Arapesh merely swear the woman to secrecy, telling her that if she does not talk to others nothing will happen to her. On the beach, initiated boys are told that if they betray the secrets of the cult they will be found hanging from a tree, eviscerated by the *tamberan*. But in the mountains this frightening threat is omitted. And the great distinction between initiated and uninitiated boys is also blurred. In a properly organised men's cult, boys who have not been initiated are severely barred from participation, but among the Arapesh, where all the motivation for such exclusion is lacking, the older men say: "Here is a good feast. It is a pity that the he who is tall should not eat it just because we have not yet incised him. Let him come in." But if critical and orthodox strangers from the beach are present, the uninitiated boys are hustled out of sight, for the Arapesh are sensitive about their own happily muddled unorthodoxy.

On one occasion in Alitoa, there were many visitors from the beach in the house of the *tamberan*, blowing the flutes, beating the slit gongs, and generally taking matters into their own hands. After all it was from the beach that the flutes had come; forty years ago the mountain people had had nothing but seed whistles with which to impersonate their supernaturals. The visitors were haughty and hungry and demanded more meat. In traditional fashion they banged on the floor of the *tamberan* house and began hurling fire-sticks down the ladder. Finally, with a great clatter, they threatened the emergence of the *tamberan*. It was just dusk. Women and children were gathered in clusters close to the *tamberan* house, cooking the evening meal, when the threat came. Frantic, unprepared, desperate, they fled down the mountain sides, children straying, falling, lost among the rocks. With my hand held tightly in hers, Budagiel, my "sister," dragged my unaccustomed feet after the rest. Slipping, sliding, gasping for breath, we tumbled on. Then came a shout from above: "Come back, it was nonsense! It was not true." And breathlessly we clambered back up the slope. On the *agehu* confusion reigned, men were rushing about, arguing, exclaiming, disputing. Finally Baimal, volatile, excitable little Baimal, always indomitable despite his slight stature, dashed forward and began beating the front of the *tamberan* house with a stick: "You would, would you? You would come out and frighten our women-folk, and send them slipping and stumbling out into the dark and wet? You would chase our children away, would you? Take that and that and that!" And blow after blow fell with resounding whacks on the thatched roof. After that Baimal had to send in some meat to the outraged *tamberan,* but he didn't mind. Nor did the community. Baimal had expressed for all of them their objection to the use of the *tamberan* as an instrument of terror and intimidation. It was the *tamberan* that helped them grow the children and guard the women! The visitors from the beach sulked, ate the meat-offering, and went home to comment upon the barbarous ways of these mountain people who had no sense of the way in which things should be done.

Sometimes the *tamberan* stays only a few days in a village, sometimes he stays several weeks. He comes to taboo coconut-trees for feasts and to lift the taboo, to preside over the second mortuary feast when the bones of an honoured man are dug up and distributed among the relatives. He comes when a new *tamberan* house is built, and most importantly, he comes for an initi-ation, when a large enclosure of palm-matting is built at one end of a village and the initiates are segregated in it for several months.

As children grow older and beyond the period when they cling in fright to their mothers' skirts, there comes to be a marked sex-difference in their attitudes towards the *tamberan.* The little girls continue to follow their mother's steps; they learn not to speculate lest misfortune come upon them all. A habit of intellec-tual passivity falls upon them, a more pronounced lack of intel-lectual interest than that which characterises their brothers' minds. All that is strange, that is uncharted and unnamed—unfa-miliar sounds, unfamiliar shapes—these are forbidden to women, whose duty it is to guard their reproductivity closely and ten-derly. This prohibition cuts them off from speculative thought and likewise from art, because among the Arapesh art and the supernatural are part and parcel of each other. All children scrib-ble with bits of charcoal upon pieces of bark, the highly polished sago-bark strips that are used as beds and as wall-plates. They draw ovals that are yams, and circles that are taros, and little squares that are gardens, and patterns that are representative of string figures, and a pretty little design that is called the "morning star." Drawing these designs becomes in later years an occupation exclusively of women, a game with which they can amuse themselves during the long damp hours in the menstrual hut. But painting, painting mysterious half-realised figures in red and yellow, on big pieces of bark that will adorn the *tamberan* house, or a yam-house, this belongs to the men. The feeling against women's participating in art and in the men's cult is one and the same; it is not safe, it would endanger the women themselves, it would endanger the order of the universe within which men and women and children live in safety. When I showed them a brown, life-sized doll, the women shrank away from it in fright. They had never seen a realistic image before; they took it for a corpse. The men, with their different experience, recognised it as a mere representation, and one of them voiced the prevalent attitude towards women's concerning themselves with such things: "You women had better not look at that thing or it will ruin you entirely." Later the men became gay and familiar with the doll, danced with it in their arms and rearranged its ornaments, but the women, schooled since childhood in the acceptance of marvels and the suppression of all thought about them, never quite accepted the fact that it was only a doll. They would take me aside to ask me how I fed it, and ask if it would never grow any bigger. And if I laid it on the ground with its head lower than its feet, some solicitous woman always rushed to turn it around. Thus through the appearances of the *tamberan* the women and girls are trained in the passive acceptance that is considered their only safety in life.

But for the small boys it is different. To them speculation is not forbidden. It is true that they have to run away now, but later, just a little later, they will be part of the performance; they will go with the men to bring the *tamberan* back to the village, they will see if the *tamberan* really eats all those plates of meat which are passed into the *tamberan* house, or whether the men and boys get some too. If they are lucky, they will be initiated with a large group of boys; for three months they will live within the initiation enclosure, while they undergo the ceremony that is called "being swallowed by the *temberan*," or sometimes "being swallowed by the cassowary." They know that the cassowary and the *tamberan* have some not very clear connection with each other. Anyway, this talk of swallowing, made up by some distant people interested in frightening women and children, holds no terror for little Arapesh boys. They have seen their big brothers emerge plump and sleek from this swallowing process, with their eyes glowing with pride and self-importance, their skins beautifully oiled and painted, new ornaments on their arms and legs, and lovely feathers in their hair. Apparently this swallowing is a very pleasant business, and the main point is to be swallowed in large numbers, in a big initiation ceremony, rather than swallowed quietly among your own relatives. So the small boys speculate together, no longer hiding with the women but going off by themselves into the bush, where they can give their tongues and their imagination free rein. As the *tamberan* cult dulls the imagination of the girls, it stimulates and quickens the imagination of the small boys. And this quickening extends to other things, to greater interest in the plants and animals of the bush, to greater curiosity about life in general. Upon the little girl of ten, sitting demurely beside her mother or her mother-in-law, the horizon of life has closed down in a way that it has not upon her brother. New responsibilities wait for him, as soon as he is grown enough to be initiated. He watches the taboos of his public hair even more assiduously, and imitates the self-disciplinary cuttings of the bigger boys even more valiantly, and wonders again and again what it will be like to be swallowed. The little girl bubbles her lips and ceases to think at all. If she does not think, if she does not let her mind wander in forbidden places, some day she too will hold a baby in her arms, a baby who will be born secretly in the bush, in a spot forbidden to men.

At last the time comes for a boy to be initiated. If he is an eldest son, son of a large household, heir to an important man, he may be initiated separately. The large initiations are held only every six or seven years, when repeated gibes between communities at big feasts have finally goaded some community into undertaking the huge work of organisation and preparation that is necessary if some twelve or fifteen boys and their sponsoring relatives are to be fed for several months in one place. Such a feast takes several years to prepare, and has its echoes throughout the lives of the group of novices, who years later, as middle-aged men, will be finding pigs to take back to that village to be distributed in final long-deferred repayment for the initiation. Meanwhile, in the six-year period between initiations, boys who were too small when the last initiation was held have grown very tall, embarrassingly so. They have gradually learned most of the secrets. They know that the voice of the *tamberan* is made by the big bamboo flutes, and may even have learned to play upon them. Altogether, it is better that a great tall boy should be initiated quietly, with a small family feast.

The essentials of the initiation remain the same: there is a ritual segregation from the company of women, during which time the novice observes certain special food taboos, is incised, eats a sacrificial meal of the blood of the older men, and is shown various marvellous things. The marvellous things fall into two classes: remarkable objects that he has never seen before, such as masks, and other carvings and representations; and the revelation, part of which usually had been revealed to him already, of the fact that there is really no *tamberan* at all, but that all of these things are done by men. The cassowary, who has been so mysteriously said to swallow little boys, is merely one of the men of a certain clan, wearing a ferocious pair of cassowary-feather eye-pieces, and having suspended from his neck a shell-covered bag in which are stuck two sharpened cassowary-bones. The *tamberan* himself is simply the noise of the flutes, the beating of the slit gongs by the men, or a general concept covering the whole set of mystifying acts. To a boy, growing up among the Arapesh means finding out that there is no Santa Claus, having it acknowledged that one is old enough to know that all this fanfare and ruffle of drums is a pantomime, devoutly maintained generation after generation because its maintenance will help to make boys grow, and so promote the well-being of the people. The incision itself, and the meal of blood that the initiates are fed, is another matter. The belief in blood and blood-letting, in the important connexion between blood and growth, is part of the very bones of Arapesh culture. And when one boy is initiated at a time, it is these aspects which are stressed. About the flutes he knows already, and one household has few other hidden marvels to show him. His initiation becomes a matter of incision and a sacrificial meal.

In the big initiations other points are emphasised: the comradeship between all of the boys, the care that is taken of them by their fathers and elder brothers, and by the special sponsors, who accompany them each day to the bathing-pool, bending back the brambles from their paths, even as their ghostly ancestors are also believed to do. The reciprocal attitudes of the boys towards their sponsors are emphasised; their sponsors weave them arm-bands that the novices must wear until they fall off, and then they will make feasts for the sponsors. In the enclosure there is plenty to eat. The older men hunt for the novices and feed them well; the period is supposed to be magically growth-promoting, and they see to it that it is actually healthful also. For the only time in all their meagerly fed lives, the young Arapesh boys become almost plump.

The anxiety of the older men about the preservation of these necessary secrets is communicated to the novices, not with intimidating threats, but by giving them a share in all the little acts of loving deception that the men practice on the women. The novices wear little leaf covers on their new wounds, and these are spoken of as their wives. The voices of these wives are imitated on pieces of whistling grass for the benefit of the listening women. A great fiction is got up about these imaginary "wives." Little bundles of firewood are prepared and hung on the paths to show the women where the tiny fanciful wives of the novices have been at work. Meanwhile, the women among themselves refer to these wives as "little birds" and probe no deeper into what is obviously some kind of a male mystery and better let alone.

The whole ceremony, formally representative of a jealous male society grudgingly admitting younger males, now too old to be kept out, has been turned into a growth-giving rite. Even the gauntlet that the initiates run betwen two rows of men armed with stinging nettles is not administered in a spirit of hazing, but so that the novices will grow. They are given no instructions that will make them hate, despise, or fear women. They are subjected to a divinatory ceremony to find out whether they have been experimenting with sex or not, something that they know is forbidden because it will stunt natural growth. The boy who is found guilty is punished by being made to chew a piece of arecanut that has been placed in contact with a woman's vulva, if possible with the vulva of the woman, usually his betrothed wife, with whom he has had intercourse. This ritual break of the most deeply felt taboo in Arapesh culture, the taboo that separates the mouth and the genitals, food and sex, is felt to be punishment enough; and while the guilty are punished, all are cautioned against similar indulgence. Sex is good, but dangerous to those who have not yet attained their growth.

So, with ceremonial and a little admonition, much singing and bathing and eating, the two or three months of the seclusion pass away. At the end, the novices, dressed most resplendently, appear before their overjoyed mothers and sisters, who far from having spent the period in anxiety about their fate, have expected to find them just as plump and well fed as they actually appear. Then each youth, dressed in his best, is taken by his father over his father's road, to the houses of all of his father's trade-friends, and also, when such women have married far away, to the houses of his father's sisters. In each house the novice is given a gift, a gift that he will some day reciprocate. He now walks, ceremonially and often actually for the first time, the road of his ancestors, the road by which tools and implements and weapons and ornaments, songs and new fashions, are imported; along this road also goes dirt stolen in anger, and loving relatives hunting for others' dirt. This is hereafter known as his road, the road over which all of these simple necessities and high excitements of life will pass.

His childhood is ended. From one who has been grown by the daily carefulness and hard work of others, he now passes into the class of those whose care is for others' growth. During his pubescence his care was for his own growth, for the observances of the taboo would ensure to him muscle and bone, height and breadth, and strength to beget and rear children. This strength is never phrased as sexual potency, a point in which the Arapesh are profoundly uninterested and for which they have no vocabulary. Now this care is shifted and he has instead new responsibilities towards those who after years devoted to his growth are now growing old themselves, and towards his younger brothers and sisters, and his young betrothed wife.

There is no feeling here that he is subservient towards those older than himself, that he chafes beneath the power of those stronger than himself. Instead, the oldest and the youngest, the ageing parent and the little child, are placed together in Arapesh feeling, in contrast to those who from puberty to middle age are specially concerned with sex and child-rearing. From puberty to middle age one occupies a special position with responsibilities towards the old and towards the young. Half of the food in the world is set apart for the elders and the children, certain kinds of yams, certain kinds of taro, certain kinds of birds and fish and meat—these are for those who are not yet concerned with sex, or whose concern with it is over. There is no feeling here that the powerful and the strong appropriate the best foods, but rather there is a symbolic division into two equal parts from which all are fed. After a big feast, the men of the locality make a special little family feast for the women whose hard labour in carrying food and firewood has made the feast possible. They often garnish the plates with tree-kangaroo, a food that the women themselves cannot eat. But when I commented on the seeming thoughtlessness of rewarding the women with meat that was forbidden them, they stared at me in surprise: "But their children can eat it." And between men and their children there is no more rivalry than this. To grow his son, to find for him the food from which he must himself abstain, has been the father's great delight during his son's childhood. Piece by piece he has built up his son's body. The Arapesh father does not say to his son: "I am your father, I begot you, therefore you must obey me." He would regard such a claim as presumptuous nonsense. Instead he says: "I grew you. I grew the yams, I worked the sago, I hunted the meat, I laboured for the food that made your body. Therefore I have the right to speak like this to you." And this relationship between father and son, a relationship based on food given and food gratefully received, is shared in slighter measure by all the old and young of a community. Every man had contributed to the growth of every child reared within the small circle of mountains that forms his world. If a young man should so far forget himself as to speak rudely or hastily to an old man, the old man may answer, sadly, reproachfully: "And think how many pigs I have fattened from which you took your growth."

As the young wax strong, the old retire more and more. When his eldest son enters the *tamberan* cult, or if the eldest child is a girl, when she reaches puberty, the father formally retires. Henceforward, all that he does is done in his son's name; the big yam-house that he built last year is spoken of as his son's; when trade-friends come, he sits aside and lets his son entertain them. The son too must bear in mind his father's increasing age by little ritual acts of carefulness. He must take care that none of the sago that is worked by himself or his brothers and sisters is given to his father and mother to eat. Sago worked by the young is dangerous to the old. The son must not eat lime from his father's lime-gourd, or step over any of his father's possessions as they lie on the floor. His young, springing manhood would endanger his father's slackening, sexless hold on life.

The father's sexless rôle is illustrated most vividly in the attitude of Arapesh middle-aged men towards women. Quarrels over women are the key-note of the New Guinea primitive world. Almost every culture has suffered in one way or another because it has failed to solve the problem. Polygynous societies permit of far more quarrelling over women than do monogamous ones, for the enterprising man, not satisfied with one wife, can always try to express his superiority by trying to attach a few more. Among the Arapesh, this quarrelling has been reduced to a minimum. Polygyny they phrase entirely in terms of inheritance, as the duty of caring for the widow and children of brothers, not as a sign of superiority over other men. Between the father-age-group and the son-age-group, there is no possibility of conflict, for all men over thirty-five or so are concerned not in finding wives for themselves, but in finding wives for their sons. The search for wives is conducted among small children, girls from six to ten, and the father's entire interest is enlisted in the son's behalf. Thus one of the ugliest results of quarrelling over women, the quarrel between a man and his son, in which wealth, power, and prestige are pitted against youth and vigour, is eliminated. As we shall see later, the Arapesh have not been able to avoid all quarrelling over women, but by phrasing polygyny as a duty instead of a privilege, and by involving the interests of all the powerful men in the marriages of the next generation, this struggle is reduced to a minimum.

Thus at the end of his adolescence the Arapesh boy is placed in his society, he is initiated, he has manifold duties to perform, unaggressively, co-operatively, assisting his father and his uncles; guarding his father in his old age and his young brother in his childhood; and growing his small, preadolescent wife.

6

the growth and betrothal of an Arapesh girl

An arapesh boy grows his wife. As a father's claim to his child is not that he has begotten it but rather that he has fed it, so also a man's claim to his wife's attention and devotion is not that he has paid a bride-price for her, or that she is legally his property, but that he has actually contributed the food which has become flesh and bone of her body. A little girl is betrothed when she is seven or eight to a boy about six years her senior, and she goes to live in the home of her future husband. Here the father-in-law, the husband, and all of his brothers combine to grow the little bride. Upon the young adolescent husband particularly falls the onus of growing yams, working sago, hunting for meat, with which to feed his wife. In later years, this is the greatest claim that he has upon her. If she is dilatory or sulky or unwilling, he can invoke this claim: "I worked the sago, I grew the yams, I killed the kangaroo that made your body. Why do you not bring in the firewood?" And in those exceptional cases when the arranged marriage falls through from the death of the betrothed husband, and the girl is betrothed again after she has attained her growth, the tie is never felt to be so close. Similarly when a man inherits the widow of a relative, he may have contributed very little food to her growth—especially if she is older than he—and these marriages, lacking the most important sanction that the culture recognises, are less stable.

The Arapesh believe that parents should be able to control their children whom they have grown, and on the same principle, they believe that husbands should be able to control their wives; they have grown them, they are responsible for them, they are older and have better judgment. The whole organisation of society is based upon the analogy between children and wives as representing a group who are younger, less responsible, than the men, and therefore to be guided. Wives by definition stand in this child-relationship to their husbands, and to their husband's fathers and uncles and brothers, in fact to all of the older men of the clan into which they marry. Before the little girl has become conscious of her sex, while she is still a slim, unformed child, the eyes of the fathers and uncles of other clans are upon her, judging her gently as a possible wife for one of their stripling lads. As it is upon the small girl that choice falls, it is about small girls that the Arapesh are most romantic; young men will comment with enthusiasm upon the feminine charm of a five-year-old, and sit about entranced by the coquettishness of some baby whose mother, for amusement, has decked her out in a grass skirt. There is no sexual emphasis in this choice; to regard children as sexual objects would be incredible to the Arapesh. It is merely that after girls are nine or ten years of age they are no longer possible objects of choice, either for one's self or for one's son, but are instead the betrothed wives of others. Not until a girl becomes a widow will she again be a person upon whose desirability one can speculate. And so mothers occasionally deck out their tiny daughters, and the conversation of a group of big boys is hushed for a moment as a small girl flips by, rustling her stiff little skirts.

When a father selects a wife for his son, he is moved by many considerations. First, there is the problem whether to choose a wife close to home, from the next village, from a clan with which his own clan has already intermarried. This is very good. It is good that brother and sister should marry brother and sister, that if one clan gives two of its girls to the other, the other clan should reciprocate with two of its daughters. This is no hard and fast rule. The Arapesh construct their marriages to last, and are not bound to any fixed system that might dictate marriages in which the young people are the wrong ages. But still the marriage nearer home is a desirable one. The men-folk of the two clans, already bound together by several ties, will urge a further tie. Against these considerations, there are the advantages of a marriage in a far-away place. This kind of marriage widens the circle of friendliness within which the next generation will walk about safely, sure of a welcome after a hard, cold journey. A tie set up by a marriage between distant places will bind those two places together for a long time to come, perhaps, with good luck, for ever. The descendants of the marriage will remember it, calling all the people from their mother's village "grandfather," and welcoming them respectfully when they come to feasts. Furthermore, if the new bride comes from a village towards the beach she may bring some special skill with her, which she will teach to her daughters and her daughters-in-law. It was thus that the secret of making the *wulus*, a *soigné* braided grass skirt, was brought to the people of Suabibis five generations ago, by a bride from Daguar. But against this choice there is the fear of sorcery. If one chooses a wife from the stranger, if one permits one's daughter to go among strangers, fear, the compulsive resort to sorcery when angered and frightened, may destroy the marriage. So the fathers and uncles balance the matter in their minds.

In the girl herself they look for various definite attributes. She should have the right kind of relatives, many male kindred, men who are good hunters, successful gardeners, slow to anger and wise in making choices. The father who chooses a wife for his son is choosing also, and as importantly, his son's brother-in-law, and his grandchildren's maternal uncles. Instead of regarding marriage as a necessary evil, as so many people do, as an unfortunate compromise which makes it inevitable that a stranger be allowed to enter the house and sit down familiarly within it, the Arapesh regard marriage as primarily an opportunity to increase the warm family circle within which one's descendants may then live even more safely than one has lived oneself. This attitude is brought out very clearly in their comment on incest. I had the greatest difficulty in getting any comment upon it at all. The only formulation on the subject that I obtained is contained in a series of rather esoteric aphorisms:

> Your own mother,
> Your own sister,
> Your own pigs,
> Your own yams that you have piled up,*
> You may not eat.
> Other people's mothers,
> Other people's sisters,
> Other people's pigs,
> Other people's yams that they have piled up,
> You may eat.

This sums up the Arapesh attitude towards selfishness, their feeling that there is an intimate connexion between a man and his surplus yam-crop that would make his eating from it rather like incest, and similarly that to appropriate for one's own purposes one's mother or sister would be of the nature of antisocial and repellent hoarding. But this set of aphorisms was given me to explain how a man who made an *abüllü* should act about his yams, and I never received it in reply to any inquiry about incest. The native line of thought is that you teach people how to behave about yams and pigs by referring to the way that they know they behave about their female relatives. To questions about incest I

---

*This does not refer to ordinary yams, but to yams that have been formally exhibited in an *abüllü* and distributed to the community for seed.

did not receive the answers that I had received in all other native societies in which I had worked, violent condemnation of the practice combined with scandalous revelations of a case of incest in a neighbouring house or a neighbouring village. Instead both the emphatic condemnation and the accusations were lacking: "No, we don't sleep with our sisters. We give our sisters to other men and other men give us their sisters." Obviously. It was simple as that. Why did I press the point? And had they not heard of a single case of incest? I queried. Yes, finally, one man said that he had. He had gone on a long journey, towards Aitape, and there in the village of a strange people he had heard a quarrel; a man was angry because his wife refused to live with him, but instead kept returning to her brother, with whom she cohabited. Was that what I meant? That, in effect, was what I meant. No, we don't do that. What would the old men say to a young man who wished to take his sister to wife? They didn't know. No one knew. The old men never discussed the matter. So I set them to asking the old men, one at a time. And the answers were the same. They came to this: "What, you would like to marry your sister! What is the matter with you anyway? Don't you want a brother-in-law? Don't you realise that if you marry another man's sister and another man marries your sister, you will have at least two brothers-in-law, while if you marry your own sister you will have none? With whom will you hunt, with whom will you garden, whom will you go to visit?" Thus incest is regarded among the Arapesh not with horror and repulsion towards a temptation that they feel their flesh is heir to, but as a stupid negation of the joys of increasing, through marriage, the number of people whom one can love and trust.

So the father, in choosing his son's wife, considers her brothers and her cousins, who will be his son's friends in the years to come. It is well if there are many of them. Look at Aden now, a man who was lonely because of a series of foolish moves. Aden's father and mother had been cousins and both had been members of vanishing lines. Aden had no relatives at all except two mother's brothers, one who was a half-wit, and one who, out of loneliness, had moved away and joined his wife's people in the next locality. And then Aden, in addition, did an unusual thing—he married two sisters. Now there is no objection to a man's marrying two sisters, and in this case Aden's wife's sister was left a widow and did not wish to marry any of the distant relatives of her former husband. She preferred to return to Alitoa and live with her sister, and finally Aden married her also. But, it was pointed out, that was a foolish thing to do for a man so precariously placed as Aden. He thereby lost the chance of acquiring a second set of brothers-in-law and was completely dependent upon his one set. When his one little child, Sauisua, grew up, no one would be anxious to choose for a daughter-in-law a girl who had so few relatives.

The father of a girl, in accepting overtures for his daughter, is moved by the same kind of consideration. He looks without favour upon a suit on behalf of a youth who has few relatives. And while the fathers of sons are always very anxious to mark little girls for their sons, the fathers of daughters are traditionally cautious, unenthusiastic, recalcitrant. The negotiations are carried on in the face of articulate lack of interest on the father's part: "I have given away enough daughters. What do I get out of it? They go and live a long way off and I never see them. Only my sons are near me, a comfort to my old age. This one I will keep. She is still very small. Her breasts show no signs of standing up. Why should I send her away among strangers?" And if the daughter is of the type who is regarded as a particularly promising wife, he will add: "She already can take her mother's place when visitors come. She hastens to light the fire and boil the pot. I will not send her away." For small girls are judged first on just this quality: Do they assume domestic responsibility quickly, are they actively and intelligently hospitable, or do they sit lazy and sullen when a guest enters the house? This quality of responsibility, far more than brains or beauty, is what is demanded in a wife, one who will grace a man's house by her deft and happy responsiveness to everyone—to himself, to his guests, and to their children. A little girl who already at six or seven "can take her mother's place" has proclaimed herself as a desirable wife. Additionally, she should be sweet-tempered, but this is regarded as almost a corollary, for bad temper among the Arapesh expresses itself in "not giving things to people." And she should have a clear skin.* A girl who has a diseased skin will usually marry, but she will be betrothed later than other girls, and the marriage will be a less advantageous one; she will have to marry a boy with few relatives. On the other hand, a boy with a chronic case of tinea will only by some strange accident ever marry at all. When he is a child, the other children will shrink away from him, calling him "skin-infected man." Already about him clings the aura of the disgruntled and the unfortunate, the kind of man who among the Plainsmen becomes a sorcerer, the kind of man who among the mountain people is over-ready to traffic in sorcery. The argument runs that men who have skin infections cannot get wives, and so, angry and disgruntled, become sorcerers. "This child has a skin infection, therefore he will be a sorcerer, or a trafficker in dirt," is already on people's tongues. The afflicted child shrinks into himself, knowing that his path is already marked out as the path of the stranger, the one who will never be accepted into the warm group by the fireside. The unpleasant colour of a tinea infection and its rancid odour touch the Arapesh at just the point where their sensuousness leaves them no room for charity.

So it is boys, not girls, who know in childhood that they will never wed. Here the Arapesh share with most primitive societies a state which contrasts sharply with that of modern civilisation.

---

*Her skin should be free from yaws, tropical ulcers, ringworm, tinea imbricats, and the local New Guinea skin infection that is a compound of penicillium and scabies. Almost everyone suffers at some time of life from one or all of these disorders, but only in certain cases do they become chronic and a permanent liability.

Every girl, unless she is horribly deformed—and very few badly diseased or deformed people survive—will be married at least once. If she is left a young widow, she will be legally married a second time even if she is not received into her second husband's bed. The fear of the child's not marrying, the desperate concentration upon marriage as a goal, is transferred in Arapesh society from the parents of the girl to the parents of the boy. He it is who may get left out altogether, who must be carefully provided for. And one of the chief causes of a son's gratitude is that his father found him a wife while he himself was still a youth and unable to provide for himself.

Selecting a wife for one's son is called "placing a carrying-bag on her head." This pantomime is usually not carried through in practice, but the point is made verbally. The little girl is taken by her parents and left in the home of her betrothed. Here her life hardly differs at all from the life that she led at home. She sleeps with her parents-in-law, works with her mother-in-law, goes about with all of the female relatives of her betrothed. She is perhaps a little shyer than she was at home, if this new home is among people whom she does not know. But most often it is among those whom she has seen already many times. Towards her young husband, her attitude is one of complete trust and acceptance. No constraining taboo marks the ease of their relationship. He is just another older male to whom she looks up and upon whom she depends. She is to him another small girl, his special small girl, whose hand must be taken in rough places on the paths. He calls out to her to light his pipe, or to feed his dog. And all of his brothers share his attitude towards her, and she includes them in the circle of her affection. With the smaller ones she romps and plays. To all of them she becomes warmly attached. Her feeling for her husband and his father and brothers is practically identical with her feeling for her own father and brothers. Ease of companionship, lack of taboo, lack of fear, characterise all of these relationships. She passes back and forth between her own home and her husband's, depending upon the demands of a feast or of taro-planting. She returns as cheerfully to her husband's home as she does to her own home. Little girls comment easily and happily upon the rhythm of their lives. So Anyuai, aged ten: "Sometimes I stay here with my father, sometimes in Liwo with my husband. They plant taro here, I come here. They plant taro in Liwo, I go to Liwo. My husband is tall, as tall as Gerud." And I asked her: "Did you cry when you first went to Liwo?" "No, I did not cry. I am very strong. My husband is good. I sleep in the house of his father and mother. Una is going to marry Magiel. Magiel is very tall. Una is smaller than I. She still stays most with her father. Miduain is going to marry Seaubaiyat. Sinaba'i calls him son-in-law. Ibanyos [Anyuai's father's other wife] and mother sit down together in one house. They make one garden. They do not quarrel. Tomorrow I will go back to Liwo."

When these long years during which husband and wife live together like brother and sister are taken into account, one of the determining factors of Arapesh attitudes towards sex is intelligible. Actual sex-intercourse does not spring from a different order of feeling from the affection that one has for one's daughter or one's sister. It is simply a more final and complete expression of the same kind of feeling. And it is not regarded as a spontaneous response of the human being to an internal sexual stimulus. The Arapesh have no fear that children left to themselves will copulate, or that young people going about in adolescent groups will experiment with sex. The only young people who are believed likely to indulge in any overt sex-expression are "husband and wife," the betrothed pair who have been reared in the knowledge that they are to be mates (or, even more unusually, a woman and her brother-in-law). As the little girl approaches puberty, her parents-in-law increase their supervision of her, both for her sake and for the sake of her boy husband.

The need for this chaperonage is based upon the Arapesh conception that growth and sexual life are antithetical, the conception which we have encountered already in the taboos that surround the birth and suckling of a child. If the little girl who is only now keeping the taboos of her small swelling breasts experiences sex, her growth will be stunted, she will be spindly and puny and, most important of all, her breasts will continue to stand up, small and stiff and inhospitable, instead of falling in the luxuriant heaviness that the Arapesh consider to be the high point of female beauty. This is a point about which little girls are very conscious. As small sisters and sister-in-law work together, scrubbing the sagoshoots between their palms before plaiting them into new grass skirts, or peeling taros for the evening meal, they talk over the relative beauty of the big girls. Budagiel and Wadjubel, they have lovely big breasts. They must have kept the taboos very stringently and never have let themselves be tempted into filching one small bite of meat. Afterwards, too, when they menstruated, they must have kept the other rules very carefully, been observant of the women's *tamberan.* What this is the small girls are not quite certain, but like the uninitiated boys they are not afraid. Because the results make one beautiful. They know that a girl fasts for four or five days at her first menstruation, but how lovely are her new grass skirt and ornaments when she appears again in the village! Anyway, Anyuai asked her husband's sister what it was like, that fasting, and her husband's sister said you slept most of the time and hardly noticed the time passing. It was warm by the fire in the menstrual hut. And look what happens to girls who have intercourse with their husbands too early. Look at Sagu for instance—Sagu, slight and straight as a fourteen-year-old, and yet she had been married twice and had a baby that died, it was so little and poor. Sagu had first been married in another locality to a boy much older than she, who had inherited his dead brother's right to her. This boy had "stolen her," that is, he had had intercourse with her before she reached puberty. Her breasts had hardened standing up and would never fall now. She had had a baby by this husband and the baby had died. Then she had run away from him and come home to her father. After all he was not the husband who had originally grown her and to whom she really owed allegiance. Her father remarried her to a man from a neighbouring clan and soon after he had married her he died. Meanwhile Sagu's little sister, Kumati, had been betrothed to Maigi, the younger brother of her second husband. This younger brother was slender and charming, and had not yet attained his growth. Sagu took a fancy to him and, guided by her atypical sex-experience, seduced him. The elders remonstrated, but Sagu had bound Maigi fast to her. He shrugged his shoulders at their threats, which two years had now demonstrated to be only too well grounded—that he would never grow to be a tall, sturdy man. So Sagu was permitted to marry Maigi, and the little Kumati, who had not yet left her father's home, was reassigned to a younger cousin of Maigi. It was all very irregular. And the little girls, scrubbing at their sago-shoots, thrust out their full little lower lips into grimaces of disapproval. Sagu had no breasts, she would likely have no children either, and Maigi would never be tall and strong. That was not the way that things should be done. If a boy waited until his wife had menstruated many times, even for as long as two years, then her breasts would be ready to fall, and the first contact with sex would loosen those delicate cords which bound the breasts to the vulva. But if that contact came first, if the girl's vein was broken—for so they phrase the hymen—before puberty, then her breasts would never develop.

The Arapesh have ways of keeping a girl small and immature, but they do not work very well. Her parents or her parents-in-law can take a little bit of her personality, a piece of a half-chewed areca-nut or a sugar-cane butt, and bind it up very tightly with a piece of croton-leaf; this they can hide in the rafters of the house, and as long as it remains fastened, so the girl will be fastened, her development retarded. The need for such magic arises when betrothing parents miscalculate the relative ages of the boy and girl. This can happen very easily, as the people pay very little attention to the ages of their children, and even the mother of a first child will say one day that the child is two moons old and the next day it is five moons old. Relative ages of children brought up in different communities, as betrothed children usually have been, are particularly hard to gauge. So sometimes the parents-in-law will be faced with the alarming fact that the daughter-in-law is maturing much too fast, that she will be mature and ready for sex-experience while their son is still underdeveloped. Then the magic may be restored to. But on the whole the Arapesh consider magic an unreliable solution of this very pressing difficulty. Observation has shown that it does not work very well, and this is an important matter. More often they solve the difficulty by rearranging the betrothals, and give the too mature girl to an elder brother of the original husband. This solution often works well. The child wife in her husband's home has regarded her husband and all his brothers in very much the same light. She has used her husband's terms in speaking to them, calling her husband's elder brother by the term meaning "elder sibling of the same sex"; she trusts him; he too has fed her, held her hand when she stumbled, gently rebuked her if she has done something incorrectly. It is a shift that is not on the whole difficult to make.

The small girls, talking over life as they sit at work, do not regard the possible shift of their betrothal as a very serious matter. On the whole, they are wedded in feeling to a group of people, not merely to one man. They have become an integral part of another family, a family to which they will now belong for ever, even after death. For unlike so many Oceanic peoples among whom the brothers claim the body of a woman at death, the Arapesh bury the wife on the land of her husband's clan, and her ghost remains with him in his *mersalai* place. Her husband and sons make a series of payments to her clan, they "buy the mother" to remain always with her husband and children.

A girl's first menstruation and the accompanying ceremonial take place in most cases in her husband's home. But her brothers must play a part in it and they are sent for; failing brothers, cousins will come. Her brothers build her a menstrual hut, which is stronger and better-constructed than are the menstrual huts of older married women; these are miserable cone-shaped little structures that they build themselves, with no floor and offering scant shelter from the cold and rain. But for this first segregation, a floor is built. The girl is cautioned to sit with her legs in front of her, knees raised, and on no account to sit cross-legged. Her woven arm- and leg-bands, her ear-rings, her old lime-gourd and lime-spatula, are taken from her. Her woven belt is taken off. If these are fairly new they are given away; if they are old they are cut off and destroyed. There is no feeling that they themselves are contaminated, but only the desire to cut the girl's connexion with her past. The girl is attended by older women who are her own relatives or relatives of her husband. They rub her all over with stinging nettles. They tell her to roll one of the large nettle-leaves into a tube and thrust it into her vulva; this will ensure her breasts' growing large and strong. The girl eats no food, nor does she drink water. On the third day, she comes out of the hut and stands against a tree while her mother's brother makes the decorative cuts upon her shoulders and buttocks. This is done so gently, with neither earth nor lime rubbed in—the usual New Guinea methods for making scarification marks permanent—that it is only possible to find the scars during the next three or four years. During that time, however, if strangers wish to know whether a girl is nubile, they look for the marks. Each day the women rub the girl with nettles. It is well if she fasts for five or six days, but the women watch her anxiously, and if she becomes too weak they put an end to it. Fasting will make her strong, but too much of it might make her die, and the emergence ceremony is hastened.

The father of the young husband now instructs him concerning the ceremonial meal that he must prepare for his wife. This contains a whole series of special herbs, and no one who has not prepared one for his wife knows how to do it. It is part of the Arapesh tradition that only as the emergency arises one learns what to do from someone who has done it before. Many young men whose wives have not yet reached puberty, and who have never acted as "brothers" to a nubile sister, have never seen a puberty

ceremony. When people refer to it, they look confused and worried, and it adds to their sense of infinite and precarious dependence upon tradition as it is carried in the minds of men older than
they are. What if there were no older men to tell them what to
do, what magical herbs to find, how to prepare them?

The father tells the youth to search for the *nkumkwebil* vine,
which is tough and hard to break, the strong bark of the *malipik*
tree, the sap of the *karudik* tree, the sap of the breadfruit-tree, the
little shrub called *henyakun*, and the cocoons of the *idugen* cater-
pillar. These are all strong things and will make the girl strong,
strong to cook, strong to carry, strong to bear children. Then the
youth is told to make a soup into which he puts parts of the
herbs, and also to cook some of them with specially strong yams
called *wabalal*. Meanwhile the women adorn the girl. She is
painted on back and shoulders with red paint. They put on her a
new and beautiful grass skirt, new plaited armlets and leglets;
they put new ear-rings in her ears. One of the women lends her
the little green horn-shaped shell and the scarlet feather that all
married women wear as a sign of their estate. Later her husband
will give her one of her own. This is thrust into the hole at the tip
of her nose that was made long ago when she was a child and
which she has kept open ever since with a piece of stick or a roll
of leaf. Now she is ready to go up on the *agehu* and appear before
the eyes of her husband and of her brothers, who have come, each
with a gift: bows and arrows, wooden plates, net bags, cassowary-
bone daggers, spears—these are the proper gifts for the men of
her kin to bring an adolescent girl.

The women put her old net bag on her head, freshly decorated with *wheinyal* leaves. They place a bright-red heart-shaped
leaf in her mouth. This leaf is also worn by novices in the *tamberan* ceremony. Her husband has been told to bring a rib of a
coconut-leaflet, and some *mebu*, the scented flowers of sulphur,
on a pair of *aliwhiwas* leaves. He waits for her in the middle of
the *agehu*, she comes up slowly, her eyes downcast, her steps lag-
ging from her long fast, supported beneath the arm-pits by the

women. Her husband stands in front of her. He puts his big toe on her big toe. He takes the coconut-rib and as she looks up into his face he flicks the old net bag from her head—the old net bag that his father placed on her head as a child when he arranged the betrothal. Now the girl drops the leaf out of her mouth and puts out her tongue, furry and heavy with her fast. Her husband wipes it off with the *mebu* earth. Then the girl sits down on a piece of sago-bark; she sits down carefully, lowering herself with one hand, and sits with her legs straight out in front of her. The husband gives her a spoon wrapped in a leaf, and the bowl of soup that he has made. For the first spoonful he must hold her hand to steady her, and so for the second. By the third she will be strong enough to hold it for herself. After she has eaten the soup, he takes one of the *wabalal* yams and breaks it in half. She eats half and half he places in the rafters of the house; this is the earnest that she will not treat him like a stranger and deliver him over to the sorcerers. Lest she do so, tradition provides him with part of her personality also. The piece of yam is kept until the girl becomes pregnant. This yam meal is an incongruous piece of ceremonial, possibly borrowed from the Plainsmen. Only the insane and the feeble-minded attempt sorcery through it.

After the girl has eaten, she sits in the centre of the *agehu*. Her brothers put their gifts down in a circle around her. Then they take coconut-leaf torches, light them, and circle the girl with fire. They do not know why they do this. It is a new custom, borrowed from the beach, but it makes a pretty showing. Beyond Alitoa, towards the plains, the people have not yet learned to do this.

For a week neither she nor her husband eat any meat. Then the girl makes a false vegetable-pudding, like the one made by a mother of a new baby. She throws it away in the bush. Then her husband goes hunting, and when he has found meat he and she make a feast for all who have helped them, for the women who have carried firewood and water, for those who beat her with nettles, for those who brought coloured clay and painted her. For a month the girl herself will eat no meat, nor drink cold water or the milk of young coconuts, nor eat sugar-cane. Then it is finished. In the future, she goes without ceremony to her menstrual hut.

This ceremony which officially ends a girl's childhood is of another order from a boy's initiation, although it has many elements in common with it—the nettles, the hygienic self-inflicted pain, the segregation, and the ceremonial emergence. But the boy passes from one way of life into another; before, he was a boy, now he is a man with a man's responsibilities and therefore he may share in the secrets of men. For the girl there is no such emphasis. For four years or so she has lived in her husband's household. She has carried firewood and water, she has weeded and planted and harvested taro and greens, she has prepared food and tended the babies; she has danced when there has been special good luck in hunting or harvesting. She has gone with groups of young people to work sago. Her tasks have been grown-up tasks that she has shared with the women. The interior of a menstrual hut is no mystery to her; since babyhood she and her brothers and sisters have run in and out of them. Her puberty ceremony is no ritual admission to an order of life, but merely a ritual bridging of a physiological crisis that is important to her health and to her growth. It is not a marriage ceremony.

Her husband's clan already regard her as one of them. They as a group have fed her, they have made her body, she is a part of them, and they have also paid for her. From time to time the husband's family have sent meat to the bride's family. Some time after her puberty the chief payment for a wife is made, some dozen rings and shell valuables, of which three or four may be actually retained by her parents, while the remainder are merely exchanged for valuables of a similar size and beauty. Actually the expenditure is not very great; the food that the husband's family have contributed over a dozen years to the girl herself is far more valuable. But these interchanges of valuables and conspicuous payments of meat are the details most often referred to, they are the outer and visible signs that this is a true marriage of long planning and long standing. When a child is born it is paid for. A couple of rings if it is a boy, one or two more if it is a girl, are given to the mother's clan. This is to establish full claim to the child; more rings are paid for a girl than for a boy because otherwise the mother's clan might exercise claims to her bride-price or to her children later, when she is grown. These payments again have but slight economic value; they are rather symbols of the child's absolute membership in the paternal clan.

After the first menstruation ceremony, the betrothed girl's life goes on as before. The parents-in-law will continue their slight, unobtrusive chaperonage. She still sleeps in their hut, and if one of the daughters of the house is at home, the young sisters-in-law may sleep together. Just below the surface of articulate recognition by the community is the knowledge that sometime soon now, in a few months, in a year, this marriage will be consummated. Meanwhile, the girl makes herself a lovely grass skirt; with young wives a little older than she is, she spends many hours plaiting the sago-shoot shreds that she has wheedled some old woman into dyeing a beautiful red. She keeps her skin bathed and shining, and wears her necklace of opossum-teeth or dog's teeth every day. No one is fairer or gayer in the whole of Arapesh than these young girls waiting, in lovely attire, for life at last to catch up with them. No definite day is set; as the months pass, the parents relax their chaperonage more and more. The girl is fully mature now. The boy is tall and well developed. Some day the two, who are now allowed to go about alone together in the bush, will consummate their marriage, without haste, without a due date to harry them with its inevitableness, with no one to know or to comment, in response to a situation in which they have lived comfortably for years in the knowledge that they belong to each other.

7

Arapesh marriage

The Arapesh do not seriously conceive of sex outside of the marriage bond. The casual encounter, the liaison, a sudden stirring of desire that must be satisfied quickly—these mean nothing to them. Their ideal is essentially a domestic one, not a romantic one. Sex is a serious matter, a matter that must be surrounded with precautions; a matter above all in which the two partners must be of one mind. To blend together the "heat" that is male— heat not in a physiological sense but in a symbolic sense, as all things that have any contact with the supernatural are said to be hot, and the "cold" again not physical coldness but antipathy to the supernatural, which is female—is a dangerous matter. It is least dangerous when it occurs within the protective circle of long betrothal, when one's young, inexperienced wife is almost a part of one's own family, when one has seen her every day for years. Then she is no longer a stranger with whom sex-relations are tantamount to a surrender of a part of one's personality into the hands of sorcerers. For the Arapesh do not connect suddenly aroused passion and affection; instead they regard these two as strictly antithetical. Therefore if a man permits himself to be seduced by a woman whom he encounters casually, in a strange village, at a feast, it is reasonable for him to conclude that she seduced him with intent to sorcerise him, as an enemy and a stranger. Only with marriage—long-established, comfortable, friendly marriage—is sex safe and valuable.

Even within marriage certain precautions must be taken. Both bride and bridegroom must ritually rid themselves of the antipathetical heat and cold that have become intermingled. If this precaution is omitted, his yams will not flourish, his eye will not find game, and she will not bear strong and healthy children. But after this first precaution they are safe together. If he goes into his yam-gardens for harvesting, he will magically rid himself of the contact with womankind, and if he dances with the *tamberan*, he must rid himself of the *tamberan* contact before he can safely approach his wife. So also after he has held a corpse or killed a man, or carved a specially sacred *tamberan* mask called an *abuting*, he will take magical precautions not to bring these dangerous contacts to his wife. When his child's fontanelle heals over, again a crisis in his life has been passed, and the ritual blood-letting will be resorted to. A woman performs her analogous ritual only after first intercourse and after the death of her husband. Likewise after the death of a wife, a man again performs the ceremony. These are all part of the orderly conduct of life, the ritual devices for making something that is dangerous into something safe and comfortable and warm—for shutting out fear from the hearts of the people.

A chance encounter, on the other hand, holds no guarantee of safety. Such an occurrence is always phrased as seduction, and, because it is the men who walk abroad and chance upon the home paths of strange women, it is thought of as seduction of a man by a woman. Fathers warn their sons: "When you travel abroad, sleep in the houses of relatives. Wherever there is a woman who is related to you, a sister, a cousin, a father's sister, a mother's brother's wife, a sister-in-law, there you will be safe. But do not go about on strange roads, with your mouth open in a wide smile. If you meet a strange woman do not stop and talk with her. Before you know it she will have seized you by both cheeks, your flesh will tremble and grow weak, and you will be delivered into the hands of the sorcerers. And you will die young and never live to see grey hairs." Besides the fear of sorcery, these chance encounters, based on flaring, surface-stimulated passion, are full of the quick burning character that mixes a male and a female nature too quickly and is dangerous to the man's and woman's appointed tasks in rearing children. Such encounters have to be ritually exorcised each time, even should they be repeated with the same woman. There is no safety, no familiar comfort, possible in them.

With this repudiation of passion perishes all the romanticism connected with the stranger, the new face, the unaccustomed gesture. It is the known, the domesticated, love that the Arapesh want, the love which is concerned with food given and received, with many years of sleeping in the same village. The slight, pleasantly romantic attitude towards very small girls fits in well with this preference; it is the child who may be reared to an all-confining domesticity who seems to them desirable. In such a setting, the unaggressive, slowly awakening sexuality of the Arapesh personality finds its best expression. Neither men nor women are regarded as spontaneously sexual. When either a man or a woman makes a definite sex-initiating act outside of marriage, where it is the situation and not the wish of the individual that is thought to give the signal to desire, some other motive rather than a simple sexual impulse is always attributed. This motive may be either sorcery or, within the narrower community, a man's desire to win as his wife a woman now married to another. For although the Arapesh have no fondness for a liaison, occasionally a man who lacks a wife will be moved by the attractiveness of another man's wife, especially if the other man is careless of her virtues himself, too much taken up with another wife. Then in order to persuade her to elope with him, to appear to be abducted by him, the man may have intercourse with the woman he hopes to win. This is the most complete earnest of his honourable intentions that he can offer her, since by so doing he lays his life in her hands; and if she does not trust him, she may be expected to provide herself with the means of his undoing. Later, if he has changed his mind and proved unfaithful to his first promises, his conscience will convince him that she has placed him in the hands of the sorcerers.

Young Alis was slowly dying of anxiety over a similar situation. Two years before, at a feast in Yimonihi, a faraway village on the road of the setting sun, he had met a Plainswoman who had seduced him. She had done so in order to persuade him to take her back with him to his mountain village, where the women wore such beautiful clothes and both men and women had lovely shell ornaments. She wished to have her nose pierced in the end and wear a feather in it, instead of having only a hole in the side of one nostril and wearing a little string of beads as was the fashion of the plains. Alis had yielded and then, his nerve failing him, he had fled back to Alitoa without her. He had remembered his young wife Taumulimen, whom he liked very much and who had not yet borne him a child. If he brought this tall avid stranger into their home, Taumulimen would probably run away. For the behaviour of these Plainswomen is well known. They are jealous and actively sexed, rapacious and insatiable. They have none of the home-loving virtues that the Arapesh cherish in women. Women, say the Arapesh, are of two kinds: those which are like big fruit-bats, the bats that nurse their young at only one breast while one breast hangs dry and empty, and which hang up outside the house in the storm and rain; and those like the little gentle bats which live safely in holes in trees, feeding and watching over their young. The Plainswomen are like the fruit-bats; the Arapesh ideal woman is like the little bat that guards its young within its home. Occasionally one of these Plainswomen, one who is a little more aggressive and a little more violent even than her sisters, will quarrel finally and irrevocably with her husband and run away to throw herself upon the mercy of the mountain people, in order to find herself a docile husband and a more polished way of life. And find a husband she does, for the Arapesh man is not accustomed to resisting the determined advances of a woman who has settled herself on his door-step. She moves in, and as often as not succeeds in monopolising all of her husband's attention, in driving away the little mountain wife who has no weapons with which to fight back. All of these things were well known to Alis, and he shuddered, partly in thought of Taumulimen and partly in remembrance of his skill as a hunter, which would surely suffer if he brought such a turbulent woman into his home. A month after he deserted her, he heard that she was dead. He did not doubt for one moment that she had placed a small bit of his personality in the hands of some sorcerer relative. But which one? There was no way of telling. No blackmail message came. Perhaps she had not had time herself to tell the sorcerer who her seducer had been. In any case, she was dead, and the sorcerers would very justifiably believe that Alis had taken similar precautions against her, and encompassed her death by sending his theft in to different sorcerers. So probably they would send no blackmail message—they would be satisfied only with his death. For a man who feels a slight malaise from sorcery, there is the help of a menstruating woman;* for one who is sure he has been sorcerised, there is an emetic. As the sorcerer smokes the bit of dirt over his unhallowed fire, the *mishin*, the life-soul of the victim, struggles to rise in his throat. In its attempt to rise, a thick white fluid is generated, which gradually wells up in the throat of the victim, choking him and permitting the life-soul to escape and travel overland into the sorcerer's waiting bamboo tube, in which it will be burnt or beaten to death. To avoid this, to exhaust the white fluid at least for a time, the victim takes an emetic called *ashup*, a brew of extraordinary bitterness. To this

---

*A man who feels that he is being subjected to sorcery may go to a menstruating woman and get her to pound him on the chest while he holds his hunting-hand aloft. Her potency will drive out the magical powers that are injuring him.

emetic Alis in his misery and fear had continual recourse. Sickened, weakened by the emetic, he ate less and less, and was gradually wasting away, paying for his wicked foolishness in sleeping with a woman and then deserting her. As he wasted, the tinea with which his young wife had been only slightly infected before spread more and more over her skin, as it seems to do when someone with a slight infection becomes worried or unhappy.

Of rape the Arapesh know nothing beyond the fact that it is the unpleasant custom of the Nugum people to the southeast of them. To people who conceive sex as dangerous even within a sanctioned relationship where both partners give complete acquiescence, the dangers of rape do not need to be pointed out. Nor do the Arapesh have any conception of male nature that might make rape understandable to them. If a man carries off a woman whom he has not won through seduction, he will not take her at once, in the heat of his excitement over having captured her. Rather he will delay soberly until he sees which way the negotiations turn, whether there is a battle over her, what pressure is brought upon him to return her. If she is not to belong to him permanently, it is much safer never to possess her at all.

This fear of exercising any compulsion extends even into the ordinary relations between a man and his wife. A man must approach his wife gently, he must make "good little talk," he must be sure that she is well prepared to receive his advances. Otherwise even she, who has been reared by his side, on his food, may become a stranger, the inimical one. There is no emphasis upon satisfaction in sex-relations; the whole emphasis for both men and women is the degree of preparedness, the completeness of the expectancy. Either man or wife may make the tentative advance that crystallises a latent consciousness of the other into the sex act. It is as customary for the woman as for the man to say, "Shall I lay the bed?" or, "Let us sleep." The verb "to copulate" may be used either with a male subject and a female object, or with a female subject and a male object. More often the phrase

"They played together" or "They slept" is used. Women express their preferences for men in terms of ease and lack of difficulty of sex-relationships, not in terms of ability to satisfy a specific desire. There is no recognition on the part of either sex of a specific climax in women, and climax in men is phrased simply as loss of tumescence. The emphasis upon mutual readiness and mutual ease is always the dominant one.

The oral sensitivity so highly developed in childhood and early adolescence is continued into adult sex life. It will be remembered that this oral play has been checked in boys at adolescence, and in spite of the partial substitution of areca-nut chewing and smoking, this requires a certain amount of self-control. At the same time, the taboo upon any careless handling of the genitals has prevented the development of masturbation. The boy comes to marriage, therefore, with his oral sensitivity somewhat muted, a strong taboo upon any mixture of oral and genital contacts, and some feeling against any type of tactual stimulation. The girl has not been dealt with so stringently; she has been permitted to bubble her lips right up to her marriage, and if she wishes, she is permitted to continue the comforting practice until she substitutes a child at her breast. The rigorous hygienic practices of the menstrual hut have insured her against feeling even first intercourse as painful. She shares with her husband the taboo against combining oral and genital contacts. It is probable that among a people in whom oral sensitivity is permitted such a highly specialised development, the existence of this taboo has very definite results in ensuring a complete genital expression of sex in adult life. The highly prized oral stimulation falls into place as foreplay, and it is interesting and significant that the Arapesh, unlike most primitive people, possess the true kiss, that is, lip-contact that is punctuated by a sharp implosion of the breath.

In their marriage structure, the Arapesh are a people who presume monogamy but permit polygyny. Polygyny is not an ideal state, a state towards which every successful man naturally aspires, but it is a condition in which one is likely to find oneself, and its causes are several. The most important contributory factor is death. When a man dies leaving a widow, there is a strong feeling that she should remarry within his clan, to which she is now felt to belong.

There is no thought of binding her over to a perpetual mourning. The Arapesh have no ideology about either the living or the dead that would dictate such a course. The dead have gone beyond the reach of all desire, there is no need to placate them with elaborate mourning or with celibate widows. A ritual device will separate the wife for ever from any contact with her dead husband. It is true that if she and her new husband fail to take the ritual precautions, then the dead husband will walk always by the side of the living one. As the live husband puts his spoon into his dish, a ghostly spoon will dip out an equal share and the dish be emptied in half the time; as the live husband puts his hand into his yam-house, a ghostly hand will draw out with him yam for yam. But this nightmare is kept as a nightmare; in real life widows take proper precautions, men who marry widows are well instructed by those who have married widows before them. And even this behaviour on the part of the ghost is not viewed as anger against the new husband, but as the existence of too close a bond between the living and the dead, one that should have been ritually severed.

There is no belief that the wife is responsible for her husband's death and so must make a long and painful ritual expiation, mourning at the dictation of her dead husband's kin. She is one of them, and the most greatly bereaved of all. They would repudiate any thought of an exacting mourning that would make her weak and ill, as they would repudiate it for their own daughters. But after all, she is not a daughter, she is a daughter-in-law, a putative wife of a member of the clan, and as such she should be married to a member of the clan, to one of the brothers of the deceased. This is especially true if she has children; it is right that they should be brought up in their father's place, to know his roads and his trees. If a woman takes her child home to her own clan, later the men of her clan will claim it because they have grown it. Unless there is some strong reason against it, therefore, a widow is remarried within her husband's patrilineal group, or sometimes to a cross-cousin of her husband. If she has been unhappy far away from home, if she has no children, if there is no one who particularly wants to marry her, if there is someone else whom she wishes to marry—for these and other similar reasons she may be allowed to go back to her own people. If she does marry outside her husband's kin, the second husband will give presents not to her kin, but to the kin of her former husband, to whom she really belongs. The first child she bears will be of mixed allegiance, belonging equally to the former husband's clan and to the clan of the second husband. Such children are said to be hard to discipline; they slip through the fingers of one set of relatives into the warm welcoming hands of the other set.

But three-quarters of the widows remarry within their husbands' group. And as women are younger than their husbands, and are exposed to far less risks from hunting and trading abroad in hostile country, most women expect to be widowed at least once. There is no insistence that a widow should marry a man older than herself; this would be particularly difficult because neither would older men have a need for more than one wife nor have they the food to support another wife. It is the young men around thirty who are called upon to marry their brother's widows and support their brother's children. The proper relative position of these inherited wives is very clear in the Arapesh minds. The true wife, the wife who really matters, is the wife to whom a man was betrothed while she was yet a child, the wife for whom he has paid rings and meat, and more importantly still, the wife whom he has grown to womanhood. She takes precedence in his home, she should be consulted first and treated with more honour. This feeling is definite enough, although very slightly expressed because the Arapesh lack most of the ritual paraphernalia of deference or precedence. The widow who enters her house should come as a bereaved and already beloved sister-in-law. For many years the two women have known each other well, more intimately even than sisters. They are pleasantly sentimental about each other. As one woman said to me, as she and her husband's brother's wife sat over a smoky fire at midnight, dyeing sago-shoots for grass skirts: "To be alone is bad. Two by two we go for water, two by two we gather firewood, two by two we dye our grass skirts." Such women have nursed each other in illness and attended each other in childbirth. If their children are nearly of an age, they have suckled each other's children. They have sat for long, drowsy days, after some heavy task was done, each with a child at the breast, singing together or making net bags, and talking quietly. One calls the other *megan*, and this is a term of affection and confidence. As I would be sitting with one woman and another woman married into the same clan would pass by, my companion would turn to me and remark beamingly, "*Megan,*" with all the pride with which a schoolgirl says, "My best friend." Cowives are supposed to have stood in this relationship for years. Now one of these two is widowed, and must go as a secondary wife into the home of the other's husband. Theoretically it is always the elder who is widowed, who enters as wife the home of the man whom she has called "younger brother."* She is supposed to come quietly, to take up a motherly rôle in the household, and even though the inheriting husband actually sleeps with her, as he very often but not invariably does, she is expected to make no strong claims, to acquit herself instead like a woman whose own life is over, who lives now for her children.

It is very convenient for a man to have two wives; when one is menstruating, he has another one to cook for him. If he lives with both, the taboo of pregnancy is relieved. If one wife has a small child, the other can accompany him on his longer expedi-

---

*Actually, she uses the term that her husband uses for "younger sibling, same sex," uniting with her husband in terminology rather than using the term for "sibling of opposite sex, woman speaking."

tions. One wife can attend to part of his gardens and the other to a different part. He can leave one wife to look after a garden with a broken fence while he takes the other wife a day's journey away to work sago. If one of his brother's wives or children is ill, he can send one wife to do her share of nursing and still have a wife to cook for him and accompany him. Men are not enriched by women's work among the Arapesh; it is rather that having two wives makes a man's life easier and also stimulates him to do more work in which each wife can share. In the scattered semi-nomadic life with so many different interests to be cared for, it is very convenient to have two wives. Lastly, by taking a second wife a man links himself more closely and personally with the members of her clan.

This, then, is the Arapesh ideal of married life: the long years of betrothal during which two young people become inextricably used to each other, and the wife learns to look up to her older husband as a guide and near-parent; the first sex-experience an unforced, entirely private experience within this long-defined relationship; the gradual strengthening of the marriage bond as children are born and the young parents observe the protective taboos together; then as the husband approaches middle age, the entrance of an inherited wife into the household, a widow with children, one whom the wife has known always and whom she trusts. If all things fell out according to their gentle but badly organised formulations, Arapesh marriage would be as happy as they conceive it to be. There would be neither quarrelling between wives, nor dissension between husbands and wives, nor elopements, which are phrased as abductions and which bring fighting between the communities involved.

But like so many New Guinea marriage systems, the Arapesh plan is largely based upon events that are outside their control. They assume that between betrothal and child-bearing there will be no deaths, that every young man will marry the wife whom he has fed, that every girl will have as her final husband the boy who gave her food when she was small. And they further assume that later when deaths do occur they will occur in an orderly fashion, the elder brother dying before the younger brother, as would be the order of natural death. Every time that a betrothed boy or girl dies, the whole delicately balanced system is disarranged, with bad results not only for the survivor of the original betrothal but sometimes for a whole series of other marriages. Similar bad results may come from miscalculation over the relative ages of the betrothed pair and a subsequent shift in relationships. In this event the girl is married to another member of the clan, whom she has not learned to trust in the same degree, and the man is presented with a wife whom he has not grown. A third complication comes when women from the plains run away and marry mountain men. In all of these cases, misery may be the result. The occasional occurrence of some physical or extreme mental defect may cause a girl to refuse to stay with a defective husband, or a man to reject a defective wife. A few concrete instances of these various unforeseen but frequent upsets of the normal order of Arapesh marriage will show how these difficulties work out.

Ombomb, a boy of Alitoa,* had had small Me'elue of Wihun marked for him as a child. She was a lanky little creature, half covered with tinea. Just before she reached adolescence, a girl from another village, fleeing a marriage that she disliked, ran away to Ombomb. Ombomb kept her and performed her first puberty ceremonial, but later her relatives took her back. Unfortunately Ombomb, who was of a violent, arrogant disposition, atypical for an Arapesh, had made a few comparisons. After this he did not accept his thin little wife with quite as much enthusiasm. She was a frightened, apprehensive girl; her fear of not pleasing her husband was so great that she fumbled all she did. She bore a child, a girl, who was thin and spindly, with an abnormally big head. Ombomb took a good deal of care of the child, conforming to

---

*Unless another village is mentioned all of these persons are members of the locality of Alitoa.

Arapesh usage, but he was very little attached to either mother or child. He was destined to be a big man, there would be a great deal of very onerous work to be done, and Me'elue was not strong enough for it. When his little daughter was about a year old, there came a message for Ombomb from his cross-cousins in a village nearer the plains: "Two strong young Plainswomen have run away and come to us. We neither of us want them. But you are everlastingly complaining about Me'elue. Come and get one and bring another man with you who would like one too. Meanwhile we will keep them here." Ombomb called his cousin Maginala, whose betrothed wife had just died. Together they went to look at the women and Ombomb, as the more aggressive, selected the wife whom he preferred. Her name was Sauwedjo. She had a narrow face with a heavy jaw and little slits of eyes. She was purposeful and angry and lustful. She wore only the little four-inch grass skirt of a Plainswoman, and she was smarting under the indignities of a plains honeymoon,* with a husband whom she hadn't liked. Sauwedjo looked at Ombomb and she found him satisfactory. He was very tall for an Arapesh, five feet ten, and had a fine head of hair that he wore beach-fashion, in a basket ring at the back of his head. He had a hot temper and a quick arbitrary manner. She went home with him, and they settled down in a concentrated sex-relationship that suited his temperament far better than the slow, child-rearing, affectionate marriage of his own people. Sauwedjo monopolised all his attention. Wherever he went, she went also. When he was given meat, it was to her that

---

*In a plains honeymoon, the newly married couple are shut up together for a month, and one is not allowed to move for any purpose without the other accompanying, both haunted by a fear of sorcery. Only after the woman is pregnant—or failing that, after several months—are they permitted to emerge. Some of the women in the plains villages on the edge of the area that practices this honeymoon look enviously across the border, where women wear proper clothes and are not so humiliated.

he gave it. She became pregnant, and still he hardly turned to
Me'elue at all. Sauwedjo's child died at birth, and although it was
a girl, Ombomb was inconsolable. People began to talk among
themselves about his treatment of Me'elue. After all, she was his
first wife, his properly paid-for and grown wife. He left her for
weeks with his gardening partners, and hardly did his share in
preparing her garden-space, or providing food for her. The tinea
spread all over her body. It attacked her face, which was now a
mere bony frame for two big unhappy eyes. Talk grew. One of his
elders rebuked Ombomb. This was not the way to treat his true
wife. Moreover it was dangerous. One did not treat one's wife as
an enemy and still permit her to live close to one's person. Also, it
made too much work for his brothers and cousins to care for his
wife and child as much as they did. After all she was not a widow.
She was his wife and the mother of his child. If he did not want
her, he had better send her home. Ombomb was sulky. He had
no intention of sending her home. He continued to spend all his
time in the house of Sauwedjo, who became pregnant again and
bore another child, a girl. His two best houses stood side by side,
one in which Me'elue slept with her child when he permitted her
to come up to the village, and one in which he and Sauwedjo
laughed and ate meat and slept side by side. There was a third one
that was falling down the hill-side for lack of repairs. Ombomb
hitched it to a palm-tree with a piece of ratan, but he never
mended it. In this way he made public and explicit the fact that
he had no fear that he would ever need a third house in which to
sleep when neither of his wives pleased him. He spoke rather contemptuously of men who couldn't keep their wives in order, who
permitted one of them to quarrel with the other. People waited.
This wouldn't go on much longer, soon there would be talk of
sorcery. Unless Me'elue died first, as seemed very probable.

  One day I was sitting with her and two of her sisters-in-law
on the ground beneath her house. She had come up to the village
to fetch something from the house. There was a halloo from the
hills. Ombomb was coming from a long journey to the beach.

The face of the neglected little wife lit up with joy. She raced up her house-ladder and fell to cooking the best soup she knew. Her sisters-in-law each gave her something from their own larders to make it more palatable. They were very sorry for her. She was the first wife, the wife whom Ombomb had grown, and why should she be thrust aside, half starved and miserable, for a bold-eyed, lusting woman from the plains? That day Ombomb ate his first wife's soup, for Sauwedjo was far away on an errand. It was very good soup. He was tired, and pleased with the result of his own expedition. He fell asleep in the house of Me'elue, and Sauwedjo, for the first night since she had married him, slept alone in the house next door. The next day he sent the frightened, eager Me'elue away to her garden and returned to Sauwedjo. But Sauwedjo did not forget or forgive. Had she run away from her own people and found a man entirely to her liking, a man who was strong and hot-tempered and easily roused, only to have this little meek skin-infected creature triumph over her, even for a night?

The next time that Ombomb went away, Me'elue came up to the village with her little girl and entered the house of Sauwedjo and took from Ombomb's net bag, which Sauwedjo had left there, a string of dog's teeth that Ombomb, in a moment of temporary remorse, had promised his little daughter. Sauwedjo came home at evening and heard that Me'elue had been there. She seized her chance. She began to make low-voiced allegations, mixed with regretful comments on her own lack of care. Ombomb would beat her when he heard that she had left his net bag, with all his most personal possessions, alone for that spiteful little opossum of a wife of his to come and cut a piece off his headband, a piece that could be used for sorcery. Everyone knew she was one for sorcery. Years before when they had first been married, Ombomb had found a piece of taro-skin hidden in the roof and had known that she meant to sorcerise him. Oh, alas, what a careless wife she was to have left her husband's net bag that way! Surely no one must tell Ombomb, or he would be angry with her. But alas, alas! that Ombomb should die, that such a fine strong man should waste away, all for a little tinea-covered wife who was of no account except to steal into other people's houses and take her husband's dirt, and his poor Plains wife's too, for she had taken a piece of Sauwedjo's necklace also. On and on she muttered, and the talk spread. Madje, poor eager, tinea-covered Madje, who had just fully realised that he would never have a wife at all, for all his adolescent industry in building himself three splendidly made little houses all by himself, felt drawn to Me'elue, afflicted like himself. He went down to the taro-gardens where she and the child were living and told her. Tearful, blazing with anger and repudiation, panting from the exertion of climbing the hill, Me'elue arrived in the village. There on the *agehu* among a group of the women, she faced her rival. "Sorcerise Ombomb? Why should I do such a thing? I am his wife, his wife, his wife. He grew me. He paid for me. I have borne him children. Am I an inherited wife, am I a stranger, that I should sorcerise him? I am his own wife, the wife whom he grew." Sauwedjo sat with the net bag in front of her, its contents spread out, the headband with the missing cord significantly on top. The eldest woman in the group acted as a kind of judge. "Did you take your child with you when you climbed into Sauwedjo's house?" "No, I left her down below." "And entered alone the house of your co-wife. Silly!" The eldest woman slapped the sobbing Me'elue slightly with the end of one of the necklaces. Sauwedjo sat saying little, suckling her child, a sly satisfied smile on her face. Me'elue sobbed on: "He does not give me food. He never looks at me nor takes food from my hand. I and my child go hungry. We eat the food of others. This stranger woman is always angered at me. If he makes a garden for me, if he cuts down trees and fences my garden, she is angry. She is too strong. She eats meat, and I and my child, we stop without anything." From Sauwedjo, bent above her child, came a contemptuous and proud: "Oh, I eat meat, do I? Tcha!" The eldest woman went on speaking to Me'elue: "You are not a woman who came here after you were

grown that we should suspect you of sorcery. You were but a little thing when you came, when we paid for you." Me'elue burst
out again: "Am I a stranger! Am I a late-acquired wife? Now I
have borne him a child, a daughter. She remains. Why should I
sorcerise him? I did not. He came down to me, he said: 'Go and
get the dog's teeth. Fasten them on the neck of our child.' So I
did so." The eldest woman says again: "You were well paid for.
Ten rings he paid for you. You are his first wife. You are not a
stranger." Me'elue, inconsequently: "And her water-bamboo. She
says I broke that too. Madje, he said so." This gave Sauwedjo a
chance to appear beneficent and generous. She replied, through
her teeth: "I did not say so. The water-bamboo that is mine, I
alone broke it." Sagu, another young sister-in-law, spoke up
pacifically: "A stranger, another, must have cut the string. There
are always Plainsmen coming to Ombomb's house. One of them
has entered and done it." But Sauwedjo would accept no such
alibi: "There have been people in the village all of the time. They
would have seen if a Plainsman entered the house. She, that one,
alone entered. Of you only have they spoken." Me'elue
responded, more breathless, more trapped, more tearful each
time she spoke: "Always, always she scolds me. They two, they
stay always together. He does not treat me like a wife. Those
dog's teeth were mine." "But," says the eldest woman reprov-
ingly, "they were in Sauwedjo's house." Me'elue stood up, frenzy
giving a certain dignity to her weak, bedraggled little body, which
looked as if she had never borne a child: "I shall take my yams,
my baskets. I shall go down below altogether. I carried only a little basket. When I returned I emptied it. It was not a big basket
to hold hidden sorcery things. When I emptied out the basket, all
would have seen it. Lately, the pigs ate my taro. I said: 'Never
mind.' I have no husband, I have no husband to look after me, to
clear the ground and to plant. I am the wife whom he paid for as
a child. I am not a stranger." And sadly, still crying, she went
down the hillside.

The feeling of the village was divided. Many people thought

that perhaps Me'elue had cut the hair-ornament. No one would have blamed her if she had. The argument that she was the true wife cut both ways, for Ombomb had treated her not like his true wife, but like a stranger. Treated so abominably, left to the care of others, never given the opportunity to give her husband food, what wonder if Me'elue had come to feel like a stranger? Who would have blamed her? On the other hand, she was a sweet and gentle person, she had borne her deposition quietly, without using obscenity against Ombomb. This in itself proved that she was good and possessed one of the virtues that the Arapesh most value in women. For a man to whom obscenity is used in public is vulnerable. If the obscenity is overheard by anyone who has a grudge against him or wishes to discipline him for some failure towards the community, it can be told to one of his *buanyins* or cross-cousins, and they can summon the *tamberan*. All the men of the community, carrying the *tamberan*, will gather at the victim's house, nominally to scare and punish his wife, who flees incontinently before the *tamberan*, while the *tamberan's* human companions scatter her rings, tear her net bag, and break her cooking-pots. But they also cut down a tree or so belonging to the insulted husband, and strew leaves on the house floor; he is shamed in their eyes, and must run away from the community until he finds a pig among some distant relations, with which he can placate the *tamberan*. Ombomb had several pigs and therefore was vulnerable, for he was preparing to make the first of a series of feasts that would lead to his being a big man. If Me'elue had chosen to hurt him, she could have resorted to public obscenity, but she had not. In actual fact, very few wives try either obscenity or sorcery. But the uneasy consciences of neglectful husbands warn them to expect treachery where there is none. And for all that Me'elue had never used obscenity, she might have taken the slyer, safer course. So the community reasoned.

On the other hand, Sauwedjo was not free from suspicion herself. She belonged to the plains, to those who are rapacious and never satisfied. Her ways were not the ways of a decent woman; she cared for sex for its own sake and had taught Ombomb to do so also. She took all the meat and left none for Me'elue. She was not content with a share of her husband, she must needs have all of him. And everyone knew that she had been angry and sullen that one time when Me'elue had cooked Ombomb's dinner for him. It was possible that Sauwedjo and not Me'elue had wished to sorcerise Ombomb. And there was a third possibility, that Sauwedjo had merely faked the whole affair, that she had cut Ombomb's headband, and a piece of her own to divert suspicion from herself, not to sorcerise Ombomb but merely to cast suspicion upon poor Me'elue and complete her overthrow. Anyway, the whole position was a scandal. Ombomb was beginning to behave altogether too much like his elder half-brother Wupale, who had thrown spears at his own relatives and left Alitoa while Ombomb was still a child, never to return. Ombomb had inherited his coconut-palms and his land, and apparently was taking after his violent ways also.

When Ombomb returned from his journey, Sauwedjo did not tell him of her accusation, shielding herself behind her pretended anxiety over her dereliction in duty in leaving his net bag unattended. But one of his brothers told him. At first he was scornful; he had told Me'elue to come and get the dog's teeth, what was this all about anyhow? But after a day or so his self-confidence wavered. He had seen the cut string. Sauwedjo had had her say. Ombomb revised his statement that he had told Me'elue she could have the dog's teeth, and said that he had merely promised them to his small daughter and the mother must have overheard. After about a week of gossip and underground comment, Ombomb went down to the gardening-patch where Me'elue lived with his old mother, but he did not see Me'elue. He told his elder brother to find her, take her home to her parents, and bring back the dirt that she had taken them. He made a croton-leaf sign and fastened it beside Me'elue's fire. This was to summon her to bring back the dirt.

Two days later, there were many people in Alitoa on their

way home from a feast. Among them was Nyelahai, one of the big men of the community, and his two wives. The elder of these was a woman whom Nyelahai had formerly called "aunt," a woman already a grandmother, whom he had taken in her widowhood to keep his house and feed his pigs. This old woman was still vigorous and touchy in her rather dull position as the pig-keeper and housekeeper of a big man. She heartily disliked the younger wife, Natun, who was the beautiful younger sister of Me'elue, Ombomb's wife. Natun represented another irregular marriage. Nyelahai had originally marked her for his younger brother, Yabinigi, and she had come to live in the household expecting to marry Yabinigi. But Yabinigi was almost stone-deaf and given to running amuck, and when Natun reached puberty, she refused to marry him. Nyelahai was a widower, with only his old pig-keeper and a small and sickly son of ten. He was old for Natun, he had regarded her almost as a daughter. His marriage to her would almost transgress the rule that the elder generation should never compete for women with the younger. But Natun was young and lovely, and furthermore, Nyelahai was very much attached to her mother, who was young and sprightly and little older than himself. He could not bear to lose the company of the daughter and the chance of the company of the mother, who, although not a widow, spent much time with her daughter. He married Natun, and he called her mother not "mother-in-law," but by the intimate term reserved for one's own mother, *yamo*. The community almost approved of the marriage. After all, Yabinigi was deaf and impossible; but they stubbornly continued to refer to Natun as "Yabinigi's wife whom Nyelahai had taken." This is the kind of quiet stubborn pressure that Arapesh public opinion applies, in the absence of any stronger sanctions for interfering adequately in the behaviour of a man as valuable to them as the oratorically gifted Nyelahai.

Nor was Natun comfortable in her new position, which was full of anomalies. The old wife, first wife in time and no wife in fact, herself in the position of having been married out of her age-group, disliked her. Natun felt uncomfortable with a husband so much her senior, a man who really was more comfortable with her mother than with herself. Yabinigi's big dog-like eyes followed her about. And now the curse that had descended upon all of Nyelahai's former offspring except the one sickly child who had survived fell on her new baby. It began having convulsions. She accused the old wife of having brought the illness from some of her own relatives, whose sick child she had been visiting. Over this accusation the two wives quarrelled, and in the course of the quarrel Natun said that presently the old wife would go and cry at her nephew Ombomb's funeral, and one look at the corpse would proclaim how he died—that is, that he had died of sex sorcery. This accusation was repeated when the people passed through Alitoa, and Ombomb and his relatives took it as proof that Natun knew that her sister Me'elue had taken Ombomb's dirt and sent it on to the Plains sorcerers. This was in spite of Me'elue's nominal theft having been a piece of headband.

Natun and Nyelahai remained in Alitoa after the crowd had departed, and Ombomb's elder brother came into the village bringing the father and mother of Me'elue to answer the accusation. Nyelahai sat by his mother-in-law and offered her areca-nut, and people smiled happily over this affectionate behaviour. Ombomb produced the cut headband and Sauwedjo's cut necklace, accused Me'elue of having taken them, and demanded their return. The father countered that many men had worn that headband, and who was to know against whom the cutting had been directed, and anyway, Sauwedjo had undoubtedly done it to cast suspicion upon his poor defenceless daughter, whom she treated very badly anyhow. Me'elue came up from the gardens after everyone had assembled. This was the first time that she and Ombomb had met face to face since the supposed theft. He hurled himself forward, demanding violently why she had done this thing. She stood by her own parents, answering very little, sad, and resigned to returning with them. A brother of Ombomb's stepped out of the group and presented Me'elue with a tied croton-leaf, which laid upon her the obligation to cease from her sorcery machinations. She and her parents, the latter reiterating that they never trafficked in sorcery, turned and left the *agehu.* Sauwedjo had won. If Ombomb became ill or died, even their own community of Wihun would turn against Me'elue and her parents, regarding them as having disregarded this public warning, one that the big men of Wihun repeated to them also.

I have told this story in some detail because it illustrates the kind of rocks upon which Arapesh marriage may drift. In this one incident, involving the two sisters, Me'elue and Natun, we have partial rejection of a fed wife by her husband, himself of aberrant and violent temperament; complete rejection of a deaf betrothed by his young betrothed wife; the marriage of a widower to a woman much older than himself, which made her status anomalous; the marriage of a man to the betrothed wife of a brother who was so much younger than himself that the father-son age grading was involved; and most disruptively of all, the entrance into the mountain community of a runaway Plainswoman with her different standards. Arapesh marriage is not arranged to stand such strains, and trouble results.

For one marriage that fails and plunges the community into acrimonious quarrelling and accusations of sorcery, the great majority succeed. And if I recount these marital tangles, I must do so with the reiterated statement that these are the unusual situations, not the pattern of Arapesh married life, which, even in the polygynous marriages, is so even and contented that there is nothing to relate of it at all. The ethnologist cannot be for ever recording: "The two wives of Baimal with their two small daughters came into the village today. One of them remained to cook dinner, and the other took the two children and went for firewood. When she returned the dinner was cooked, Baimal came in from hunting, they all sat around the fire until chilliness drove them inside, and from within the house where the whole family sat together came the sounds of low laughter and quiet conversation." This is the texture, the pattern, of Arapesh life, quiet, uneventful co-operation, singing in the cold dawn, and singing and laughter in the evening, men who sit happily playing to themselves on hand-drums, women holding suckling children to their breasts, young girls walking easily down the centre of the village, with the walk of those who are cherished by all about them. When there is a quarrel, an accusation of sorcery, it breaks through this texture with a horrid dissonance that is all the sharper because the people are unaccustomed to anger, and meet hostility with fear and panic rather than with a fighting *élan*. In their panic and fright, people seize firesticks and hurl them at each other, break pots, cast about for any weapon that comes casually to hand. And this is specially true because Arapesh marriage has no formal pattern that takes account of anger and hurt. The assumption is that the mild, gentle husband, eight years or so older than his docile and devoted wife, will live with her in amity. Her own kin keep no sharp surveillance over her. It is not customary for her to run home to her father or brother over some slight disagreement. Her husband is now as close to her as her own blood-relatives, as much to be trusted and relied upon. He and she are separated by no differences in temperament; he is simply older and wiser than she, and equally committed to the growing of food and children.

But if he should die or turn his attention entirely to another wife, the wife goes through the drastic experience of a second weaning, an experience that her brother has undergone in some measure when he is weaned from his second great attachment, his father, but which she has been spared. From a small toddler, balancing a huge net bag from her forehead, she has been surrounded by loving care; she has passed from the home of her father-in-law to the home of her husband without a wrench. There have always been older women with her whose constant companion she has been. Her marriage has been no sudden, frightening shock, but the gradual ripening of a tried affection. Widowhood comes as the first break in the security of her life. Not since her mother left her alone with women who had no milk has she known such misery. And perhaps because this experience of bereavement comes to a woman so late, after she has spent so many sheltered years, she is likely to react with more violence than does the eleven-year-old boy, raging after his father's departing steps. Widowhood is, of course, a major weaning experience, when the husband on whom she has depended is entirely removed by death, but Me'elue suffered something of the same sort when Ombomb, whom she had been reared to love and trust, turned to Sauwedjo. All the threads upon which her life had been suspended were rudely torn away. This experience of losing a husband or a husband's affection is the one that brings self-consciousness to Arapesh women. It is at this crisis rather than at adolescence that a woman sees herself pitted against her environment, wanting that from it which it is unwilling or unable to give her.

Very occasionally this awakening may come at adolescence. This is particularly true if one or other of the betrothed pair has some defect. Then the parents may keep the young people a little apart until, with the girl's adolescence, she must finally take up her residence in her husband's home. In such cases her dependence upon him is not the result of actual day-by-day contact, but rather a contented identification of herself with all other betrothed girls and young wives in their attitudes towards their husbands. When she finds her husband, then, to be deaf, or foolish, or diseased, she may fling away from the shock and refuse to go on with the marriage. This was what happened to Temos, the daughter of Wutue. Wutue was a quiet, frightened little man; he spent all of his time gardening in the bush, and his young relatives came and gardened with him, while he himself went about very little. During the period when Temos was ten or eleven, her mother died, and although she was already betrothed to Yauwiyu, she was kept much at home with her widower father. Yauwiyu was an empty-headed, very unstable youth. Wutue was himself a little afraid of the boy, and anyway he needed Temos at home to care for her younger sisters under the unusually isolated conditions of the life that they led. And before Temos reached adolescence, another of the ubiquitous Plainswomen came on the scene, and married herself to Yauwiyu. Temos as a young, not yet adolescent girl entered her husband's house, to find a jealous, ranting Plainswoman there before her. Nor did she like Yauwiyu, with his silly grin and boorish gaiety. Before she reached adolescence, she ran home to her father, and refused to have anything more to do with Yauwiyu. She had learned to storm and rage in the manner of her Plains cowife, and Wutue was now a little afraid of her also. He and his brother consulted, and finally decided that it might be well to betroth this unrestful child to someone who had the age and wisdom to supply that contrast between husband and wife which the Arapesh depend upon age alone to produce. They selected Sinaba'i, a mild, middle-aged widower, father of two children, a man who had not hoped to find himself another wife, since he was a member of a vanishing clan and there were no widows to come his way. The house of Sinaba'i, one that he shared with his young cousin Wabe, stood just opposite the house which Wutue shared with his nephew Bischu when they two came into Alitoa. Temos had known Sinaba'i all her life. Now she spent part of her time working with his young daughter in his gardens. His gardens were not plentiful. Sinaba'i was too sympathetic, too willing to yield to every suggestion, too compliant to everyone's demands, to provide even the Arapesh minimum of individual effort. He lived in half of a house that really belonged to Wabe, who lived in its other end.

Now Wabe was having troubles of his own. He was the elder brother of Ombomb, and he was more violent, more sulky, and less well adjusted than his younger brother. The Arapesh convention that sex-desire is something which arises in marriage, but does not spring up spontaneously, was not congenial to Wabe. While his young affianced wife, Welima, was still pre-adolescent, Wabe had yielded to the importunities of his Wihun cousins—the same cousins who had held Sauwedjo until Ombomb could come and fetch her—to play the part of abductor in the capture of Menala, a girl who had been betrothed to a man of another village. Menala's kin were disgruntled with her betrothed husband. He had not acknowledged the marriage by a payment of rings, he never sent any meat to his wife's people, he did not come to help them with their gardening or house-building, he had taken another wife who mistreated Menala. For all this the kin of Menala were angry.

But according to Arapesh custom, a wife's kin do not take her away from her husband unless they wish to provoke a genuine fight. The wife's people have given the child to the husband's people; the husband's people have fed her, she is theirs. The payment of rings and meat about which there is so much conversation is not really regarded as the binding element, for even though the payment has not been made the wife's people usually do not feel justified in taking their daughter back.* It must be remembered that the Arapesh do not make the sharp distinction that so many peoples make between blood-relationship and relationship by marriage. A brother-in-law is as close to one as a brother; to find that he has turned against one is a devastating, a maddening experience. Under such conditions, a woman's husband's elder brother is more likely to take her part, to protect her if her husband neglects her, to rebuke her husband as a parent does a child, than are her own relatives. This condition makes for peace and family solidarity among the Arapesh. There is a lack of the continual bickering between in-laws, the continual cross-

---

*Very occasionally a daughter will be taken back as part of a real feud; so the men of Banyimebis took their sister as a way of showing their contempt for a man who had become a proselyte to a strange religious cult that came up from the beach. He had lied and tricked the people, and they were angry; the brothers of his wife were particularly angry to have had their sister involved in a fraud. They took her back. But in such cases, the taking back of the wife is merely a secondary aspect of a quarrel about something else. And even this is infrequent.

purposes between husband and wife that result when each one has antithetical kin-dictated interests at heart. For a wife to stand upon the same footing in a clan as a sister or a daughter guarantees her a solid position that is lacking among peoples whose marriage systems are differently organised. But if she is mistreated, if her own kin are actually disgruntled with the marriage, then a difficulty arises, for it is as complicated for an Arapesh to take back his own sister as it would be for him to assist his brother's wife to escape from his brother. If such a situation arises, it is necessary to stage an abduction. The kin of the mistreated or restive wife suggest quietly to some enterprising bachelor, widower, or disgruntled husband, of a different hamlet and, if possible, of a different locality, that he carry off their sister. In most cases the sister is a party to this plan; when the abducting party seize her as she goes for water or firewood, accompanied by a child or so to serve as witnesses, she will only pretend to struggle and scream; secretly she will acquiesce.

It was such a plan as this which was presented to Wabe. Here was a strong young girl whom he knew slightly and of whom he approved, who was being neglected and underfed by an unappreciative husband. The brothers of Menala arranged for the abduction and Wabe and his cross-cousin surprised the girl on the road accompanied by a child, and carried her off with them. She resisted, but this was regarded as appropriate pantomime. Wabe brought Menala home to live with him, into the house with his mother and his not yet adolescent betrothed wife, Welima. Now Menala was stupid—easy-going, good-natured, but stupid. She never quite realised that Wabe had not actually abducted her against her will. His harsh, excited hold on her arm became more of a reality to her than the neglect by her betrothed husband, to which her brothers may have been oversensitive. She settled down uneasily in Wabe's house; she made firm friends with Welima, who had been shy and nervous before the advent of the new wife. But she continued to remember that Wabe had carried her off against her will, and she used to mention it, resentfully at times, until Wabe began to believe it himself, and occasionally boasted of his prowess. Meanwhile, when they came up to the main village, Wabe and his wives shared one end of their house with Sinaba'i, the widower, and his children. Menala, uncertain and ill at ease with the violent Wabe, turned for comfort to the mild, middle-aged, stupid Sinaba'i, still wifeless, although the truculent little Temos had been promised him presently. Finally, Inoman, dull-witted half-brother of Wabe, reported to Wabe that he had overheard Menala and Sinaba'i making love to each other when they thought they were alone in the house.

Wabe was in a furore of anger and fear. How long had this been going on? Had Menala delivered him into the hands of the sorcerers? What about his yam-crop? For the yams of a man whose wife commits secret adultery are annoyed by it and slip away from his garden. He forced a confession from Menala and wanted to fight with Sinaba'i. But here an elder of the clan stepped in. Wabe and Sinaba'i were "brothers." Quarrelling over such a matter was inappropriate. Since Sinaba'i and Menala liked each other, it was obviously better that they should marry than that Wabe should keep a wife who did not wish to remain with him. Let Sinaba'i give Temos to Wabe, in spite of the fact that Temos and Wabe were cousins and their marriage therefore incorrect, and let him take Menala. And let Sinaba'i return all the presents of meat that Wabe had made to Menala's brothers. This Sinaba'i would never do. Everyone knew that, and Wabe stipulated that if he failed to do so, the first child born to Menala and Sinaba'i should be given to him. To this they agreed good-naturedly enough. Temos now became Wabe's destined wife and moved her fire from Sinaba'i's end of the house to Wabe's, again to adjust to a new future husband. Menala moved into Sinaba'i's end and they settled down to produce the child that would some day belong to Wabe.

Peace reigned except in the heart of Temos, who was reduced to a frantic state of insecurity by this third change. Twice she had been uprooted, and twice, so it seemed to her now, by other women. She forgot how stupid and foolish Yauwiyu was, and remembered only the cold sound of his Plains wife's voice. Then when she was just accustoming herself to the idea of marrying Sinaba'i, who was really a flabby, almost old, man, not at all the kind of husband that a young girl might look forward to, Menala had come and wrecked it all again. And now, in Wabe's house she found a third woman, the young Welima, who had watched with wide-eyed alarm and lack of comprehension all of these developments, these strange manoeuvrings of Wabe whom she adored, of Menala who was her trusted companion, and of Sinaba'i who was like a father to her. Temos decided to hate Welima, as a possible cause of a new disruption. This was all the easier because Menala, whom she also hated, remained firm friends with Welima.

Both girls reached puberty, and Wabe made their puberty ceremonials close together. Welima hid in Menala's menstrual hut, afraid to share a hut with Temos. When Wabe was kind to Welima, Temos stormed, and when he was kind to Temos, Welima wept and suffered from headaches. He built a separate house for Temos, and still another house as a refuge for himself. Welima continued to live in the house with Sinaba'i and Menala, and after Menala's baby boy was born, she devoted herself to this child. Temos became pregnant and miscarried after a storm of temper. She accused Wabe of having come to her unpurified from dancing with the *tamberan*. Wabe refused to make the customary payments that accompany a pregnancy, demanding bitterly why he should pay for blood upon the ground. He was harassed and unhappy and jealous. One little incident annoyed him particularly. A cousin of his had sent him half a wallaby. He told his wives to cook it. They immediately fell into an argument as to who was to cook it, Temos claiming the right to do so because the dog that had caught it belonged to her father's brother's son; but Welima and her mother-in-law had fed the dog's mother, so that in native thinking Welima was justified.

Finally the two fell to tussling. The fire went out, and Wabe took away the meat and cooked it himself.

Wabe, Temos, and Welima might be said to be suffering from polygyny. But one circumstance alone could not have produced the difficulties; the advent of Yauwiyu's Plains wife; Temo's father's peculiar hermit-like temper and his insistence upon her staying with him in his temporary widowhood; Menala's brothers' oversensitivity or unusual interest in political machinations; Menala's stupidity and inability to sort out structural and personal happenings and so distinguish between a formal abduction and a genuine act of violence; the peculiar form that the solution of the difficulty took in dictating an exchange between Temos and Menala—all of these factors had contributed to produce a difficult social situation among three people, two of whom were singularly unable to stand it, for neither Wabe nor Temos had the gentle, friendly temper to which Arapesh culture is adapted.

But even in these unusual and unhappy marriages, the influence of Arapesh standards can be clearly seen. Me'elue clung to Ombomb and lived patiently on his brother's bounty, as a rejected daughter might live on at home. And the difficulty resulting from one man's seducing his house-mate's wife was solved—not by a break-up of the living arrangements, but by an exchange of wives and the promise of a baby.

In their married lives it may be said that the Arapesh suffer from overoptimism, from a failure to reckon up the number of mischances that may wreck the perfect adjustment between a young man and his child wife. The very simplicity and sweetness of the ideal make the actual conditions of disruption and interruption more difficult to bear. The boys are not trained to habits of command and an attitude that expects submission from women because women are inherently different. They are trained merely to expect that their wives will obey because they are much younger and more inexperienced. Women are not trained to obey men, but merely to look up to their particular fostering husbands. When either men or women find themselves in a situation in which this condition does not obtain, they are at a loss. The husband still expects his wife to obey him but he has no idea why, and frustrated anger and purposeless quarrelling may result. It is the spectacle of gentle and well-meaning people caught in a net that they possess no culturally sanctioned weapons to sever, and in which they can only flounder and splutter. The ones who splutter and flounder most are the wives whose allegiances have been broken, girls like Temos who have been handed about from one potential husband to another, or young widows who are not old enough to settle down to the resignation that is the only well-defined rôle for a widow.

One case of adultery in middle age will serve to illustrate further the Arapesh attitude towards such occurrences within the family. Manum and Silisium were brothers. Manum was the elder, Silisium was the more intelligent. Both had adolescent children. And at this late date, the long association between Homendjuai, the wife of Manum, and her husband's brother Silisium developed into a sex-relationship. The native account was typical: "Once, on the road to Wihun, the two played. Manum suspected, but said nothing. Once, after a feast at Yapiaun the two played again. Manum guessed, but he did not speak. Finally a third time the two played. Then Manum was finally angry. He said: 'She is my wife. He is my brother, my younger brother. This is not right. I will stop it.' He set a woman of his kin to questioning Homendjuai. Homendjuai confessed. Then Manum spoke angrily to his brother, and Silisium was ashamed that he had taken his elder brother's wife, and Silisium ran away and took refuge from his brother's anger. He went to his wife's people, and his wife went with him. Manum, meanwhile, wished to beat Homendjuai. But Homendjuai's mother and aunt were visiting them, helping Homendjuai in her garden. If he had beaten Homendjuai, she could not have cooked for them. So he did not beat her. In a few days Silisium returned and gave a ring to his brother. After all, they were brothers; between brothers there can be no long anger." So Sumali, the brother of Homendjuai, told me the story, and a few days later I heard further comment from a group of young people from Ahalesemihi, the village of Manum and Silisium. They giggled at the idea of such middle-aged people becoming so involved in love-making, and while the adolescent son of Homendjuai merely grinned at such foolishness, the son of Silisium hung his head because after all Silisium was younger than Manum. These adulteries within the clan are those which are most congruent with the whole Arapesh ideal of familiar love, and they make much less trouble than the situations in which old and established relationships between a betrothed pair are upset by death, or by the entrance of a Plainswoman with a different standard of life.

Nowhere in Arapesh culture is their lack of structure, their lack of strict and formal ways of dealing with the interrelations between human beings, more vividly illustrated than in their marriage arrangements. Instead of structure they rely upon the creation of an emotional state of such beatitude and such tenuousness that accidents continually threaten its existence. And if this threat on occasion materialises, they manifest the fright and rage of those who have always been protected from hurt or unhappiness.

8

the Arapesh ideal and those who deviate from it

We have now followed the Arapesh boy and girl through early life, through puberty, and into married life. We have seen the way in which the Arapesh mould each child born within their society to an approximation of what they conceive the normal human personality to be. We have seen how they lack the conception of human nature as evil and in need of strong checks and curbs, and the way in which they conceive the differences between the sexes in terms of the supernatural implications of male and female functions and do not expect any natural manifestations of these differences in sex-endowment. Instead they regard both men and women as inherently gentle, responsive, and co-operative, able and willing to subordinate the self to the needs of those who are younger or weaker, and to derive a major satisfaction from doing so. They have surrounded with delight that part of parenthood which we consider to be specially maternal, the minute, loving care for the little child and the selfless delight in that child's progress towards maturity. In this progress the parent takes no egotistic pleasure, makes no excessive demands for great devotion in this world, or for ancestor-worship in the next.

The child to the Arapesh is not a means by which the individual ensures that his identity will survive his death, by which he maintains some slight and grasping hold upon immortality. In some societies the child is a mere possession, perhaps the most valuable of all, more valuable than houses and lands, pigs and dogs, but still a possession to be counted over and boasted of to others. But such a picture is meaningless to the Arapesh, whose sense of possession even of the simplest material objects is so blurred with a sense of the needs and obligations of others as to be almost lost.

To the Arapesh, the world is a garden that must be tilled, not for one's self, not in pride and boasting, not for hoarding and usury, but that the yams and the dogs and the pigs and most of all the children may grow. From this whole attitude flow many of the other Arapesh traits, the lack of conflict between old and young, the lack of any expectation of jealousy or envy, the emphasis upon co-operation. Co-operation is easy when all are wholeheartedly committed to a common project from which no one of the participators will himself benefit. Their dominant conception of men and women may be said to be that of regarding men, even as we regard women, as gently, carefully parental in their aims.

Furthermore, the Arapesh have very little sense of struggle in the world. Life is a maze through which one must thread one's way, battling neither with daemons within nor daemons without, but concerned always with finding the path, with observing the rules that make it possible to keep and find the path. These rules which define the ways in which sex and growth may and may not be brought in contact are many and complicated. From the time that a child is six or seven he must begin to learn them, by early puberty he must be taking responsibility for their observance, and by the time he is adult a careful meticulous observance, which will make yams grow beneath his hand, game come to his traps and snares, and children spring within his household, will be established. There is no other major problem in life, no evil in man's own soul that must be overcome.

Upon those who do not share this mild and loving attitude towards life, the Plainsmen, the Arapesh project the responsibility for all their misfortunes, for accidents and fire, for illness and death. Their own supernatural guardians, the *marsalais*, punish lightly and always for a breach of one of the rules by which men live in comfort with the forces of the land, or because men have failed to keep separate the natural potency of female functions and the supernatural forces that aid and abet men. But the Plainsmen kill for profit and for hate; they take advantage of slight breaches in the warm wall of affection by which an Arapesh community is usually encircled; they convert this slight ill feeling into illness and death, a result that no one of the Arapesh himself intended. That the Arapesh feel this lack of intention is evident whenever there is a death. Then by processes of divination it is possible to place the blame upon the member of the community who originally opened the way to sorcery by sending the dirt to the Plainsmen. But the Arapesh shrink from such an imputation. They perform the divination, but find no one guilty. That quarrel was healed long ago; they cannot believe that the anger which was then generated was of a strength to bring about death. No, the death is the hostile act of a disgruntled blackmailer or of some impersonal anger in another community far away, a community that, losing one of its own people, has paid the blackmailer to revenge the death upon someone whose name they will never even know. When one of their young men dies, the Arapesh avoid placing the responsibility for his death and attempting to wreak revenge within their own community; instead they in turn pay the Plainsmen to kill another such young man, in some distant community, so that they may obey the traditional forms and say to the ghost: "Return, thou art revenged." Those who are distant, who are unknown, who because one has never seen them or given them fire or food are believed to be capable of any evil, are the ones whom it is possible to hate; they and the arrogant, swaggering, bullying sorcerers who boldly advertise their inhumanity, their willingness to kill for a price. Thus, with the aid of the

Plainsmen and of this formula of distant, impersonal, and magical revenge, the Arapesh exile all murder and hate beyond their borders, and make it possible to call any one of fifty men "brother" and eat trustfully from the same plate with any one of them. At one blow they demolish the hierarchy of distinctions between near relative, far relative, friend, half-friend, affinal relative, and so on, the gradations of trust that distinguish most communities, and they make instead absolute categories of friend and enemy. This absolute dichotomy leads, as we have seen in the discussion in Chapter 3, to the compulsive resort to sorcery practices whenever slight expressions of hostility occur. This resort to sorcery can be explained by the way in which they have built up a trustful, loving attitude, an attitude that can be shattered at a blow because no blows are received in childhood to habituate the growing child to ordinary competitive aggressiveness in others. As a result, in adult life on those occasions when hostility becomes overt, its expression is random, unpatterned, uncontrolled. The Arapesh do not reckon with an original nature that is violent and must be trained to peace, which is jealous and must be trained to sharing, which is possessive and must be trained to relinquish too fast a hold on its possessions. They reckon instead on a gentleness of behaviour that is lacking only in the child and in the ignorant and an aggressiveness that can only be aroused in the defence of another.

The last point is vividly illustrated in the quarrels when a woman is abducted. In formal compliance with the firm belief that no brother-in-law would take back his sister, it then becomes a quarrel between two communities, the community into which the woman was married and the community by which she has been abducted. It is not the husband who habitually takes up the quarrel, demanding the return of his wife, the vindication of his rights, and so forth, but one of his relatives, and more often one of his maternal relatives, who can speak entirely disinterestedly. A mother's brother or a mother's brother's son will rise up in wrath: "What, should I stay quiet when the wife of my father's sister's son is taken from him? Who grew her? He. Who paid rings for her? He. He, indeed! He, my father's sister's son. And now he sits, his wife gone, her place empty, her fire dead on her fire-place. I will have none of this. I will gather people together. We will take spears and bows and arrows, we will bring back this woman who has been stolen away"— and so on. Then this disinterested and therefore properly enraged defendant of the injured man will gather a group of the husband's relatives and go to the community that has stolen the women. The fight that follows has already been described. It is again phrased always as: "Then La'abe, angry because his cross-cousin was wounded, threw a spear that wounded Yelusha. Then Yelegen, angry that his father's brother's son, Yelusha, was wounded, threw a spear that hit Iwamini. Then Madje, angry that his half-brother was wounded"—and so on. Always there is the emphasis that one fights not for one's self, but for another. Sometimes anger over the abduction of a relative's wife will take a more arbitrary form, and the vindicator of his relative's rights will carry off some other woman married into the abducting community and give her away to someone else. Such acts of virtuous highway robbery are regarded by the Arapesh as overstatement, extravagant action, which is, however, based upon such sound principles of anger on behalf of another that they hardly know what to do about it. But the phrasing of anger as anger for someone else, not for one's self, is again a maternal phrasing. The mother who engages in quarrels on her own is disapproved, but the mother who will fight to the death for her young is a figure that we ourselves invoke with approval from the pages of natural-history annals.

In the matter of the acceptance of leadership and prestige, the Arapesh phrasing again presupposes a temperament that we regard as properly womanly. The promising young male is prevailed upon to assume the very distasteful and onerous task of being a big man for the sake of the community, not for his own sake. For them he organises feasts, he gardens and hunts and raises pigs, he undertakes long journeys and establishes trade-partnerships with men of other communities, that they, his brothers and his nephews and his sons and his daughters, may have more beautiful dances, fairer masks, lovelier songs. Against his will, with promises of early retirement, he is thrust into the forefront, and bidden to stamp about and act as if he liked it, talk as if he meant it, until such time as age releases him from the obligation of imitating a violent, aggressive, arrogant person.

In the relationship between parents and children, and between husband and wife, there is again no reliance upon any contrast in temperament. Age, experience, the responsibility of the parent greater than that of the child, of the older husband greater than that of the younger wife—these are the points emphasised. A man will listen with equal readiness to chiding by his mother or by his father, and there is no feeling that it is by virtue of his maleness that a man is wiser than a woman. The marriage system, the more slowly developing pace that is permitted women, their long period of great vulnerability while they are bearing children, which defers the age when their relationship to the supernatural is almost identical with that of a man—all these contrive to preserve the sense of an age-contrast, a contrast in wisdom and responsibility, between men and women.

In the sex-relationship, in which so much argument, resort to considerations of anatomy, and analogies from the animal kingdom have gone to prove that the male is the natural initiator and aggressor, the Arapesh again recognise no temperamental difference whatsoever. A scene that culminates in intercourse may be initiated by "his holding her breasts" or "her holding his cheeks"— the two approaches are regarded as equivalent and one as likely to occur as the other. And the Arapesh further contravene our traditional idea of men as spontaneously sexual creatures, and women as innocent of desire until wakened, by denying spontaneous sexuality to both sexes and expecting the exceptions, when they do occur, to occur in women. Both men and women are conceived as merely capable of response to a situation that their society has already defined for them as sexual, and so the Arapesh feel that it is necessary to chaperon betrothed couples who are too young for sex-relations to be healthful for them, but they do not feel that it is necessary to chaperon young people in general. Unless there is deliberate seduction with ulterior, non-sexual motives, sex-responses take a slow course, follow on the heels of affectionate deep interest, do not precede it and stimulate it. And with their definition of sex as response to an external stimulus rather than as spontaneous desire, both men and women are regarded as helpless in the face of seduction. Before the affectionate and amorous gesture, which comforts and reassures even as it stimulates and excites, a boy or a girl has no resources. Parents warn their sons even more than they warn their daughters against permitting themselves to get into situations in which someone can make love to them. In that case, "Your flesh will tremble, your knees will weaken, you will yield," is the prophecy. Not to choose, but to be chosen, is the temptation that is irresistible.

This then is the Arapesh ideal of human nature, and they expect each generation of children born to them to conform to it. The reader schooled in a knowledge of humanity that makes this picture seem like a day-dream of an age of innocence will inevitably ask: "But is this true of all Arapesh? Are they a race among whom there are no violent, no possessive, no strongly sexed individuals, a people incapable of developing the ego to a point at which it is ruthless to all other interests except the interests of the self? Have they different glands from other peoples? Is their diet so insufficient that all aggressive impulses are blocked? Are their men feminine in physique as well as in their imputed personalities? What is the meaning of this strange anomaly, a whole culture that assumes men and women to be alike in temperament, and that one a temperament which we consider to occur most often and most appropriately in women, a temperament, in fact, that is regarded as inconsistent with the true male nature?"

Some of these questions can be answered categorically. There is no reason to believe that the Arapesh temperament is due to their diet. The Plainsmen, who speak the same language and share much of the same culture, have a diet which is even more circumscribed and lacking in proteins than that of the mountain people. Yet they are a violent, aggressive people; their whole ethos contrasts strongly with that of their mountain neighbours. The physique of the average Arapesh male is not more feminine than that of the males of the other peoples whom I shall presently describe. Nor do the Arapesh present a uniform temperamental picture which would suggest that a local type has been developed by inbreeding, a type of peculiar gentleness and lack of aggressiveness. There are highly developed individual differences, far more conspicuous individual differences than in cultures like that of Samoa, where the assumption is that human nature is originally intractable and therefore must be systematically moulded to a set form. The Arapesh acceptance of human nature as good and altogether desirable, their lack of realisation that there are many human impulses which are definitely antisocial and disruptive, makes it possible for aberrant individuals to flourish among them.

Also their easy-going acceptance of the individual's own wishes in regard to choice of work increases the range of individuality. All men garden to some extent, but beyond that a man may spend much time hunting or never hunt at all; he may go on trading-expeditions or never stir from his own locality, he may carve or make bark paintings, or he may never take a carving tool or a brush in his hand. In none of these matters is any social compulsion exercised. The fostering duty of all persons towards the young, the obligation to provide food and shelter for them, and in a few cases to assume the additional responsibility of leadership, these are insisted upon. Otherwise the growing boy is left to his own devices, the growing girl may learn to make netted bags and elaborate grass skirts, to be proficient in the plaiting of belts and arm-bands, or she may remain innocent of these arts. It is not technical skill or special brilliance that the Arapesh demand either in men or in women; it is rather correct emotions, a character that finds in co-operative and cherishing activities its most perfect expression. This premium upon personality rather than upon special gifts is shown particularly if one examines the history of the bones of the dead. The bones of men who have been valued are exhumed and used for hunting, yam-planting, and protective fighting magic. It is not, however, the bones of the hunter that are used for hunting magic, or the bones of the truculent that are used to give protection in a possible fight, but rather the bones of the gentle, wise, reliable man, which are used indiscriminately for all these purposes. It is upon character, in the sense in which they understand it, that the Arapesh feel that they can rely, not upon anything as erratic and unpredictable as special skills. So while they permit the development of a gift, they put no premiums upon it; the specially fortunate hunter or the gifted painter will be remembered for the degree to which his emotions were congruent with the dominant ethos of the people, not for his full traps or brightly coloured bark paintings. This attitude decreases the influence that a specially skilled individual might have in changing the culture, but it does not detract from his own individual expression during his lifetime. Dealing with no established tradition of great skill, he must work out his own methods and so is offered a greater field for his individuality.

Neither among Arapesh children nor among Arapesh adults has one a sense of encountering a dead level of temperament. Individual differences in violence, in aggressiveness, in acquisitiveness, are as marked as they are among a group of American children, but the gamut is different. The most active Arapesh child, schooled to a passivity, a mildness, unknown to us, will be far less aggressive than a normally active American child. But the difference between the most active and the least active is not thereby reduced, although it is expressed in so much milder terms. It is not, in fact, as much reduced as would probably be the case if the Arapesh were more conscious of their educational aims, if the passivity and placidity of their children were the result of constant purposeful pressure, which would definitely cheque and discourage the too active and aberrant child. It is possible to contrast here the point of activity with the point of loving trust of all those persons whom one calls by a relationship term. Here the Arapesh do definitely train their children, and the difference between Arapesh children in this respect is less than among children in other cultures where no such training is given. That is, although the range in actual temperamental differences among the children born into any society may be approximately the same, that society may and will alter the interrelations between these differences in several different ways. It may mute expression all along the line or stimulate expression all along the line, so that the children retain the same relative position in regard to a trait, but the upper and lower limits of its expression have been altered. Or culture may skew the expression of temperament, it may select one temperamental variant as desirable, and discourage, disallow, and penalise any expression of contrasting or antithetical variants. Or culture may merely approve and reward one end of the scale and discipline and thwart the other, so that the result is a high degree of uniformity. The Arapesh may be said to produce the first type of result in the passivity that descends upon all of their children like a pall, due to the lip-bubbling, the tiring cold life and the contrast of the warm fire at evening, the lack of large children's groups, the encouragement in children of a receptive, non-initiatory attitude. All children are exposed to these influences and they respond to them differentially—the gamut is changed, but the differences in any group of children remain more or less constant.

In their attitudes towards egotism of any sort, either of the type that seeks recognition and applause or of the type that attempts to build up a position through possessions and power over others, the Arapesh take the second position. They reward the selfless child, the child who is constant in running hither and yon at the beck and call of others; they disapprove of and reprove the other types, as children and as adults. Here one variant of human temperament, and that a rather extreme variant, is definitely encouraged at the expense of other types, and the interrelations within a group of children are changed in a different way. As I have already mentioned, in the attitude towards relatives, in their stress upon the importance of food and growth, the Arapesh culture has the third effect; it tends to make all Arapesh much more alike in these respects than their original temperamental position would dictate; it shortens the gamut and does not merely change the position of its upper and lower limits.

There thus grow up among the Arapesh, in each generation, groups of children whose temperamental position has been moulded and changed in these various ways. As a group they are more passive, more receptive, more enthusiastic about the achievements of others and less inclined to initiate artistic or skilled occupations themselves, than are most primitive people. Their trust in each other, their all-or-none type of emotional response that makes every person into a relative to be loved and trusted or an enemy to be feared and fled, is extreme and stands out in very strong contrast to many other peoples. There are certain types of individuals—the violent, the jealous, the ambitious, the possessive, the man who is interested in experience or knowledge or art for its own sake—for whom they definitely have no place. The question remains as to what happens to these disallowed persons in a community that is too gentle to treat them as criminals, but too set in its own milky-mouthed way to permit any real range to their talents.

Those who suffer most among the Arapesh, who find the whole social scheme the least congenial and intelligible, are the violent, aggressive men and the violent, aggressive women. This will at once be seen to contrast with our own society, in which it is the mild unaggressive man who goes to the wall, and the aggressive, violent woman who is looked upon with disapproval and opprobrium, while among the Arapesh, with their lack of distinction between male and female temperament, the same temperament suffers in each sex.

The men suffer a little less than the women. In the first place their aberrancy is not recognised quite so soon, because of the circumstances that result in the boys having more temper tantrums than the girls. The girl who throws herself down in a fit of rage because her father will not take her with him becomes therefore more conspicuous, she is rebuked a little more because she deviates from the behaviour of other small girls, and she learns at an earlier age either to trim her sails or to rebel more whole-heartedly. Judgment is also passed upon her character at an earlier age than it is upon a boy's. While her brother is still roaming, unbetrothed and free, in search of a bandicoot's track, she is already being judged as a possible wife by her future husband's parents. While a boy remains in his own home, where his parents and near relatives have become inured to his fits of rage or sulks, a girl passes at an early and impressionable age into a new home where everyone is more acutely aware of her emotional deficiencies. The sense of being different from others, of being a disapproved person, settles therefore a little earlier upon a girl; it is likely to make her recessive and sulky and liable to sudden inexplicable outbursts of rage and jealousy. The fact that at no age is her conduct regarded as normal, as possibly promising, distorts her personality earlier and more definitely.

Such a girl was Temos, violent, possessive, jealous; in her series of unfortunate marriages she had encountered all of the circumstances with which she was least fitted to cope. She became therefore almost obsessive in her hostilities; she followed her husband about everywhere, she quarrelled continually even with the small children in the village, who muttered behind her back: "Temos is bad. She does not love to give to others." Yet Temos was merely an egocentric girl who was more possessive and exclusive in her sentiments than Arapesh society voted to be appropriate.

Boys, on the other hand, are free to develop a tempestuous and touchy personality right up into adolescence, and even here there is some chance of their escaping social disapproval because of the fantastic Arapesh belief that leadership and aggressiveness are so rare that they need to be encouraged, cultivated, and finally overstimulated in adult life. So an arrogant, ambitious boy may pass for one who will be willing to lead; and if his aggressiveness is combined with sufficient shyness and fearfulness—a not infrequent combination—he may pass into young manhood with the stamp of social approval upon him and be selected by the community as one of those whose duty it is to become a big man. In rare cases, he may actually become a big man before the community realises that his stamping and shouting are not good play-acting but genuine, that his threats against his rivals are not mere idle and appropriate bluster, but are accompanied by thefts of their dirt and continuous attempts to deliver them into the hands of sorcerers. This had been the case with Nyelahai, and Alitoa found itself saddled with a loud-mouthed, malicious man, who took delight in the sorcery traffic, and went up and down the countryside abusing his neighbours. He was not quite a big man, so they said, for his mouth was too ready with angry abuse, although he had done the things that make one a big man. And Nyelahai had none of the serenity and ease of the men who had had greatness thrust upon them; he walked restlessly up and down the community, nicknamed by his wives as "One-who-walks-about"; he was constantly being accused of sorcery, he beat his wives, and put a curse on his younger brother's hunting, and was not at home in his own world. This was because he was in actuality what he should only have been in mere theatrical imitativeness. Only too naturally, he was a confused person and gave all the appearance of stupidity. His culture had said he must bluster and shout, and when he blustered and shouted, they turned their backs upon him in shame.

But Nyelahai's case was the unusual one. More often, the violent, aggressive boy, the boy who in a head-hunting, warlike society would be covering himself with glory, the boy who in a culture that permitted courtship and conquest of women might have had many broken hearts to his credit, becomes permanently inhibited in his late adolescence. This was so with Wabe. Tall, beautifully built, the heir of one of the most gifted family lines in Arapesh, Wabe at twenty-five had retired from taking any active interest in his culture. He would help his younger brother, Ombomb, a little, he said, but what was the use, everything was against him. His *buanyins* had all died, Menala had been unfaithful to him, Temos had borne him no child but a blood-clot, Welima's relatives resented the way he treated her and no doubt were doing black magic to prevent his finding any meat—although they were the people who would be the recipients if he caught any—his dog was dead; all of his real and imaginary difficulties were jumbled together into a paranoid construct that left him gloomy, jealous, obsessive, confused, and useless to his community. One war-party, one good fight, one chance for straight, uncomplicated initiative, might have cleared the air. But there was none. He began to believe that other men were trying to seduce his wives. People laughed, and when the accusation was repeated, they grew a little remote. He decided that his gardening partners were using black magic for theft—a magic that is a mere matter of folk-lore and of which no one knows the formulas—on his yam-gardens. One month he accused Welima's relatives of being responsible for his bad luck in hunting, the next month he became jealous of Alitoa men and ordered his wives to pack up, and much against Temos' will, went to live in Welima's village. His behaviour was jerky, irrational, changeable, his temper dark and sullen. He was a definite liability to his society, he who had the physique and the intelligence to have been very useful to it. His capacity to lead was high. If we wished a convoy of cargo taken to the coast, or a far-away village stimulated into acting as carriers for our goods, Wabe was the man for the job. He was the man who naturally gravitated to the service of the white man, an ideal boss boy in a hierarchical scheme. In his own culture, he was a loss both to himself and to his community. Of all the men in the locality of Alitoa, he was the one who approached most strongly to a western-European ideal of the male, well built, with a handsome face with fine lines, a well-integrated body, violent, possessive, arbitrary, dictatorial, positively and aggressively sexed. Among the Arapesh, he was a pathetic figure.

Amitoa of Liwo was Wabe's temperamental counterpart among women. Raw-boned, with a hawklike face and a sinewy body that lacked all the softer signs of feminity, her small high breasts already shrunken although she was a scant thirty-five, Amitoa had found her life a stormy one. Her mother before her had been a violent, tempestuous person, and both Amitoa and her sister showed the same characteristics. She was betrothed at an early age to a youth who died, and she was inherited by a man much older than she, a man enfeebled by illness. Now although Arapesh girls prefer young men, this is not on grounds of physiological potency, but rather because they are less grave and decorous, and less exacting in the matter of household duties. Amitoa alone, of all of the Arapesh women whom I knew well, was articulately conscious of sexual desire and critical of a husband in terms of his ability to satisfy it. She alone knew the meaning of climax after intercourse, while the other women to whose canons she had to adjust did not even recognise a marked relaxation, but instead described their post-intercourse sensations as diffused warmth and ease. Amitoa despised her timid, ailing husband. She mocked her husband's orders, she flew out at him savagely when he rebuked her. Finally, enraged at her insubordination—she who was a mere child whose breasts had not fallen down, while he was an older man—he tried to beat her, seizing a fire-brand from the fire. She wrested it from him, and instead of giving blows he received them. He took up an adze and this also she seized. He screamed for help, and his younger brother had to rescue him. This was a scene which was to be repeated again and again in Amitoa's life.

The next day she ran away to Kobelen, a village nearer the beach with which her own village had extensive ceremonial relationships. Following the fashion of the Plainswomen, whom she had seen enter her native village and find a welcome, she went from one man to another, demanding to be taken in. She had intuitively adopted a procedure that had been developed by women like herself. But she was not a Plainswoman, she was one of their own people. The people of Liwo and the people of Kobelen had been friends for generations; no wild undisciplined woman who came unsolicited into their midst should upset that, so the old men said. The younger men hesitated. Amitoa, with her flashing eyes and decisive expressive manner, was very aggressive, but very attractive. It was true enough that such women made bad, jealous wives, and were moreover too strongly sexed to permit yam magic to flourish peacefully in their vicinity. Still . . . They dallied with the idea of taking her in. She went back to Liwo to visit her brother, who scolded her roundly for her desertion of her husband. When he tried to use force, she ran away again to Kobelen. There the counsels of prudence had asserted themselves in her absence. She sat among the women of her father's trade-friends' household, and no one would take her for a wife. Again she returned, furious, baffled, to Liwo, where people sent word to her husband. He and his kin had meanwhile consoled themselves with a magical explanation. The Plainsmen had made *wishan*, the species of secondary black magic by which one member of a community is acted upon through the dirt of another, and had caused her to run away. As one member of her husband's clan related it long afterwards:

"People said to my uncle: 'Your wife has come on top. Go and get her.' He got up, he took his two younger brothers. They went down. They waited at the river. Amitoa and another woman and her father's elder brother came down to bathe. Amitoa went to loosen her grass skirt to bathe. My uncle seized her hand. She called out to her uncle: 'Uncle, they are taking me.' Her uncle said: 'What, did he pay for you and feed you? Did men of Kobelen pay for you? Is it another man who is taking you? If it were another man, you could shout. But it is your husband.' The other woman screamed: 'They are carrying off Amitoa.' My uncle called out, 'Come, bring the spears.' They all ran away and my uncle brought Amitoa back. She was heavily adorned, as had always been her custom. She wore many bracelets, many earrings. She sat down in the centre of the village and she wept. My uncle said: 'It is I, your husband, who brought you back. Had it been another, you could cry.' She stayed. She conceived. She bore a female child. Amitoa wanted to strangle the child. The other women held her fast. She wished to run away. My uncle beat her. He made her stay. He made her suckle it. She became pregnant again. The child was a male. She bore him alone and she stepped on his head. If there had been another woman present the child would have lived. Had he lived he would have been as old as my younger brother. Then they buried the dead child."

This simple account sums up, with the cool impersonality of a young man who was a small boy at the time, the struggle that Amitoa went through in her fight against the traditional placid role of women. Behind the first attempt at infanticide, its failure, her rejection of the child and unwillingness to suckle it, and her successful lonely delivery in the bush that made it possible for her to kill her second child, there were years of anguish. She was an intelligent, vigorous, outgoing person, interested and alert. The unhappiness and despair of her conflict between her own violence and the prescribed gentleness of her culture baffled her as much as it did others. They would say in one breath that she should have been a man because she liked action and as a man she would have had more scope, and in the next that as a man she would have been undesirable, a quarreller and a fomenter of trouble.

When her little girl was five, Ombomb, her cousin, whose temperament was very akin to her own, helped her elope and marry Baimal, also of Alitoa and a widower. He tried to persuade Amitoa to take the child with her, arguing in a manner more characteristic of Ombomb than of Arapesh thought that then perhaps he could share in the bride-rings. But Amitoa refused, arguing that as her husband, now really an old man with a bad sore, had grown her, Amitoa, and paid rings for her, he should be left the daughter. She never saw her daughter again; she did not wish to see her. Her daughter was after all a child whom she had wished to kill and whom she had rebelled at suckling.

Amitoa became passionately attached to Baimal, to Baildu, the elder of Alitoa, to her new village in all of its ramifications. She was loud and continuous in her praises, in her disparaging comments upon the community of her former husband and its headman. She bore Baimal a daughter, Amus, to whom both of them were devoted, but the child's life was made miserable by continual conflicts over her allegiance. Since she was an only child, Baimal tended to take her about with him. If she cried to accompany him, Amitoa quarrelled with him furiously. He was inclined to slip away quietly or to advise the five-year-old Amus to stay with her mother. He could not understand what the quarrels were about or why his wholly traditional and gentle behaviour aroused such storms in Amitoa's breast. The night that the *tamberan* chased all of the women from the village* Amitoa was suffering from an attack of fever and Baimal begged her not to dance, saying it would make her ill. She met his solicitude by putting on heavier ornaments and preparing to dance. Baimal, already strung up and nervous from his onslaught on the *tamberan*, lost his temper and ordered her not to dance, saying that she was ill, and furthermore too old to deck herself out like a young girl. For this remark Amitoa attacked him with an ax, and his younger brother, Kule, arrived just in time to save him from serious injury. Amitoa took refuge in a sister-in-law's house, weeping noisily and uttering again and again a sentiment that is almost unknown among the Arapesh—that she hated all men, as such, that she was through with matrimony, and meant to go and live in her own village by herself. All the while she was furiously working into a cord a series of mnemonic knots, which she said indicated the number of times that Baimal had beaten her. Baimal

*See above, p. 65.

appeared on the scene for a moment to exhibit his wounds. He was a sensitive, valiant little person, devoted to Amitoa, wholly without malice or genuine violence, and very much perplexed by the whole affair. This quarrel was one of many. Amitoa was, in middle age, more fortunate in Baimal's devotion than she had been in her young girlhood. She was still, however, a wild creature, without any genuine place in her cultural tradition.

The adjustment of these violent natures, of Wabe and Ombomb, or Temos and Amitoa and Sauwedjo, varied in accordance with the accidents of their early upbringing and of their marriages. Wabe had been reared by his maternal relatives, gentle, retiring, friendly people, who succeeded in making him feel so alien that he never came to take an active part in his culture. His younger brother Ombomb had been partly reared by the violent half-brother who had fled from Alitoa years before. Ombomb had what Wabe lacked, a partial sanction for his arrogant, violent, possessive nature. The addition of a wife who was bred in such a tradition and pursued her own ways without any conflict or sense of guilt again strengthened his position, while Temos' violence and possessiveness, which were as atypical as his own, rather reinforced the weakness of Wabe's. The possibility of marrying a Plainswoman always complicated the fate of mountain men with such temperaments, and the presence of Plainswomen in the community gave Arapesh mountain women models that their culture had not trained them to follow with safety and would not permit them to essay. These aberrants' own misunderstanding of their cultures was further aggravated by the existence of very stupid people among themselves—such as Menala, who further complicated Wabe's life by accusing him of a wilful act of violence that had actually been carried out in strict accord with the rules of the culture, in which he had co-operated with her brothers in breaking up a marriage of which they disapproved.

Further flicks to the suspicions and maladjustments of aberrant people are given by the stupid and malicious people in the society who purloin dirt for no reason at all, or try to practise the little bits of black magic that are Arapesh heritage from former times or other cultures. Such a man was Nahomen, of a very low-grade intelligence, incapable of understanding more than the rudiments of his own culture and practically insensible to moral appeal. He and his brother Inoman, who displayed the same personality traits, would seize on pieces of other people's food arbitrarily, with a sly, half-witted malice, and one or two acts of this sort would serve to shake the faith of men like Wabe or Ombomb in the safe world in which they had been assured that they lived. Continually battling within themselves with attitudes and impulses that their society either declared to be non-existent or implicitly disallowed, such as jealousy, a strong desire to mount guard over their own property and define the limits between it and other people's possessions, and definite sexual urges that were not mere responses to defined situations—it was only natural that all the overt contradictions in the social order should strike them most forcibly. The single cases in which a woman had attempted to seduce them stood out far more sharply in their minds than the hundred times that they had passed lonely women upon the road and received only a shy and friendly greeting.

Among the aspects of the culture that confused them most was the insistence upon reciprocity. The Arapesh ideal of a man is one who never provokes a fight, but who if he is provoked will hold his own, give as much as he takes and no more, and so re-establish the equilibrium that is lost. This premium on a level relationship between all men is carried into every aspect of life, but ordinarily it is not carried to extremes. In the revenge for the dead, we have seen how it was translated into revenge upon some far-distant and anonymous person. In revenge between villages, a long time is permitted to elapse, and the most fortuitous happening is interpreted as revenge. So in the case of the final elopement of Amitoa. The clan of Suabibis of Liwo had paid for her and grown her; when Baimal of the Totoalaibis clan of Alitoa married her, he committed a hostile act against Suabibis, a matter about which Suabibis muttered and grumbled. Three years later Tapik, a woman who had been grown from early childhood by Totoalaibis, ran away and married a man of Suabibis. Totoalaibis attempted to get her back by force and failed. It was then decided that Tapik should be regarded as a return for Amitoa, and years later, whenever Amitoa threatened to run away the men of Totoalaibis would invoke this fact, as if it had been a sister-exchange, as an argument that her running away would be illegal.

So it is also with all the payments to a mother's brother or to a mother's brother's son, which are demanded at initiation, when one is in disgrace, or when one's blood has been shed, or at death. These payments are always returned later when the mother's brother finds himself in similar circumstances. So on any given occasion, say a death, it will be said, "Rings are paid to the mother's brother and the mother's brother's son, and to the sister's son," and no mention is made that one is a new payment, for which the mother's brother makes a specific demand, and the other is a repayment. But crystallised in the ritual of the *rites de passage* are the demands that the mother's brother makes, the special song he sings to his nephew after initiation, the type of mourning that he wears when his nephew dies. The man whose natural bent is towards initiating demands upon others rather than towards a mere preservation of equilibrium seizes upon these cultural gestures; he is loud in his demands upon his sister's son, and dilatory in his repayments. Similarly, the Arapesh share with the adjoining tribes the institution of the familial curse, in which a father, an elder sister, a brother, a mother's brother, can invoke the ancestral ghosts in a curse that will prevent a man's working and finding game, and which will prevent a woman from having children. The power of this curse depends upon the fact that the person who puts it on is the only person who can take it off. So if a man offends his mother's brother in any way, his mother's brother's position is only strengthened by cursing his nephew if only he himself can remove the curse. The Arapesh have made this curse nugatory in most cases by blithely ignoring this structural point. In the first place, they permit anyone who is called "mother's brother," traced through any line of blood-kinship, however remote, to perform the ceremonies of cursing and "uncursing," and furthermore, they believe that one man can take off a curse that another put on. Only in the most extreme cases is it impossible to find such a person, and the mother's brother's curse is therefore relatively meaningless. It is, however, still invoked by violent and bad-tempered people, who do not pause to reckon with the modification that the culture has introduced. People like Wabe and Ombomb are for ever cursing and believing that they have been cursed; they serve to keep alive in the culture these structural aspects which are no longer relevant, which the culture itself had practically outlawed long ago, just as some forgotten anti-witchcraft act or blue law can be invoked among ourselves by a paranoid personality.

The violent aberrant personalities, either men or women, have therefore a very difficult time among the Arapesh. They are not subjected to the rigid discipline that they would receive among a people who deal seriously with such temperaments. A woman like Amitoa who murders her child continues to live on in a community; similarly a Suabibis man who murdered a child in revenge for his own son's fall from a tree was not disciplined by the community, nor by the child's relatives, because they lived too far away. The society actually gives quite a good deal of lee-way to violence, but it gives no meaning to it. With no place for warfare, for strong leadership, for individual exploits of bravery and strength, these men find themselves treated as almost insane. If they are very intelligent individuals, this curious mute ostracism, this failure by their fellows to understand and recognise their demands, merely sends them into sullen recessive fits, blunts their minds, ruins their memories, as they find themselves increasingly unable to explain why people have acted as they have in any given instance. When they think about their society they attempt to reinstate the formal relationships, such as those of a genuine claim of the mother's brother over the sister's son, and to ignore all the blurring, softening distortions that the society introduces in practice. They state with a beautiful clarity points of social structure that would make sense to them, but which are not borne out by the actual facts. Intellectually they are lost to their society, always seeking to project their own violent and aberrant temperamental choices upon it. If in addition circumstances are adverse, if their pigs die or their wives miscarry or the yams fail, far from being merely a loss to society, they may become a menace, and substitute overt murderous activity for glowering suspicion and impotent rage.

Such a man was Agilapwe, a hard-faced, vitriolic old man who lived on the side of a cliff across the valley from our house. On his leg was a great sore from which he had suffered since childhood—a red and running demonstration of someone's hostility towards him. The Arapesh exempt sores from their theories of sorcery; unlike all other forms of illness and death, sores can be caused within their own safe society, by hiding dirt in the roots of wild taro, and in one or two *marsalai* places of evil omen. If the sore causes death, then the theory is advanced that there must have been additional and unlocated dirt in the hands of the Plains sorcerers also, and the community is absolved from responsibility for the death. Now the normal course of bad tropical sores is a reasonably quick healing, or occasionally a rapid degeneration of the affected limb, which ends in death. When sores occur, people use the ordinary reasoning applied to sorcery. They ask who was likely to have been angered and who had an opportunity to purloin a bit of dirt, and what route they would have taken in disposing of it. The displacement of the responsibility for these minor ailments is merely upon a distant community of the mountain or beach people, not upon the Plainsmen, so that a mountain man suffering from a sore suspects that his dirt has been buried in a *marsalai* place in the beach villages of Waginara or Magahine; a beach man in turn suspects the mountains, the *marsalai* place of Bugabahine or the wild taro patches of Alitoa. It was believed that a particularly tough and imperishable part of

Agilapwe's personality—for example, a bone that he had once gnawed—lay rotting in one of these *marsalai* places, long ago forgotten, with the man who had hidden it there dead these many years. Meanwhile, Agilapwe lived on, an angry man. There was never a fight but he was part of it, never a dispute but he wished to be in it. His wife wearied of his behaviour, for the Arapesh say of a bad man: "If his wife is a good woman, she will leave him." They count it as no virtue to stay faithful to one whose conduct has alienated him from society.

His wife ran away to Suapali while she was still a young girl, and this is the account that tradition has preserved: "Agilapwe thought her brother Yaluahaip of Labinem had helped her. Yaluahaip was in his garden. He had an ax. Agilapwe had a spear. Agilapwe went inside the garden. He looked at Yaluahaip. He asked him: 'Where is your sister?' Yaluahaip answered: 'I do not know.' 'You are a liar, she has run away.' Yaluahaip said: 'If she had run away I should know it.' Agilapwe said: 'Yes, she has run away for good. You can't lie to me. I know it.' Yaluahaip answered: 'Oh, brother-in-law, if she has run away, I will find her.' Agilapwe started forward. He seized Yaluahaip's ax. He cut his shoulder open. The ax stuck fast. Agilapwe pulled at it but it was fast. Now Agilapwe took up a spear. He threw it at Yaluahaip. Yaluahaip dodged. His wife climbed over the fence and ran away. Yaluahaip ran away. They both fled. Agilapwe chased them. He lost their tracks in the bush. He went up on the hill-top. They weren't there. He ran back to the garden. They weren't there. The man had run away far below. His wife hunted for him. She thought he was dead. She found his blood. She tracked him. She found him. She held him by the arm. The two ran and ran. They came to our place. She called out to my father: 'Elder brother-in-law, your brother is all cut up.' My mother came down. She washed the wound, she put lime on it, she bound the jagged edges together with a vine. They brought him into the village. They made two supports for him. He leant against one and rested his arm on the other. He was a fine strong man, but Agilapwe had wounded

him. They slept. In the morning they went and built a house in
the bush. They built a high bed in it. They carried him there and
hid him. At night Agilapwe would go prowling about trying to
find him. If he had found him, he would have killed him. Later
when they all went to a feast they took Yaluahaip with them and
hid him near by. The wound healed. Father wished to take an
avenging party to Manuniki [the home of Agilapwe], but it was
impossible. The flock of white parrots who lived there always flew
up and gave warning. Agilapwe stood up above and hurled spears
and stones down. Afterwards Agilapwe married a woman whom
my father called sister's daughter and the quarrel was healed. No
rings were ever exchanged."

This gives a fair picture of the violent, unreasonable rages to
which persons like Agilapwe were subject, and the attitude of
their chance victims towards them. Later Agilapwe aggravated his
rift with the community by purposefully cultivating the rapidly
reproducing wild taro all over his rugged mountain side. More
and more frequently people with sores accused Alitoa of sorcery.
The people of Alitoa hamlet tore down their *tamberan* house,
which was said to be making the ground in the centre of their village supernaturally hot, and they rooted up all the wild taro that
grew on their hill-sides. But in Manuniki, just across the gorge,
Agilapwe lived on, trafficking in sorcery, gloating over his wild
taro, and beating the victory-call on his slit gong whenever any
news of a death reached him. Like several other of the violent
misfits in the community, he had also taken a partial refuge in
art, and his fantastic, dour paintings adorned several *tamberan*
houses.

Persons like Wabe and Agilapwe, Amitoa and Temos, by
their conspicuous aberrancy serve to distort for growing children
the picture of Arapesh life. Their own children and those brought
up close to them may take their conduct as patterns and so
become confused in adult life. The picture of a gentle community
in which all men are loving relatives is not quite so vivid to the little boy who has just seen his mother bind up Yaluahaip's wound.

The quiet responsive non-initiatory nature of men and women is blurred for those who watch Amitoa take an ax to Baimal, or Wabe beat both his wives and declare that he wishes he was rid of the pair of them. By the insistence that all people are good and gentle, that men and women alike are neither strongly nor aggressively sexed, that no one has any other motive except to grow yams and children, the Arapesh have made it impossible to formulate rules for properly controlling those whose temperaments do not conform to the accepted ideal.

The Western reader will realise only too easily how special an interpretation the Arapesh have put upon human nature, how fantastic they have been in selecting a personality type rare in either men or women and foisting it as the ideal and natural behaviour upon an entire community. It is hard to judge which seems to us the most utopian and unrealistic behaviour, to say that there are no differences between men and women, or to say that both men and women are naturally maternal, gentle, responsive, and unaggressive.

part two

the river-dwelling Mundugumor

FINDING THE MUNDUGUMOR

It will be remembered that the underlying purpose of my field studies in New Guinea was to discover to what degree temperamental differences between the sexes were innate and to what extent they were culturally determined, and furthermore to inquire minutely into the educational mechanisms connected with these differences. I left the Arapesh with a disappointed feeling. I had found no temperamental differences between the sexes, either when I studied their cultural beliefs or when I actually observed individuals. The inference was that such differences were purely a matter of culture, and that in those societies in which the culture disregarded them they did not occur. The Arapesh had been selected for study for a variety of ethnographic and practical considerations that had no relation to my special problem. This is always unavoidable, because by the time that enough is known about any primitive society to assure the investigator that it is relevant to a particular line of investigation, that culture has already been thoroughly studied. In the present state of research among primitive peoples, when cultures with thousands of years of history behind them, cultures that are unique and can probably never be duplicated in the future of the human race, are breaking up, no one trained in ethnological research can retread the footsteps of another investigator if he can by any possibility combine his special problem with a complete investigation of a new culture. This obligation was intensified in my own case by the fact that two field-workers were together, and we wished to have the scope of an entirely unknown culture for our combined and separate researches. So I left the Arapesh pleased with the temper of the people and interested in the consistency of their culture, but with little additional knowledge about my own problem.

From the Arapesh we decided to undertake a journey up the Sepik River to escape the ardours of mountain living with its attendant difficulties of transport. Again our choice of a tribe had to be arbitrary and was governed by considerations remote indeed from the problem of differences in sex temperament. Two other ethnologists had preceded us in this general region. Dr. Thurnwald had recorded the culture of the Banaro on the Keram River and Mr. Bateson was at that time studying the Iatmül culture of the middle Sepik River. The villages on the lower Sepik were in a partially disintegrated state, owing to mission influence and overrecruiting. We had hoped to make our way into one of the inland tribes north of the Sepik, whose culture adjoined the Plains Arapesh, and so to make a study of a continuous strip of territory from the Sepik to the Pacific Coast. When we reached the government station at Marienberg, a day's journey from the mouth of the Sepik, consultation of government maps showed that it would be impossible to get our goods and equipment into that country at present. To aid us in selecting a possible alternative site we had only a map, the knowledge that we had gained from the publications of Dr. Thurnwald and Mr. Bateson, and the information the government patrol officer could furnish us in regard to the condition of villages, whether they were missionised, over-recruited, whether they were under complete or partial government control. Our choice was very simply determined. We selected the nearest tribe that was accessible by water which was unmissionised, and which seemed to be least likely to have been extensively influenced, either linguistically or culturally, by either the Iatmül or the Banaro. The most accessible tribe of this type was the Mundugumor, reported in the government records to have been well under control for over three years. They were located a half-day's voyage up the Yuat River. We had never heard either of the tribe or indeed of the swift muddy river on which they dwelt. The patrol officer at Marienberg had only recently come to the Sepik and could tell us nothing about them. A party of recruiters passing through Marienberg extended us their sympathy when they heard we were going up the Yuat and advised us to lay in a good supply of buttons, as the Yuat people had a liking for them. With this, and no further information, we landed our goods in Kenakatem, the first Mundugumor settlement, and the one that the government census books showed to be the centre of the largest locality.

I have stressed these points at some length, because the astonishing way in which the emphasis of the Mundugumor culture contradicts and contrasts with the emphasis of Arapesh culture will be bound to strike the reader at once. If I had grasped the full implications of my Arapesh results and cast about to find the New Guinea culture that would throw them most into relief, I could not have bettered the choice of Mundugumor. That two peoples who share so many economic and social traits, who are part of one culture area and live separated by only about a hundred miles can present such a contrast in ethos, in social personality, is in itself of great interest. But when it is realised that whereas the Arapesh have standardised the personality of both men and women in a mould that, out of our traditional bias, we should describe

as maternal, womanly, unmasculine, the Mundugumor have gone to
the opposite extreme and, again ignoring sex as a basis for the establishment of personality differences, have standardised the behaviour of
both men and women as actively masculine, virile, and without any of
the softening and mellowing characteristics that we are accustomed to
believe are inalienably womanly—then the historical accident that led
us to study them rather than some other people is the more remarkable.

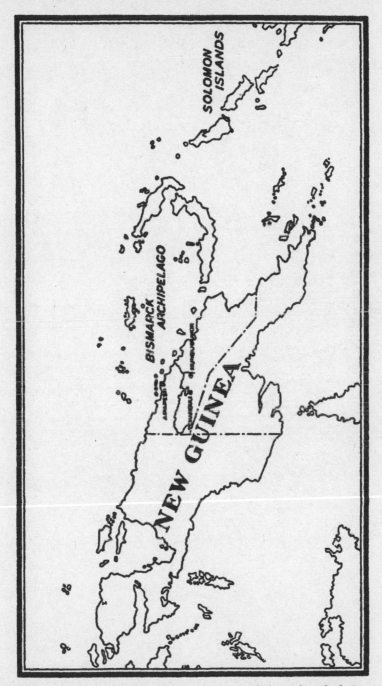

Where the Arapesh, the Mundugumor, and the Tchambuli Live

9

*the pace of life in a cannibal tribe**

In coming from the gentle Arapesh people to a group of cannibals and head-hunters we made a transition between two ways of life so opposed to each other that every step by which we gradually learned the structure and emphases of Mundugumor life was puzzling and astonishing. When we left the Arapesh the old men warned us: "You are going up the Sepik River, where the people are fierce, where they eat men. You are taking some of our boys with you. Go carefully. Do not be misled by your experience among us. We are another kind. They are another kind. So you will find it."

Although the reader has merely to shift his attention from one set of values to another, while we had to shift our actual

---

*The Mundugumor had been under full government control for about three years. When this control outlawed war, head-hunting, and cannibalism, Mundugumor life stopped dead, like a clock of which the mainspring is broken. But the memory of that way of life which they had so recently and unwillingly forsaken was still vivid and green; small children of eleven and twelve had all taken part in cannibal feasts. In this section I shall use the present tense to describe the life as it had been lived up to three years before we came to the people.

adjustments to the daily life of a native people, nevertheless he will find that transition as difficult as we found it. During our first weeks among the Mundugumor there was much that was startling, much that was incomprehensible. The violence, the strangeness of the motivations that controlled these gay, hard, arrogant people, came to us abruptly, without warning, as we studied their customs and watched their lives. In this chapter I shall present some of these startling comments, these strange occurrences and unexpected phrasings of life, as abruptly, as inexplicably, as they were presented to us. So perhaps the reader will be better prepared to understand the pattern of their lives, as it emerged from the first shock and perplexity of contact.

The Yuat River is a swift-flowing, treacherous tributary of the Sepik, which has cut its way through a patch of quite high ground and joins the Sepik at the village of Yuarimo. At low water the banks stand ten feet high, and high water comes, with a rush, rising several feet in a night and in some years, but not in all, flooding the clay floors of the hamlets. The current is so swift that a motor boat makes very little progress against it, and the natives never attempt to swim the river. It is a turbid colour; floating twigs and trunks and bits of land, and packets of bark that the natives remark upon as probably containing a new-born child which has been tossed away unwashed, rush by the spectator very quickly. For twenty miles below the first hamlet of the Mundugumor people, the river-banks stand high and empty, good coconut and tobacco land in a country where reliable dry land is very scarce. But such is the terror in which the Mundugumor people are held that no other people will venture to occupy this land. It stands, a clear empty swath across which the Mundugumor head-hunting parties must go to attack the Andoar people of the mouth of the Yuat River, a people who, like themselves, are head-hunters and cannibals.

The Yuat divides the country of the Mundugumor in half. Just a few generations ago, so the people say, there was no river here but only a slight trickling stream, which finally widened until it was necessary to bridge it, and then, in their great-grandfather's time, it suddenly swelled to its present terrifying width and swiftness, now impossible for them to bridge. It was then that they, a bush people, unaccustomed to the water, unskilled at swimming, and unlearned in the art of canoe-making, had to become in some slight measure a river people. They still live in fear of the river, and the people who dwell directly upon the banks are obsessed by a haunting fear that one of the children will fall in. They dread someone's drowning, because it will contaminate the river as a supply of drinking-water for months, compelling everyone to carry their water a long distance from springs in the bush. The canoes, which they have copied from their neighbours at the mouth of the Yuat, are simple dug-outs, with shovel-shaped sterns. They paddle them clumsily and apprehensively under shelter of the banks, and only cross the river when absolutely necessary. In flood-times they make clumsy round dug-outs that look like great wooden bath-tubs in which they can paddle short distances, in and out among the coconut- and areca-palms.

The Mundugumor now number some thousand people, and at one time must have numbered fifteen hundred or so. They are divided into two groups, those who live in the four hamlet-clusters on the two banks of the Yuat, and a section who live in the two hamlet-clusters to the west and who are still unused to the river. When the latter come to visit their acquaintances in the river villages, they are likely to swamp a canoe and get a ducking that is exceedingly inconvenient for them, since any one of the river people who can call the clumsy one "sister's son" can then plunge himself hastily into the water near the bank, and the visitor must then give him a feast for his courtesy in imitating his misfortune. Although the two groups of the Mundugumor speak the same language, they no longer feel themselves as one people; the river life has divided them. Formerly it was regarded as taboo for a Mundugumor to eat anyone who spoke the Mundugumor language. But after the river intervened and the two groups became alienated in their way of life, some of the river people, so their descendants say, tried eating a member of the bush group, and since they suffered no ill effects therefrom they continued to do so. As they were now free to eat each other, marriage became less desirable between the two groups, and the people of the four river localities married among themselves, or the men took as wives captives and runaway women from the miserable inhabitants of the swamp-lands that lay to the east of them.

The Mundugumor wander far afield not only in search of enemies to ambush, but in search of trade-acquaintances and valuable objects. From the mountains at the far-off head waters of the Yuat they receive shell ornaments, ax-blades, bows and arrows, and hunting magic. This hunting magic had to be repurchased from the upper river in almost every generation, they explained, for no father will take the trouble to see that his young son observes the necessary meat taboo so that he can inherit it. From the emaciated, half-starved, rickety peoples who inhabit the eastern swamps, they buy cooking-pots, carrying-baskets, mosquito-bags, fans, and now and again a flute fetish to which is fastened the image of a supernatural's face, wrought from clay and gum and shell. These are images of the spirits of the bush, in which the Mundugumor believe also. From the bush people they also purchase a strange, grotesque image of a snake, an object exceedingly dangerous to women. The men perform a special dance with these snake carvings between their legs, but the principal use for them is to conceal them in the fishing *barads** of the next hamlet, to ruin the health of the neighbouring women who may come upon them in the course of their fishing.

For these miserable swamp people the Mundugumor preserve a contempt tinged with a sense of their usefulness as makers of pots and baskets. They said they were careful not to kill all of them, for then there would be no makers of pots left alive. They

---

*Barad is a pidgin-English term that applies to any narrow water-way, either natural or artificial, which connects two bodies of water. Many of them are specially dug as canals, or for fishing purposes.

comment upon the advantage of having trade-connexions with two groups of mosquito-bag-makers; if one group becomes too depleted by head-hunting, they can always get mosquito-bags from the others. Sometimes they make temporary alliances with groups of the swamp people, in order to ensure a large head-hunting party. For Mundugumor head-hunting is not a matter of taking risks—the ideal is a party of a hundred men who go out to ambush a hamlet sheltering only two or three men and some women and children. For such extensive expeditions it is necessary to have allies, and children are exchanged with neighbouring tribes, the youngsters living among them as hostages until the raid comes off. The little Mundugumor children sometimes spend several months at a time in a swamp village, learning the language and the secret roads, and complaining bitterly of the miserable diet of rancid sago and smoked sago-grubs and the foul, evil-smelling drinking-water that flows in thousands of small trickles about the grassy clumps upon which the swamp people build their houses. Children are used as hostages because if there is treachery between the allies and the hostages are killed, after all it will only be a child, and in most instances a male child—who is less valued than a female child—who pays the penalty.

For the manufactures of the impoverished swamp-dwellers, the Mundugumor trade tobacco, areca-nut, and coconuts, which grow abundantly upon their rich high land. This rids them of the necessity of doing any manufacturing themselves and frees the men for head-hunting and theatrical spectacles, and the women for gardening, tobacco-curing, and fishing. Only an occasional Mundugumor woman plaits the little vase-shaped creel that the fishing women wear suspended from the back of their necks as they go fishing. These basket-makers are the women who were born with the umbilical cord twisted around their throats. Males so born are destined to be artists, to continue the fine tight tradition of Mundugumor art, the high-relief carving on the tall wooden shields, the low-relief stylised animal representations on the spears, the intricate painted designs on the great triangles of bark that are raised at yam-feasts. They it is who can carve the wooden figures that fit into the ends of the sacred flutes, embodiments of the crocodile spirits of the river. Men and women born to arts and crafts need not practise them unless they wish, but no one who lacks the mark of his calling can hope to become more than the clumsiest apprentice.

From the Andoar people at the mouth of the river the Mundugumor import new dances occasionally, for the Andoar people are near enough to the great Sepik water-way to share in the interchange of dances and ceremonies that the lower Sepik villages import from the islands along the coast. Now and then an ambitious Mundugumor man, anxious to stress his own importance further, will import a new and more ferocious mask and give a ceremony at which all of the young men of his hamlet-cluster are initiated into the mysteries of the new cult. Occasionally the Mundugumor would raid an Andoar house and come away with a trophy spear-thrower, which, however, they never learned to use, for the spear-thrower is the weapon of the practised canoeman. When Andoar canoes went up the Yuat on trading-journeys, the Mundugumor stood on the shores and hurled spears at them, compelling the Andoar people to leave hostages among them until the boats returned from the up-river trading.

But principally Andoar represented to them a final resort for the man or woman who had been too grievously insulted. Such a one could take a canoe and float down the river to Andoar. The Andoar people would come out into midstream, capture the canoe, and eat the angry suicide. Sometimes also a Mundugumor was lost in the river. Often the corpse would become entangled in the weeds at the river-bottom, and defy all searching until decomposition brought it to the surface. Sometimes, however, it would drift down the river, and the people of Andoar would salvage it. They would give it an expensive burial, for which the Mundugumor people would have to make them even more expensive return presents. This was regarded as a great nuisance by the Mundugumor, who were always likely to scant their mourning observances even for their greatest men. Tradition prescribed that the corpse should be slowly smoked and that the mourners should cluster in the closely shuttered house while the steady decomposition took place. But the Mundugumor said that the children held their noses and fled before the stench of their father's decaying flesh, and the widows were only too likely to have already chosen new husbands, so many a man was bundled unceremoniously into the earth on the plea that the survivors were not strong enough to undertake the long mourning. To have to pay heavily for burial rites performed by an enemy was maddening, and the vengeful people at the mouth of the Yuat knew it well when they gleefully salvaged a corpse from the muddy waters.

On their own high fertile land, which they hold by virtue of a greater ferocity and recklessness than any of their neighbours, the Mundugumor live among themselves in a state of mutual distrust and uncomfortableness. There is no village with a central plaza and a men's club-house, such as occurs in so many parts of New Guinea. Each man seeks to live unto himself within a palisade in which cluster a number of houses: one for each wife, or perhaps for each two wives, a special, badly thatched hut for his adolescent sons, where they sleep, miserable and mosquito-bitten, not even worthy of a mosquito-bag among them; a house of his own where he eats his meals, choosing arbitrarily and capriciously from the plates of sago seasoned with fish or sago-grubs that each wife prepares for him, and an extra house in which to store slit gongs, receive visitors, and hang up tobacco. This compound, containing nine or ten wives, a few young and dependent males, sons or sons-in-law, and a few unaggressive nephews, is only attained by about one man in twenty-five. Such a household, however, is the ideal, and the man with two or three wives, or sometimes with only one wife and some stray old female relative to swell his *ménage*, will clear himself a little secluded patch in the bush and take care to approach it by a circuitous path, so as to preserve the secret of its location. In every locality there are men

of mixed extraction, of foreign mothers, who have kept up kinship allegiances to other localities of other tribes. These men are
the professional traitors, ever ready to lead a raiding party to some
ill-defended house—and it is from these men that the roads are
supposed to be kept secret, for the success of a raiding party
depends upon the ability to go directly to the house of the victims, strike quickly, and get away.

There are other reasons for scattering the residences about in
the bush. Brothers cannot live close together, for a younger
brother only speaks to an elder when necessary and then with the
greatest circumspection and respect. Two brothers are ashamed
to sit down together, and a younger brother may not address his
elder brother's wife. These prohibitions do not veil the hostility
that exists between all the males of a household, between father
and son as well as between brothers. Sometimes a man builds a
house near one of his mother's brothers, until he or his host
becomes involved in some small civil war that breaks up the temporary living-arrangements. Between the women, the bush is
divided in partial hostility also; women retain a special power
over the spirits of the bush, and a married woman from another
place usually goes fishing with her sister-in-law and shares the
catch; otherwise the sister-in-law may curse her fishing. The bush
is threaded with little artificial ditches for dip-net fishing, and
about them clusters a great amount of fear; a *peleva*, the snake
carving of the swamp people, may be hidden there, a curse, either
of a sister-in-law or of a former owner who, disgruntled at dying,
may curse the *barad* that he had dug, and all who fish there afterwards. And one of the numerous crocodiles may take a bite from
a stooping woman's buttocks. But the *barads* are full of fish, and
the sleek, well-kept skins of the women testify to many a glutton-
ous meal in the early morning before returning to the compound.

There is no place where a group of men can sit down together
except upon the rare occasions when a ceremony is on foot. Ceremonies are individually organised with some prominent man as
leader, who makes his son's initiation into one of the series of

fetish-object cults the excuse for the undertaking. He usually builds a fair-sized home in which the paraphernalia of the ceremony can be assembled.

But feasts are oases in a life that is riddled with suspicion and distrust. In ordinary times only women gather in chattering groups to comment cattily upon each other's brightly coloured grass skirts, or laugh at the older women who stubbornly insist upon dressing in the modes of an earlier period. Out of feast-times it is not unusual for a brother to go armed against a brother; a man hears of a relative's visit to his compound with apprehension or anger; children are trained to feel uncomfortable in the presence of most of their relatives; and the sounds of angry voices are frequent in the by-paths and clearings on the edge of the river.

10

*the structure of Mundugumor society**

There is no genuine community in Mundugumor; there are a series of named places in which individuals own land, and in which they reside more or less irregularly, living in different small residential constellations that represent temporary alignments of male kin or of men related by marriage. The society is not organised into clans, as is the Arapesh, so that a group of related individuals form a permanent unit, bound together by common blood, a common name, and common interests. Instead Mundugumor social organisation is based upon a theory of a natural hostility that exists between all members of the same sex, and the assumption that the only possible ties between members of the same sex are through members of the opposite sex. Instead therefore of organising people into patrilineal groups or matrilineal groups, in either one of which brothers are bound together in the same group as either their father or their mother's brother, the Mundugumor have a form of organisation that they call a *rope*. A

---

*For the illustrations of malfunctioning in this chapter I am directly indebted to Dr. Fortune's notes.

rope is composed of a man, his daughters, his daughters' sons' daughters; or if the count is begun from a woman, of a woman, her sons, her sons' daughters, her sons' daughters' sons, and so on. All property, with the exception of land, which is plentiful and not highly valued, passes down the rope; even weapons descend from father to daughter. A man and his son do not belong to the same rope, or respect the same totemic bird or animal. A man leaves no property to his son, except a share in the patrilineally descended land; every other valuable goes to his daughter. Brothers and sisters do not belong to the same rope; one is bound in allegiance to the mother, the other to the father.

Furthermore the social ideal is the large polygynous household, in which a man has as many as eight or ten wives. In such a household there is a definite division between the group composed of the father and all of his daughters and the group composed of each mother and her sons. Between own brothers the attitude is one of rivalry and distrust. From early adolescence they are forced to treat each other with excessive formality, avoid each other whenever possible, and abstain from all light or casual conversation. Between brothers there is only one possible form of close contact; they can fight each other and abuse each other publicly. Half-brothers must observe the same avoidances in a slightly less stringent form, but half-brothers are divided also by the fierce competitive enmity that exists between cowives, their mothers, the spirit that makes one wife refuse to give food to the child of her husband by another wife. Fathers and sons are separated by early developed and socially maintained hostility. By the time a boy is ten or twelve his mother is old and no longer a favourite wife; his father is casting about for a young wife. If the older wife objects, the husband beats her. The small boy is expected to defend his mother in these scenes, to defy and abuse his father.

This is the situation within the compound of the successful man, the man who has succeeded in getting the largest number of wives. A large number of wives means wealth and power. A man can command certain services from his wives' brothers and, more importantly, the wives themselves by growing and curing tobacco furnish him with wealth, for tobacco is the most important trade-article. These compounds are not situated in a village,* but hidden away in the bush, and the head of the compound looks with great suspicion upon the visits of any adult males unless they come to transact definite business with him.

Although brother and sister do not belong to the same rope, and are trained from childhood to recognise separate allegiances, there is another institution that runs counter to the rope arrangements, and that is the insistence upon a form of marriage based upon brother-and-sister exchange. Every man is supposed to obtain a wife by giving his sister in return for some other man's sister. There is theoretically no other way in which he can legally obtain a wife, although in actual practice occasionally a wife is paid for with a valuable flute. Brothers therefore have pre-emptive rights over their sisters, and they are trained by their mothers to appreciate this right at its full value. Men without sisters have to fight for their wives, and a family that consists of a large number of sons and no daughters is doomed to a long career of fighting, for only after an elopement and a fight is it possible to compound for the theft of a woman by the payment of a flute. As the number of brothers and sisters is seldom adjusted to the equitable exchange of a man's own sister for a wife of the proper age, the brothers are constantly at odds with each other to enforce their claims on the sisters. An eldest brother, especially if the father is dead, may trade all of his sisters for wives and leave all of his younger brothers unprovided for. The existence of polygyny as an ideal of power means inevitable conflict between brothers, no matter how many sisters they have, and when there are fewer sisters than brothers, this conflict is sharpened. Rivalry is complicated further by the fact that old men can marry young women.

---

*Under government instigation the natives were building houses closer together, but they only lived in them part of the time.

In theory, individuals are not permitted to marry out of their generation, but the Mundugumor respect none of their own rules, and the violent social personality that has been fostered in both men and women breaks out in direct sexual rivalry between father and son. The son can trade his sister for a wife; with his sister he can buy a sexual partner. But so also can the father. Instead of permitting his son to use his sister to obtain a wife, the father can use her himself; he can trade his adolescent daughter for a young wife. The father has already a strong sense of possession in his daughter. She belongs to his rope, not to her brothers' rope. She gardens with her father, works in the bush with her father, uses kinship terms calculated through her father. When she talks, bears the name of one of her father's female ancestors. Her father has the closest supervisory rights over her; he may sleep in the same sleeping-basket* with her until she marries, and accompany her if she gets up in the night. He comes to regard her as his property, of which he can dispose as he wishes. Every growing boy has dinned into his ears by an anxious mother the possibility that his father will rob him of his sister, and so of his future wife. The mother has many and sufficient reasons for favouring the exchange of her daughter for the son's wife rather than for a new wife for her husband. Her daughter has long ago been removed from her control by the father; with a pert smile, the little girl has used the kinship terms that her father has taught her. Often after the mother has carried up an especially tasty dish for the father's evening meal, it is the daughter, not the mother, who is bidden to creep into her father's sleeping-bag for the night. When the father and mother have gone into the bush to select house-posts, there

---

*These mosquito-proof baskets are plaited of sago-shoots or bast. They are cylindrical bags from ten to fifteen feet long, distended by bamboo hoops, and accommodating two to four sleepers comfortably. One end is closed permanently and the other end is fastened up after the sleepers have entered the basket.

has always been a competition to see which one would see a strong straight tree first. If the father sees it first, he cries out: "That is for my daughter!" If the mother sees it first, she cries out: "That is for my son!" As the children have grown older, the mother has worked the sago-logs that her small immature son has cut; if the daughters work sago at all it is from the logs that their father has cut with his stronger, more skilled arms. The mother would like to see the daughter out of the way, and in her place a daughter-in-law who will live in her house and be under her control, whom her son will trust her to guard against his father. All her strongest motives, her dislike of the bond between her husband and her daughter, her fear of having that bond translated into the appearance of a young rival wife in the compound, her practised solicitude for her son—all are directed against letting her husband exchange the daughter for a young wife.

A set of complementary motives controls the father. He dislikes his small son just in proportion as the son is sturdy and masculine. The whole structure of the society defines the father and son as rivals. The son's growth is an earnest of the father's decline. The father's jealous regard for his daughter is outraged by his son's claim upon her, and he has a deep-seated hostility to permitting her exchange at all unless that exchange is made at his behest and results in direct sexual satisfaction to himself. Within his compound, as his sons mature, he sees a set of hostile camps developing; in each hut a disgruntled, superseded wife and a jealous aggressive son ready to demand his rights and assert against him a claim to the daughters.

In greater or lesser degree this pattern of hostility between father and son, between brothers, and between half-brothers is repeated in every family group in Mundugumor. Even if a man has but one wife, the expectation of hostility, the conflict over the sister, remains. It will readily be seen what uncertain ground such a social system is on which to base an ordered society. There is no genuine community, no nucleus of related males around which the society can permanently crystallise. The *tamberan* cult, which in other parts of New Guinea unites all the adult males in the community as over against the women and the young boys, has been robbed in Mundugumor of most of this integrating rôle. There is no permanent *tamberan* house that can shelter cult objects, or in which the men can gather together. There is no men's club-house of any kind. Instead of a village or tribal cult, there are several cults, a cult of water-spirit flutes, a cult of bush-spirit flutes, and cults of different imported masks that are regarded as supernaturals. Each of these sacred objects is owned by an individual and passes down a rope. The owner of a croco-dile flute keeps the flute wrapped up in his own house. Initiation has ceased to be a process by which all the boys of a certain age are admitted into the community of adult males. Instead, the sacred flutes, and the ceremonies of initiation without which no one may look at the flutes, have become part of the game that big men play for prestige and fame. A big man, a man with many wives and consequently the necessary wealth, can take it upon himself to give an initiation feast. He builds a large house for the occasion, and all of the boys and young men who have never seen this particular kind of sacred object are rounded up and forced to undergo the particular torture which goes with that sacred object: cutting with crocodile-teeth or burning or beating. These feasts are given very irregularly, at the whim of a big man. Many of the uninitiated are full-grown and married. The initiation has noth-ing to do with the attainment of growth or status or the right to marry. It is all organised about the idea of exclusion and the right of those who have been initiated to taunt and exclude those who have not been. Those men who as young boys congratulated themselves if they escaped to the bush and missed the rough man-handling that the older men give them at initiation, as young men slink away in shame and fury before the cry of : "Get out, you can't see this! You have never been initiated." To escape this indignity they finally consent to be initiated.

Nor does the initiation serve to reaffirm the solidarity of the men as over against the women. Girls in Mundugumor are given a choice. Do they wish to be initiated and observe the food taboos consequent upon initiation—for girls are subjected to none of the ordeals of scarification—or do they wish to remain uniniti- ated spectators who eat what they wish during the year following the initiation? About two-thirds of the girls elect to be initiated. Any initiation, then, represents a ceremony in which a miscella- neous and mixed age-group of boys and girls is initiated by an individual feast-giver and a group of men who are temporarily associated with him. It does not make for a sense of age, sex, or community responsibility. It does make for a very real awe of the sacred flutes, an awe that in practise is reserved, however, for the special flutes of one's own family line, not for the flute that was used in the initiation. There is no translation into group-feeling even of the awe-inspiring, the shared experience of seeing for the first time, under circumstances of great solemnity, the staring mother-of-pearl eyes of the shell-encrusted idol. Each boy will henceforth honour the flute of his own line if it possesses one, or strive to obtain one if there is none in existence.

The religious cult is thus as powerless to integrate the group permanently as are the lines along which descent is organised. The Mundugumor did, at some period in their history, as is demonstrated by the existence of maxims and rules that are mainly honoured in the breach, make some attempt to intertwine the intractable ropes into some sort of co-operative society. This was done by the establishment of mutual obligations between the descendants of an inter-marrying pair of brothers and sisters. The son of the sister scarified the grandson of the brother, who in turn scarified the grandson of his scarifier, and in the fourth generation the children of the two lines were supposed to marry. This elaborate and impractical system of preserving obligations through five generations, and expecting to have at the end of the process two brother-and-sister pairs of the right age to marry, is never carried out in practice.

The only consequence of the existence of such a traditional system is to intensify the conviction of every Mundugumor that he is doing wrong and that he is being wronged by others. The right to scarify a boy is financially profitable; the scarifier receives pigs and rings from the novice and the return on this investment comes when the one-time novice, now grown to adult years, is called upon to scarify the grandson of the man who performed the operation on him a generation before. Similarly, when a woman pierces a girl's ears and receives gifts for it, it is expected that some day that girl will pierce the ears of the granddaughter of the woman who is now being paid, and in return receive handsome presents. But this meticulous observance of obligations through three generations is too difficult for the aggressive individuality of Mundugumor. Quarrels, removals, the desire to pay off debts by asking someone else to perform the lucrative ceremony—all these interfere. As a result a great number of people are always angry because someone else has been asked to perform the ceremony that they have inherited the right to perform. As for the proper marriages that should reunite two ropes after four generations of reciprocity, these never take place. They are remembered in phrase and maxim and are invoked by those members of Mundugumor society who rebel against the disorganised state of its social life. The memory of what is assumed to be the orderly way in which the ancestors did things serves to give everyone a sense of guilt, to colour all their activities with the kind of angry defiance that is most characteristic of Mundugumor social relations. It is the usual attitude in a host of situations. A father who plans to defraud his son by using the daughter to obtain a wife for himself quarrels with his son upon some pretext and forces him to run away from home; a man who intends to ask some recent ally to scarify his son will accuse the proper scarifier of sorcery or of theft or of an attempt to seduce his wife—anything to produce a coolness under cover of which he can more comfortably betray his obligations. Thus these fantastic provisions for social co-operation between kindred over several generations not only do not operate to integrate the society, but actually contribute to its disintegration.

Between a boy and his mother's brother there are often friendly relations. It is true that he does not belong to either the same rope as his mother's brother or the same landowning group. But the mother's brother is always willing to shelter his nephew if the boy gets into trouble with his father. The relationship between brothers-in-law is one of strain in almost all instances, characterised by shame, embarrassment, and hostility, a hostility that is often the residual of an actual armed encounter when one eloped with the sister of the other. That the elopement was compounded afterwards by the exchange of another woman or by the payment of a flute does not entirely wipe out the memory of the encounter. So giving his nephew help against the latter's father is congruent with the mother's brother's other attitudes. A boy's own mother's brother is felt to be a very close relative, so close that he will perform the scarification ceremony without pay. Mean and stingy people trade upon this, and so save the price that they would have to pay a more distant mother's brother— that is, a mother's male cousin—to perform the same ceremony. In later life men are very often found living and temporarily co-operating with their mother's brothers or their mother's brothers' sons, whom they learned to know during the runaway days of childhood.

In order to understand how the society can exist at all with so much mutual hostility and distrust among all the related males, so little structure upon which genuine co-operation can be based, it is necessary to consider the economic and ceremonial life. The Mundugumor are rich; they have a superabundance of land, their fishing *barads* are filled with fish; generation after generation of their forbears have planted coconut-trees and areca-palms. They have plentiful supplies of the sago-palms; their gardens grow the tobacco so highly valued by their neighbours. Their palm-trees are so plentiful that they say casually that the flying foxes plant them. Compare this abundance with Arapesh conditions, in which every coconut-palm is named and its genealogy lovingly remembered. Furthermore, this economic life requires practically no co-operation between households. What work the men do can easily be done alone. They make yam-gardens, and they cut down sago-palms for sago-working and to rot upon the ground so that the edible sago-grub will flourish in the rooting trunk. The women do everything else. The men can quarrel and refuse to speak to each other; they can move their houses, most of which are flimsy, hastily constructed affairs, up and down the locality; they can sulk by their firesides, or plot revenge with a new set of associates—the work of the household goes on uninterrupted. Distances are short, the ground is level, there are canoes to go longer distances up and down the river. Cheerfully and without overexertion, the strong, well-fed women conduct the work of the tribe. They even climb the coconut-trees—a task from which almost all primitive New Guinea exempts grown women.

Upon this basis of women's work, the men can be as active or as lazy, as quarrelsome or as peaceful, as they like. And the rhythm of the men's life is in fact an alternation between periods of supreme individualism, in which each man stays at home with his wives and engages in a little desultory labour, even an occasional hunting-excursion with his bow and arrows, and the periods when there is some big enterprise on foot. The competitiveness and hostility of one Mundugumor for another are very slightly expressed in economic terms. They quarrel principally over women. They may occasionally quarrel over land or fishing-rights, but the food-supply is plentiful and economic competition does not play any great rôle. If a man wishes to demonstrate his superior wealth he may choose to give a yam-feast to a man who has been his enemy, and so heap coals of fire upon his head. The man to whom the feast is given will have to return it in kind or else lose prestige. But for such a feast a man draws mainly on his own garden and the gardens of immediate allies.

We have already referred to the initiation feasts given by big men. There are also exchanges of food made between a pair of big men, and there are the victory-feasts that follow a successful head-hunting raid. The leaders in all of these undertakings are known to the community as "really bad men," men who are aggressive, gluttons for power and prestige; men who have taken far more than their share of the women of the community, and who have also acquired, by purchase or theft, women from the neighbouring tribes; men who fear no one and are arrogant and secure enough to betray whom they like with impunity. These are the men for whom a whole community will mourn when they die; their arrogance, their lust for power, is the thread upon which the important moments of social life are strung. These men—each community of two or three hundred people boasts two or three—are the fixed points in the social system. They build their compounds well and firmly. There is a strong palisade around them; there are several strong houses; there are slit drums too big to be moved about easily. Meanwhile, less important men, men with fewer wives and less security, quarrel among themselves, move about, now living with a cousin, now with a brother-in-law, now with a mother's brother, until a quarrel over a woman disrupts the temporary alliance, which is based upon no economic necessity. These less important men shift their allegiance from one of the established big men to another, or begin to work with a man who, though still young and possessed of only three or four wives, is rising rapidly to a position of power. In this atmosphere of shifting loyalties, conspiracies, and treachery, head-hunting raids are planned, and the whole male community is temporarily united in the raid and the victory-feasts that conclude them. At these feasts a frank and boisterous cannibalism is practised, each man rejoicing at having a piece of the hated enemy between his teeth.

During periods when no raids are in progress, a big man may decide to give one of the large ceremonies. The uncertain constellations form about the two main parties to the feast, and a truce is called to all intra-community quarreling. There must be no wife-stealing, no surreptitious spear-throwing, during this time of preparation. A big feast involves not only a good supply of yams, which are not an important element in Mundugumor diet but are reserved for these display occasions, but also a large amount of ceremonial paraphernalia. For one kind of feast a great model crocodile twenty feet long is constructed of bark, and painted with elaborate designs. For another type, a bark triangle some thirty to forty feet high is painted and raised against the coconut-trees. Sometimes new flute figures are carved, and must then be decorated with real hair, shells, seeds, opossum-fur, feathers, and tiny crocheted garments. Shields and spears must be refurbished for the dance, or new ones carved.

All of this labour, under the protecting shadow of the truce, is done with the greatest good spirits. Men are called together each morning by the sound of flutes; all day a group sits crocheting, stringing shells, or chewing charcoal under the arrogant direction of the master artist, who has superseded the leading head-hunter as dictator for the occasion. Little boys and men who have never seen the ceremony are shooed contemptuously away. At noon the women bring great heaping dishes of food, well garnished with fish and sago-grubs. For several weeks men who ordinarily distrust each other's every move, and hesitate to turn their backs to one another for an instant, work together, while the more level heads scheme to bring advantage to themselves out of the temporary lull in hostilities. Finally the feast is given, the dance is over, the truce is finished, and the normal conditions of hostility and quarrelling reassert themselves until the next big feast or head-hunting raid draws the people together again.

11

the development of the individual Mundugumor

The Mundugumor man-child is born into a hostile world, a world in which most of the members of his own sex will be his enemies, in which his major equipment for success must be a capacity for violence, for seeing and avenging insult, for holding his own safety very lightly and the lives of others even more lightly. From his birth, the stage is set to produce in him this kind of behaviour. When a Mundugumor woman tells her husband that she is pregnant, he is not pleased. It makes him a marked man. When he goes among a group of men who are carving a slit gong, they will officiously and with broad grins brush up the chips lest he tread upon any of them, which would be bad for the child, whom he does not want, and for the slit gong, from the manufacture of which he is thus publicly excluded. If he fences a garden, someone else will insert the posts; if he gathers ratan in the bush, some impudent small boy will warn him to pluck only the green ratan or the child will stick fast in his wife's womb. These taboos, which might unite him to his wife in care for the child if having a child were something to look forward to among the Mundugumor, are used by his associates to aggravate his annoyance with his wife. He abuses her for having become pregnant so quickly, and curses his anti-pregnancy magic that he had set in motion in vain. If he has intercourse with her after she is known to be pregnant, he runs a further risk; she may have twins, the second child being the result of more male stimulation, which is all that a male is believed to contribute, semen that, by continual stimulation of a blood-clot, causes it to develop into a child. The father's interest, therefore, instead of being enlisted on the side of the child is already enlisted against it. And the pregnant woman associates her pregnancy with sexual deprivation, her husband's anger and repudiation, and the continual risk that he will take another wife and temporarily desert her altogether. This latter he is particularly likely to do if the new woman who attracts his attention has to be fought for—as is usually the case. Whether she is the wife or the daughter of another man, the new husband first has to elope with her, then defend her against the party of enraged men who will come to fight over her, and finally compensate them for her either with a woman from his kindred or with a valuable sacred flute. During the course of such proceedings he naturally does not confide in his pregnant wife, and she often finds herself stranded with some one of her own relatives while her husband is careening off after a rival. So to the mother, even more than to the father, the coming child is unwelcome. The first highly charged days of marriage in which an active interest in sex held them both together have given place to anger, hostility, and very often to charges of infidelity, as the husband refuses to believe that he is responsible for this unwelcome event.

This attitude towards children is congruent with the ruthless individualism, the aggressive specific sexuality, the intrasex hostility, of the Mundugumor. A system that made a son valuable to a man as an heir, as an extension of his own personality, might combine the Mundugumor personality type with an interest in parenthood, but under the Mundugumor rope and marriage system, a man has no heirs, only sons who are hostile rivals by definition, and daughters who, defend them as he will, will eventually be torn from him. A man's only hope of power and prestige lies in the number of his wives, who will work for him and give him the means to buy power, and in the accident of the occurrence of some mild characters among his brothers. The phrase "a man who has brothers" occurs every now and again in their remarks, and this means a man who, by a stroke of luck, has some weak-willed, docile brothers who will follow his lead, and instead of disputing his progress will form a more or less permanent constellation about him in his middle age. Allies whom he can coerce and bully in the days of his strength, not sons who will come after him and by their strength mock his old age, these are his desire. A wife who becomes pregnant has therefore hurt a man at his most vulnerable spot; she has taken the first step towards his downfall by possibly conceiving a son. And for herself, she has shifted her husband's active sexual interest into angry frustrated resentment—for what? Possibly to bear a daughter, who will be her husband's, not hers.

Before the child is born there is much discussion as to whether it shall be saved or not, the argument being partly based upon the sex of the child, the father preferring to keep a girl, the mother a boy. The argument is weighted against the mother, however, because her father and brothers also prefer a girl. Boys in the kin-group lead to trouble if there are not enough girls to purchase wives for them; and, even if they have a sufficient number of sisters, aggressive boys are apt to carry off additional women who will have to be fought over. The chance of survival of a Mundugumor child increases with order of birth, the first child having the poorest chance. Both father and mother are less intensely upset by the advent of later children, and also once a son is born it is absolutely necessary that he should have a sister to exchange for his wife. This feeling that one's very social existence depends upon having a sister was vividly illustrated when a Mundugumor woman offered to adopt one of our Arapesh boys.* The earnest of

---

*This woman was far easier and more good-natured than is usual in Mundugumor and she took a great fancy to the personality of our most typically Arapesh boy.

the offer was that she promised him—with her husband's approval, of course—one of her daughters as a sister, thus assuring him a proper position in Mundugumor society. A girl-child, therefore, has a better chance of survival than a boy; she is an advantage to her father, to her brothers, and also to the entire kin-group on both sides, who, if she is not requisitioned at home, may use her to compensate for one of her cousin's wives.

There is also some feeling that once one son is kept, he might as well have brothers. If a child survives long enough to be washed instead of being bundled up in the palm-spathe upon which the delivery took place and thrown into the river, it will not be killed afterwards, although it may be treated most summarily and exposed to many risks to which young children are not subjected among most primitive peoples. Also if a man deserts his wife during her pregnancy, his chances of having a son survive are much higher, for he will not be there to command her to kill it. In a polygynous household, furthermore, each rival wife insists upon having a son, and the husband is enmeshed in a net of cause and effect from which he seldom entirely extricates himself.

Thus while the motivations that control husband and wife during first pregnancy in a marriage of choice are all opposed to preserving the child, they are not the only considerations which influence the keeping or killing of new-born children. These attitudes do indeed set the tone of Mundugumor feeling about birth, but they are not allowed sufficient sway to prevent Mundugumor society from reproducing itself.

Besides the circumstances that lead to keeping the first child, and the considerations which then result in keeping other children, there are two other factors making for increase in population: the birth of twins and the custom of adoption. As if in mockery of their dislike of children, Mundugumor women have an extraordinarily strong tendency to twin birth; the twin birth-rate is far in excess of that for any of the other known tribes of that part of New Guinea. Both twins are seldom killed. If they are two boys or a boy and girl, it is the boy that is not kept; in the event of two girls, both are kept. One twin, however, is always adopted, as a Mundugumor mother does not customarily undertake to suckle two children. In addition to adopting one of a pair of twins, ordinary adoption is a very common occurrence. Even women who have never borne children are able in a few weeks, by placing the child constantly at the breast and by drinking plenty of coconut-milk, to produce enough or nearly enough milk to rear the child, which is suckled by other women for the first few weeks after adoption.* There is a great deal in favour of adoption. Pregnancy and birth are avoided, and the lactation taboo upon intercourse, under penalty of contracting a skin disease, need not be observed, as the suckled child has no relationship to father and mother. Although it is usual to adopt a girl, rather than a boy, the wife is compensated for this by the better relationship to her husband, and by avoiding the aspects of motherhood that she most dislikes. Many of these adopted children had been already condemned to death when the foster-parent appeared on the scene; such children are spoken of as "one who was adopted unwashed from the palm-spathe of birth." It must be remembered also that if a sister is to be of any use to a brother the sibling pair should be near of an age. If she is much older than her brother, she will elope before he is old enough to marry. Even if a half-grown girl is given in return for her, the small husband of ten or eleven will not be able to keep his gawky bride, who will mature only to be carried

---

*The Mundugumor say that the breasts of some, but not of all, women will secrete milk under the stimulating effect of a child's suckling, combined with drinking large quantities of coconut-milk. I was able to compare the weight and health of two sets of twins, one of each pair being suckled by its own mother, the other by an adopted mother in whose breasts milk had been artificially stimulated. One was a case of a two-year-old child entirely suckled by the adopting mother; the other of an infant of four months, whose adopted mother had only within the last month had enough milk to feed it entirely without aid from other women. In each case the adopted twin showed as high a development as the twin suckled by its own mother.

off by some older man. Sometimes a man who has several sons and no daughters, and a wife who is unwilling to adopt daughters, will bespeak the child of a sister by undertaking part of its care. Under the influence of the theory that girls are very difficult to obtain, this petition for a sister's child is more often made before birth. The petitioner then sends food regularly to the pregnant woman, but the child turns out to be the wrong sex half the time and the father of sons finds himself in the uncomfortable position of having assumed a quasi-paternal responsibility for still another boy.

It is into such a highly charged world, a world constantly disposed to hostility and conflict, that the Mundugumor infant is born. And almost from birth, unless it is an adopted child and the constant stimulating of its suckling is needed for the first few months to produce milk, the child's preparation for an unloved life is begun. Very little babies are kept in a carrying-basket, a closely woven, rough-plaited basket, semicircular in profile, which the women wear suspended from their foreheads as the Arapesh women wear their net bags. (And as the Arapesh call the womb by the word for net bag, so the Mundugumor call the womb by the word for carrying-basket.) But whereas the Arapesh net bag is flexible, adapting itself to the child's body and exerting pressure to curl the body in upon itself in a pre-natal position, and is furthermore so slight that it interposes no barrier between the child and its mother's warm body, the Mundugumor basket is harsh and stiff and opaque. The child's body must accommodate itself to the rigid lines of the basket, lying almost prone with its arms practically pinioned to its sides. The basket is too thick to permit any warmth from the mother's body to permeate it; the child sees nothing but the narrow slits of light at both ends. Women wear the babies only when they are walking from one place to another, and as most of their expeditions are short, to their own fishing *barads* and sago-bush, they usually leave them at home, hung up in the house. When a baby cries it is not fed at once; instead some bystander resorts to the standard method of soothing restless infants. Without looking at the child, without touching its body, the mother or other woman or girl who is caring for it begins to scratch with her finger-nails on the outside of the basket, making a harsh grating sound. Children are trained to respond to this sound; it seems as if their cries, originally motivated by a desire for warmth, water, or food, were conditioned to accepting often this meagre remote response in their stead. If the crying does not stop, the child is eventually suckled.

Mundugumor women suckle their children standing up, supporting the child with one hand in a position that strains the mother's arm and pinions the arms of the child. There is none of the mother's dallying, sensuous pleasure in feeding her child that occurs among the Arapesh. Nor is the child permitted to prolong his meal by any playful fondling of his own or his mother's body. He is kept firmly to his major task of absorbing enough food so that he will stop crying and consent to be put back in his basket. The minute he stops suckling for a moment he is returned to his prison. Children therefore develop a very definite purposive fighting attitude, holding on firmly to the nipple and sucking milk as rapidly and vigorously as possible. They frequently choke from swallowing too fast; the choking angers the mother and infuriates the child, thus further turning the suckling situation into one characterised by anger and struggle rather than by affection and reassurance.

As soon as children can sit up they can no longer be left safely in their baskets, although they can be carried about in them. If the basket is hung up on the wall, the child kicks and twists around in it, and is in danger of falling out—and making more trouble. For it is in these terms that the Mundugumor greet all illness and accident, even in little children. All such things are matters for exasperation and anger, as if the personality of the parent were invaded and insulted by the illness of the child. In the case of a death the whole community is similarly enraged. To have to attend to a sick child makes a mother sulky and resentful.

As might be expected, only the strongest children survive. Those who will not use the few minutes vouchsafed to them to drink enough milk to last them through the next few hours perish for lack of the careful solicitous wooing towards life that Arapesh mothers give their punier children. So the husky, independent infant begins to kick in his basket and has to be taken out of it, and laid on the floor of the house or carried about upon the mother's back. It is, of course, not safe to leave a crawling child alone in a house the floor of which is raised some four or five feet from the ground upon piles. Children of one year to two years are carried about on the mother's back. If a crawling child cries hard it is lifted up and placed firmly astride the mother's neck. A child is only given the breast in case it is believed to be really in need of food, never to comfort it in fright or pain. Here again the contrast with the Arapesh is striking; if an Arapesh child that has been weaned for several years is screaming from pain or fright, the mother will offer the child her slack, dry breast to comfort it; the Mundugumor mother will not even offer a still suckling child her full one. This attitude was particularly noticeable when I gave native babies castor-oil; all other native women in New Guinea of whom I have had any experience will give a crying child the breast as a solace after the child has been given castor-oil. The Mundugumor woman merely claps the child on to the back of her neck and goes on with her work or her conversation, completely disregarding its screams, except, in the case of an older child, for a slap or so. Nor is the child supported in this precarious position by a firm and friendly hand; instead it is taught to maintain a strong hold on its mother's bushy hair, and thus keep itself from falling.

As soon as a child can walk it is set down most of the time, and permitted to fend for itself. But it is not allowed to wander far because of the fear of drowning, an event which upsets the entire routine of the village for months, since, as has been noted, the water in which it drowns becomes taboo for drinking purposes. The Mundugumor uneasiness in the presence of water does not suggest to them that children might be trained not to fall into the river. With water-conditions incomparably simpler and safer than those under which the natives of the main river live, the fear of drowning is much greater. This fear makes the supervision of children far more of a chore than it need be; the mothers have to remain more tense and attentive, and are for ever screaming at wandering children, or snatching them back violently from the river-bank. So the Mundugumor child is given a first association with the territory beyond his home as a dangerous place, an association that is reinforced by all the kinship prohibitions which he learns later. And from the time that he learns to walk, his mother's hostility to suckling him becomes even more pronounced. He is now free to run up to her, to cling about her leg or attempt to climb up her lap in order to get at her breasts. It never occurs to him, unless he is so ill that he is almost unconscious of what he does, to attempt to lie in his mother's lap. But he will attempt to reach her breasts, only to be thrust away, as often as not, and slapped, as the mother tries to discourage his suckling. There are no weaning methods that substitute a food, lovingly given, for a breast which has been made specifically unpalatable. Children are weaned by being progressively pushed away by their mothers; they no longer sleep with them in the long plaited sleeping-bags; their mothers never hold them or carry them in a position from which they could get at the breasts. The milder women put bitter sap on their breasts. After weeks of a losing battle, the child settles down to eating sago-soup, and expects even less of comfort from its mother. In infancy, the mother's resentment and impatience were demonstrated to the child by her tense, uncomfortable standing position, her haste, the relief with which she put the child from her. The whole weaning process is accompanied by blows and cross words, which further accentuate the picture of a hostile world that is presented to the child. A few Mundugumor children suck a pair of fingers or the back of the hand; this is individual behaviour, not a recognised habit-pattern followed by all children. A child so occupied is fretful, with an anxious, peevish look on its face, and gnaws as its fingers rather than sucking them or using them to stimulate its lips or tongue.

A little child must observe a series of food taboos until, when it is about two years old, a father's sister feeds it the tabooed foods in a special ceremonial meal. These taboos instead of focusing parental care upon the child are used to formulate enmity. When a child that has not yet been released from its taboos falls ill, someone is accused of having purposely fed it the tabooed foods, as a way of injuring its parents. When a Mundugumor parent can regard the child as an extension of the parental ego, then, and then only, does the term "my child" have an emphasis that lacks ambivalence.

Although there is some difference between a woman's treatment of a boy and a girl, this difference is against such a general background of maternal rejection that to an observer the treatment of both seems hostile and harsh. The little girls are taught from earliest childhood that they are desirable. Baby girls a few weeks old are laden with shell ornaments, ear-rings two or three inches long, and necklaces and belts of shells as big as slices of lemon. Thus conspicuously are they set off from their brothers, who go about in a naked, unadorned state. The women's interest in dress includes occasionally dressing up their small daughters in highly coloured and very diminutive grass skirts; the children have not been trained to take care of these skirts and they rapidly soil them, whereupon an enraged mother rips off the damaged skirt and tells the small girl that she can go naked for her bad behaviour. The little girl is also accustomed to being paraded about in the arms of a vain but unsolicitous father, and being commented upon and chucked under the chin or poked at by the other men.

Little boys go naked until they are seven or eight, when under present conditions they put on loin-cloths. The Mundugumor men seem earlier to have gone naked until after they had acquired head-hunting honours, at which time they assumed a pubic covering made from a flying-fox skin, ornamented with a pendant covered with nassa-shells. About ten years ago, and before they were brought under government control, they obtained cloth from the lower-Sepik peoples and the entire male population over seven or eight put on loin-cloths. It is interesting that although the custom of wearing clothing is three generations old in Alitoa and only half a generation old in Mundugumor, Mundugumor men showed far more shame over any exposure than did Alitoa men, and small boys clung more vigorously to their loin-cloths.

The first lessons that a Mundugumor child learns are a series of prohibitions.* It must not defecate in the house. It must not wander out of sight. It must not go into the house of its father's other wife and ask for food. It must not cling to its mother, in fear or in affection. It must not cry unless it wishes to be roundly slapped. It must not make demands for attention except on the very occasional adults who are fond of children. Within every child's circle of kin there are likely to be one or two of these persons, a mild, unassuming paternal uncle, or some remarried widow who lives a quiet, unaggressive life, not competing with her cowives or thinking it worth while to be disagreeable to their children. Whether the child can actually turn to such refuges, however, depends upon the relations between his own parents and the kind relative; if these are at all strained, he will be forbidden to enter the house of the kind person. While children are still very small, four or five years of age, they are taught to classify their kin, the boy being taught by his mother, and the girl by her father. The importance of this point in separating parent from child of the same sex, and in separating brother from sister, can hardly be exaggerated. Mundugumor kinship behaviour is very different from Arapesh behaviour, where a child is taught practically identical behaviour towards every person, male or female, old or young, whom he calls by a kinship term. Instead, the Mundugumor divide the kin up into those persons with whom one jokes, those whom one avoids in shame, and those whom one treats with varying shades of ordinary intimacy. A joking relative

---

*The people make an extraordinarily frequent use of the imperative form. When I think of a Mundugumor verb it is always the imperative form that leaps into my mind, in strong contrast to my memory of Arapesh, in which imperatives were very seldom used.

is not a person with whom one may joke if one wishes, but rather a relative towards whom joking is the correct behaviour, a kind of behaviour that is as culturally fixed as shaking hands.

Perhaps it will make the matter clearer to imagine what it would be like if one were taught in America to shake hands with one's uncles and kiss the hands of one's aunts, while when one met a grandparent, one took off one's hat, threw away one's cigarette or pipe, and stood rigidly at attention, and upon meeting a cousin the correct behaviour was to thumb one's nose. Imagine further that in a small, inbred rural community, relationships were traced a very long way in every genealogical line, and so not only one's mother's sisters and one's father's sisters but all of their first and even second cousins of the female sex were called "aunt," until there were some twenty or thirty relatives of varying ages in the community, all of whom had to have their hands kissed, and an equal number at whom one thumbed one's nose. It will be seen also that in such a large group, one's "aunts" and "uncles" and "cousins" would be of all ages, and would occur in the same school or the same play-group. This approximates the normal condition in a primitive society that insists upon different treatment for different classes of relatives. In Mundugumor everyone must be continually on the alert and ready to respond with the appropriate behaviour. A failure to joke is more serious than a failure of an American to greet properly an acquaintance upon the street. It may easily be as serious as a failure to salute a superior officer, or to acknowledge a possible employer's friendly greeting. And whereas the American can walk down the street only watchful to distinguish between those whom he knows and those whom he does not, and only sufficiently attentive to the form that his greeting takes to regulate its boisterousness or its familiarity, in many primitive societies much more elaborate behaviour is demanded.

So a Mundugumor child is taught that everyone who is related to it as mother's brother, father's sister, sister's child of a male, brother's child of a female, and their spouses is a joking relative with whom one engages in rough-house, accusations of unusual and inappropriate conduct, threats, mock bullying, and the like. If a man meets his father's sister—and this applies not only to his father's own sister but to all the women whom his father calls sister, and whom we should call first, second, sometimes third cousins of his father—he slaps her on the back, tells her she is getting old, will probably die soon, has a frightful-looking bone ornament in her nose, and he tries to pull some areca-nut out of her carrying-basket. Similarly when a man meets a brother-in-law, any man whom his wife calls brother or any man married to a woman whom he calls sister, he must be shy and circumspect, not ask him for an areca-nut or offer to share food with him, but greet him with great coolness tinged with embarrassment. The world is early presented to the child as one in which there are a large number of such fixed relationships, with a separate behaviour-pattern appropriate to some and highly inappropriate and insulting to others, a world in which one must be always upon one's guard, and always ready to respond correctly and with apparent spontaneity to these highly formal demands. It is not a world in which one can walk about happily, sure of a friendly smile, a pat on the head, a piece of areca-nut from everyone, in which one can relax and be gay or sad as one wishes. Even gaiety is not in any sense a relaxation for a Mundugumor; he must always be gay on the right occasions and addressing the right persons; he must always be watchful that none of the persons towards whom, or in the presence of whom, such behaviour would be incorrect are anywhere about. This gives a tight-rope quality to all jest and laughter; Mundugumor laughter is bright, but not happy; it has a harsh sound as it crackles in its defined tracks.

In these respects, however, Mundugumor society is very like many other primitive societies, and somewhat like very highly formalised parts of our own society, such as the army and the navy, where there are strict limits to the amount of jesting and familiarity that are permitted between, or in the presence of, men of different rank. But the rope system of the Mundugumor adds

other complications. It will be remembered that along one rope
are ranged together a man, his daughter, and his daughter's son,
and that his wife, his son, and his son's daughter belong in
another rope. These rope organisations are partly defined by the
possession of names which help to identify a woman with her
paternal grandmother and a man with his maternal grandfather.
In the theory which underlies this structure, a man is socially
identical with his maternal grandfather and may apply the same
kinship terms to his grandfather's generation that his grandfather
himself uses; this includes calling his maternal grandmother
"wife." Such use of kinship terms is congruent with the ideal
marriage that reunites the ropes, but is so meaningless in the present disorganised state of Mundugumor society that the people
now phrase this tendency to identify members of alternate generations by saying that a boy is permitted to joke by using his
grandfather's terms. They thus convert a formal structural point
into a point of licence, and small boys—grown men do not have
living grandfathers with whom they can identify—strut about
referring to old men and women as their sisters and brothers,
wives and brothers-in-law. As a girl is supposed to take over the
social identity of her paternal grandmother, she has to learn the
details of her kinship from her father, who knows it better than
would her mother, and the same thing holds for a boy—it is his
mother who can instruct him in his rope relationships. But here
again what is in form a simple point of structure the Mundugumor phrase as a girl's helping her father and a boy's helping his
mother.

By means of their rope relationships husbands and wives
habitually insult each other. In a small inbred community, it is
obvious that individuals will be related to each other by more
than one genealogical path. So a man's wife's uncle may be also a
second cousin of his mother's to whom he would normally refer*

---

*Despite the enormous importance given to kinship terms among them,
the Mundugumor never use the terms in direct address.

as "mother's brother," rather than by the term that means "elder male relative-in-law." If the husband wishes to insult his wife, he may continue to do this in her presence, and this is tantamount to denying that he is married to her. Similarly, a woman by insisting upon her distant blood-connexion to one of her husband's relatives may insult and infuriate him. The psychology underlying this formal kind of insult is often seen in remarks made within a family group in our own society, when a woman who is angry with her husband may refer to him, in addressing her children, as "your father," with strong disassociation in her voice, or a son may say of his father to his mother: "That's the kind of thing your husband would do." The Mundugumor have simply seized upon this convenient form of insult and standardised it. As a result, a father's teaching his daughter her kinship is regarded not primarily as orienting her in rope membership, but as making points against his wife. The father is particularly careful to seek out those persons who are related in most contrasting ways to himself and to his wife, so as to ensure that every time his daughter opens her mouth to refer to them she will be making a conspicuous point against her mother. The mother retaliates by instructing the son in the same way.

In addition to all of these complications, the Mundugumor have a very strong feeling, amounting almost to a feeling of incest, against marriages between the generations, that is, against a man's marrying any girl whom he would classify as a "daughter," even though she be the daughter of a male fourth cousin. It is felt that the fact that she is classified in the same generation with his daughter should be enough to forbid the marriage. In actual practice, however, such marriages and others of like nature, such as a man's marrying a woman whom he would call "mother" or "aunt," do occur, and whenever they occur the interrelationships of a large number of people are upset. Since normally if no such marriage occurred there would be no choice of generation between the terms that one applied to any member of the community, whenever there is such a choice, people feel uncomfortable, ashamed, angry, as in the presence of incest. They stare at each other angrily, drop whatever form of kinship behaviour they used before, whether jesting, intimacy, or formal shyness. They say: "He was my mother's brother, until he married my sister. Now I should call him brother-in-law. But I do not. I stand up and stare." This stare, which is substituted for all other forms of behaviour, is one of anger and of shame, and is the behaviour that characterises one's attitude towards fully a third of the community.

This then is the world into which the growing boy seeking to classify those whom he sees every day is introduced. He learns that such and such a man or boy is a "mother's brother," which means that one is due for a rough-house whenever he appears on the scene. This is also true, with slightly less physical hazing, of those whom one classifies as "father's sister." He learns that the terms which his mother teaches him to use irritate his father. He learns that he and his sister do not classify people in the same way and have not equal freedom in entering the same houses. This he finds is also true of himself and his half-brothers. He further learns that with his own brother he must be stiff and distant, so that the presence of his own brother, of his sister, of his father, of any of his father's brothers, or of any of the relatives who are classified as affinal relatives, all cramp his behaviour in relation to those relatives with whom he is supposed to jest. He also learns that, by using the genealogical paths by which he can identify with members of his grandfather's genealogy, he can address grown men haughtily by terms which make them inferior in age and generation to himself. As he grows a little older, he learns that all the girls whom he calls "sister" yet who are not his own sisters, but merely his first or second cousins, stand in a special jesting relationship to him that calls for the continual interchange of very broad scatalogical comments, which they will reciprocate in kind. These are girls whom he should not marry; but if he does marry them, the social conscience will not be very much shocked, the interrelations between generations will not be upset and no one will have to "just stand up and stare." But if a man does marry such a woman, he will immediately have to drop all this light scatalogical conversation, which is inappropriate between husband and wife. The chance that he may perhaps marry one of the girls to whom he is commenting upon their lack of personal hygiene adds piquancy to this jesting, rather of the order that might be duplicated among ourselves by a man's flirting with a woman who he suspects may become his mother-in-law. All of this interplay the small boy or girl sees and assimilates.

What houses a child may enter, whom he may ask for food or water, whom he may accompany on expeditions, are all regulated by these multiple considerations plus the state of his parents' actual personal relationships with others, owing to recent quarrels and disagreement. And all of these points are phrased negatively: "You may not enter this house," not, "You *may* enter this one." It is small wonder that kinship and personal relationships make a child nervous and apprehensive, and that he comes to associate the whole problem with discomfort, trouble, misunderstanding, and quarrels. The fact that his mother's brothers do offer him a refuge against his father, that his father's brothers may in some cases also offer him shelter, are pleasant facts in an unpleasant context, and only serve to re-emphasise the conflict that is all about him.

Children's play-groups are also invaded by the question of kinship, for, exercising the licence of "mother's brothers," older boys are continually pinching, pushing, threatening, teasing, bullying, smaller children. This is the sole invasion of little children's casual associations by the adult world, unless they stray towards the water and are shrieked at and perhaps beaten. For the rest, little children wander about playing with bright inedible orange fruits that litter the ground, balancing them in the air, or throwing them at each other. Or they play endless little games with their hands, with pieces of stick, or with their toes, the emphasis always being on the skill with which the trick is performed, one child attempting to emulate and outdo another. Into this competitive but unorganised group come the older children, armed with licence to oppress, a licence that they use to the full. If, however, a twelve-year-old "mother's brother" has reduced a four-year-old "sister's son" to tears, one of his own brothers passing near may make this the excuse for thrashing him soundly in theoretical defence of the small sufferer, who is his "sister's son" also. By every turn and twist the rules of kinship are used among pre-adolescents to give licence, licence to tease small children, licence to insult one's father or mother, and licence to humiliate older people. This may in some measure compensate them for the amount of shame that they have been taught to feel about in-law relationships and relationships connected with irregular marriages. By the time the boys are eight to ten years old, patterns of group-play among boys—Mundugumor children never play in two-sex groups—are entirely based on kinship. A spectator who did not realise this would watch with astonishment the endless display of physical violence, which is returned in kind with no show of resentment. A blow given by a "mother's brother" or a "sister's son" cannot be resented, and so the small boys grow accustomed to stand a great deal of knocking about and harsh treatment. Only when two brothers become involved in a tussle does the emotional tone change.

The girls, on the other hand, never form a play-group, and have no such set patterns of social behaviour. There are several features of the social structure that are favourable to girls' maintaining more comfortable relations among themselves. This does not mean that sisters are always friendly; the general atmosphere of struggle, competition, and jealousy is too great for that. There is no insistence upon sisters behaving formally and distantly to each other, and half-sisters belong to the same rope. Also there is a close relationship between a girl and the girl for whom she was exchanged; they are spoken of as the "return," one of the other, and there is no emphasis upon rivalry or injury, as there is so often between brothers-in-law. Finally the ordinary marriage picture, the social ideal, is that of one husband and several wives.

Although these wives get on rather badly together, although they refuse to feed each other's children and are constantly struggling to be the chosen one who is summoned to the husband's sleeping-basket, nevertheless they form one of the most permanent semi-co-operative organisations in Mundugumor. They live in the same compound, they see each other constantly, and no formalised avoidance or jesting behaviour separates them or regulates their conduct. They call each other "sister" and reproduce the constellation of daughters around the father of the polygynous household. The element of extreme discomfort that characterises irregular marriages enters the compound when a man marries a widow with a daughter and later marries her daughter, or when he marries a girl who has previously been betrothed to one of his sons. Here the violation of the generation taboo is felt very strongly indeed, and a mother and daughter who are the wives of the same man may refuse to speak to each other, or may resort to such violent public abuse that the more easily shamed one will commit suicide. Still, there are sometimes twelve or fifteen women in a compound, and the tendency, in the absence of fixed rules of conduct between them, is towards forming shifting alliances within which the degree of enmity is at least less than it is towards the other parties or trios. All of this provides a groundplan that makes it possible for a group of girls to sit about quietly talking or making grass skirts without the restrictions imposed by an insistence upon avoidance, jesting, or shyness. The very little girls follow their older sisters about, and imitate this busy cheerful behaviour.

The child learns in his experience in the random group of small children a sturdy degree of independence, to return blow for blow, to value his physical liberty. From earliest childhood both boys and girls have been accustomed to resent and fight interference. Very small Mundugumor children resent above everything else having their arms held tight; to be held still in the presence of something that frightens them drives them almost to frenzy. A confining arm does not mean safety; it means a cut-off escape. The only protection that is ever offered to children is the position on the parent's shoulder, where they cling high above the world, and by their own efforts. When they grow a little older, even this succour is denied them and the frightened or angry child retreats into an empty mosquito-net, and lies there, thinking of revenge, until his tears have dried. No gentleness or coddling has ever come their way to make them docile. As they grow older, little girls attach themselves with strong partisan feeling to some older girl or woman in their small locality; little boys do the same. Meanwhile, their relationships to their parents become more and more tense. Seven-year-old boys will defy their fathers and leave home. Their fathers will not pursue them. But as the girls approach adolescence they are watched with a jealous care, a humiliating surveillance that infuriates them. And behind this difference in the treatment of boys and girls lies no theory that women differ temperamentally from men. They are believed to be just as violent, just as aggressive, just as jealous. They simply are not quite as strong physically, although often a woman can put up a very good fight, and a husband who wishes to beat his wife takes care to arm himself with a crocodile-jaw and to be sure that she is not armed. But as a rule women have no weapons; they are not taught to use weapons, and pregnancy will reduce them to reason if nothing else does. For these reasons, although women choose men as often as men choose women, the society is constructed so that men fight about women, and women elude, defy, and complicate this fighting to the limit of their abilities. So little girls grow up as aggressive as little boys and with no expectation of docilely accepting their rôle in life.

Thus long before a boy is adolescent he understands the behaviour required of him, and resents it. His world is divided into people about each of whom there is a series of prohibitions, cautions, restrictions. He thinks of his kinship to others in terms of the things that are forbidden to him in relation to them, and in terms of hostile attitudes which he may take up: the houses that he may not enter, the boys whom he may not tease or punch because they are his "brothers-in-law," and the little girls whose hair he may pull, the boys whom he may bully, the men from whose baskets he may purloin areca-nut or tobacco. He knows that one way or another he will have to fight over his wife, either fight his father who will wish to take his sister, or his brother who will wish to take his sister, or some prospective brother-in-law who will steal his sister, or if he has no sister, or loses her, he will have to steal a wife and fight her brothers. The little girl knows that she will be the centre of such conflicts, that the males of her family are already considering her with an eye to their matrimonial plans, that if she is exchanged as a young pre-adolescent girl she will enter a household where the quarrel will merely be shifted—instead of her father and brothers quarrelling as to which one is to exchange her, her husband and his father and brothers will fight over which one is to have her.

When a boy or more rarely a girl is eight or nine, he or she may have the experience of being sent as a hostage to a strange tribe while arrangements are being made for a head-hunting raid. Although all children do not have this experience, and some have it more than once, it is nevertheless significant of the sturdiness of the children's personality that any one of them is felt capable of undergoing such an ordeal. Frightened, not comprehending the language, amid strange faces, strange sounds, strange smells, eating strange food, the small hostage may have to remain for weeks or even months in the hostile atmosphere. And occasionally such child-hostages are sent into Mundugumor hamlets, where they are teased and bullied by the Mundugumor children. Every child has before him, therefore, the possibility of which he knows by hearing other children's tales and because of the stranger children that he has himself maltreated.

Some time before he is adolescent, many a Mundugumor boy will be called upon to despatch a captive for the cannibal feast. This is not a privilege or an honour. The father does not capture or buy* a victim so that his son may wear homicidal decorations—as is done in other parts of the Sepik region. A child does the killing lest the men of other villages should say: "Have you then no children, that grown men among you despatch your captives?" No decorations are given to the child for this kill and unless he takes other heads, it will become a matter for reproach: "You! As a child you killed a captive who was tied fast. But you have killed no one since. You are no warrior!"

As a result of all this Spartan training, pre-adolescent Mundugumor children have an appearance of harsh maturity and, aside from sex-experience, are virtually assimilated to the individualistic patterns of their society by the time they are twelve or thirteen. Initiation comes to girls as somewhat of a privilege granted to them in proportion as they are aggressive and demanding, to boys as a penalty that they cannot escape. It serves to blur the difference in the amount of freedom allowed girls and boys, for while the adolescent girls merely file in to observe the sacred objects, the adolescent boys are rounded up with blows and curses and scarified with crocodile-skulls, a sadistic exercise that obviously pleases their tormentors. Initiation does not come at any stated period, but is a matter of the time when a big man gives an initiation ceremony, so that it occurs several times in the life of a boy or girl from twelve to past twenty or so. These are not *rites de passage*, rituals that tide the individual over changes in his life; they are merely something to which one's society subjects one, if one is a boy, permits one, if one is a girl, at a time when one is still young and immature.

The actual experience of seeing one of the sacred figures or masks is a dignified and awe-inspiring one. The ceremony is pre-

---

*Victims were sold or exchanged in the eventuality of the capturing group not wishing to eat a member of another group with whom they were on fairly intimate terms. Here, as in all the discussions of war, head-hunting, and cannibalism, it must be remembered that the present tense is used merely stylistically, and that the government has suppressed these practices.

pared for days in advance; all quarrelling and shouting is hushed in the hamlet, flutes play in the morning and evening, everyone's attention is directed to a common end. The initiates are solemnly led into the presence of the sacred figures, which have been disposed to the best advantage in a nearly dark house. They are instructed in the food taboos which this privilege imposes upon them, and these are the only restrictions that are borne willingly by the Mundugumor. But to enter and see the sacred flutes with their tall, thin shell-encrusted standards surmounted by a manikin figure with a huge head, wearing a diadem of shell and hundreds of graceful and valuable decorations from the midst of which its mother-of-pearl eyes gleam—this is an experience of major importance. About these sacred flutes, the hereditary possession of a rope, the almost-equivalent of a woman, these flutes upon which all the artistic skill of the best carvers and the cherished shell valuables of a whole group of men have been lavished, is centred the pride of the Mundugumor. Of their lands, of their houses, of their loose possessions, they are careless, prodigal, and often generous. They are not an acquisitive people, interested in piling up possessions. But of their flutes they are inordinately proud; they call them by kinship terms, they offer them food with a great flourish, and in a final burst of shame and anger, a man may "break his flute," that is, take it apart and strip it of all its lovely ornamentation, and take away its name. That the young people are allowed to see these objects finally only amid blows and gleeful·abuse is simply one more stress on the hostility that exists between all males. For the girls, with their right to choose their rôles, it intensifies their sense of independence. For both sexes, initiation is likely to be a pivot of quarrelling on the part of their parents, and to come only after their pride has smarted under exclusion.

youth and marriage among the Mundugumor

It is characteristic of Mundugumor conditions that it is not possible to discuss the development of children as an orderly process in which all young people of a certain age have similar experiences. Because there is no systematic sheltering of the young, no tender parental tempering of the wind to the immature, no social concern with rearing and disciplining children, there is an enormous discrepancy between the social positions of two youngsters of the same age. One boy of eleven may have spent three seasons as a hostage in strange tribes, may have fought with his father and left home only to return sulkily to try to defend his sixteen-year-old bride, in whose presence he is resentful and ashamed. Another boy of the same age may still be his mother's pet; he may have been spared any hostage experience, spared a conflict with his father because he is much older than any of his sisters and so no question of their marriage has yet come up; the father, having no daughters to work with him, may still work with his wife, so that the boy is not yet an economic mainstay of his mother. One may have been initiated, the other not. Groups of boys who have undergone such strikingly different experiences have very little coherence. Sometimes a group of boys will play games, games in which there are always two sides and vigorous competition. Or they may band together in outlaw activity, going off to live in the bush, steal from the gardens, hunt and cook their own game. They do this very seldom, but each boy remembers with enthusiasm these nights in the bush, and the glee over stolen food that was somewhat dampened by a fear of the bush *marsalais*.

A boy's usual occupation is that of helping his mother or some elder male relative, usually not his father or his brother, in finding wood for house-building or woodwork, in hunting pigeon, felling sago-palm trunks to make grub-traps, or gathering breadfruit for a feast. All of this activity is casual and desultory, never planned except when a feast is on foot. An adolescent boy may spend a great deal of time with some one young man, as a brother-in-law, for several weeks, then some slight insult may alienate them altogether, and the pair be seen together no more.

Girls of this age are also divided by their experience; some are married and living in the houses of their mothers-in-law, some have been successfully kept at home by jealous fathers. While the betrothed girls may be fretting over the indignity of having husbands too young to copulate with them, or too old to be desirable, the unbetrothed girls are fretting because their fathers follow them about everywhere and never permit them any privacy. Temporary alliances are sometimes formed in pursuance of love-affairs, but for the most part each pair of Mundugumor lovers acts in complete secrecy. The implications of a love-affair are so dangerous that it is inadvisable to trust anyone. In the face of all Mundugumor conflicts about arranged marriages there exists a violent preference for individual selection of one's mate. Children who have been accustomed to fight even for their first drops of milk do not docilely accept prescribed marriages arranged for other people's convenience. Almost every girl, betrothed or not, goes about with her skin polished and her grass skirt gay and stylish, with her eye out for a lover, and boys and men are watchful for the slightest sign of favour. The love-affairs of the young unmarried people are sudden and highly charged, characterised by passion rather than by tenderness or romance. A few hastily whispered words, a tryst muttered as they pass on a trail, are often the only interchange between them after they have chosen each other and before that choice is expressed in intercourse. The element of time and discovery is always present, goading them towards the swiftest possible cut-and-run relationship. The words in which a slightly older man advises a boy give the tone of these encounters: "When you meet a girl in the bush and copulate with her, be careful to come back to the village quickly and with explanations to account for your disappearance. If your bow-string is snapped, say that it caught on a passing bush. If your arrows are broken, explain that you tripped and caught them against a branch. If your loin-cloth is torn, or your face scratched, or your hair disarrayed, be ready with an explanation. Say that you fell, that you caught your foot, that you were running after game. Otherwise people will laugh in your face when you return." A girl is similarly advised: "If your ear-rings are torn out of your ears, and the cord of your necklace broken, if your grass skirt is torn and bedraggled, and your face and arms scratched and bleeding, say that you were frightened, that you heard a noise in the bush and ran and fell. Otherwise people will taunt you with having met a lover." Foreplay in these quick encounters takes the form of a violent scratching and biting match, calculated to produce the maximum amount of excitement in the minimum amount of time. To break the arrows or the basket of the beloved is one standard way of demonstrating consuming passion; so also is tearing off ornaments, and smashing them if possible.

Before she marries, a girl may have a number of affairs, each characterised by the same quick violence, but it is dangerous. If the matter is discovered the whole community will know that she is no longer a virgin, and the Mundugumor value virginity in their daughters and brides. Only a virgin may be offered in exchange for a virgin, and a girl whose virginity is known to be lost can be exchanged only for one whose exchange value has been similarly damaged. However, if a man marries a girl and then discovers she is not a virgin, he says nothing about it, for his own reputation is now involved and people would mock him. Sometimes the bush meetings are varied by an accepted lover's slipping into the girl's sleeping-basket at night. Fathers may, if they wish, sleep with their adolescent daughters until they marry, and mothers have a similar right to sleep with their sons. Particularly jealous fathers and particularly possessive mothers exercise this privilege. Often, however, two girls are allowed to sleep together in a basket; if one of the pair is away, the other temporarily has the basket to herself. If she receives a lover in her sleeping-basket, she risks not only discovery but actual injury, for an angry father who discovers the intruder may fasten up the opening of the sleeping-bag and roll the couple down the house-ladder, which is almost perpendicular and some six or seven feet in height. The bag may receive a good kicking and even a prodding with a spear or an arrow before it is opened. As a result, this method of courtship, although very occasionally resorted to by desperate lovers in the wet season when the bush is flooded, is not very popular. Young men relate with bated breath the most conspicuous mishaps that have befallen their elders, mishaps so uproariously humiliating and damaging to pride and person that they have become sagas of mirth. While the lover from another hamlet will therefore seldom risk a tryst within the house, new relationships between people temporarily housed together are often set up in this way, where the risk is much smaller.

The mosquito-basket plays a constantly recurring rôle in the lives of the Mundugumor. As an infant a child is carried into the basket with its head pinioned firmly under its mother's arms for fear that its neck will be broken. Later in life, frightened children and sulking adults hide in their mosquito-baskets. Angry parents eject their children from the mosquito-basket to spend a cold, mosquito-tormented night outside. Fathers fasten the openings of their adolescent daughters' baskets with a spear, and force their adolescent sons to sleep on an exposed platform with no protection whatsoever. All ideas of secrecy, concealment of hurt pride, tears, anger, or sexual delinquency centre about the mosquito-baskets, which afford a degree of privacy unusual in native society. Whereas a bush encounter between lovers is violent and athletic, a tryst in a basket must be in absolute silence and comparative immobility—a form of sex-activity that the Mundugumor regard as much less satisfactory. In later married life, men who are actively interested in their wives accompany them habitually into the bush, ostensibly to assist them in their work, actually to copulate with them under the courtship conditions in which a rough-and-tumble battle is permitted. The delights of these bush encounters may be enhanced by copulating in other people's gardens, an act that will spoil their yam-crops. These expeditions of married couples into the bush are a form of permissible exhibitionism; people will remark with a cheerful leer: "Oh, he has gone to *help* his wife cut sago. He *helped* her yesterday, too." The swing between extreme reticence and such unabashed frankness runs through all Mundugumor behaviour. At one moment a woman will refuse to wear any ornaments given her by her husband and insist upon wearing no ornaments except those which her father or brother has given her; at another she will be shouting frank abuse and strong personal claims on her husband to one of her cowives. A man who is accustomed to receive when leaving a ceremonial group the parting injunction: "Don't stop to copulate with your wife. Hurry back, we all know what you are likely to do": will turn suddenly sullen with rage when he discovers that two small boys have been peering at his wife and himself from behind a log. He may be so angry that he will attempt to kill the boys by sorcery. The changes between a deep sense of personal inviolability and privacy and the coarsest, most Rabelaisian references to all of one's activities are continually being rung under cover of the various joking relationships. As a result, all conversation, especially about matters pertaining to sex, has the character of playing ball with hand-grenades. The point of the game is to make the most unbearable comment that the butt will bear without resorting to a spear, sorcery, the destruction of his own property, or suicide. It is against such a background of overt comment and frank sadistic enjoyment of other people's discomfiture that young lovers must walk warily, with ready alibis for their wounds.

In the quick, violent love-affairs of the young a strong possessiveness develops rapidly, especially on the part of a girl in her first affair. The married men have more affairs than the married women. A girl's first lover is very often a married man. She will try to persuade him to elope with her; very often she will take the matter into her own hands and run away to him in spite of his prudent demurrer. Very rarely she may have a sympathetic and easy-going father, or her lover may have a younger sister unbetrothed and available for the necessary return wife for her younger brother, and in this case it may be possible for her to tell her father that she has chosen such and such a lover. The affair may then be arranged quietly between the parents of the lovers, and the girl will go with slight ceremony to the house of her lover. At this time she may carry the shell-covered sacred flute that is her dowry, which she will pass on to her son, or this flute may not be given to her until the birth of her first son. If, on the other hand, the girl is betrothed, or her lover has no sisters who can be given in exchange for her, then a fight is inevitable. A day for the elopement is set and the lover gathers about him as many of his male kin as he can enlist. The girl runs away to a spot they have agreed upon and the party of the man gathers there to defend her. She carries with her, if she has one and if she can manage to do it, the sacred flute, which otherwise her angry male relatives will try to keep from her. Her relatives pursue her, and a battle is fought, varying in bitterness according to the chances of a return payment, and in proportion to her father's or brother's possessiveness about her. About one-third of Mundugumor marriages begin in this violent fashion.

The third form of marriage is the arranged marriage between very young adolescents, arrangements that usually follow one of the two forms of marriage by choice, but which sometimes, if there are two sibling pairs anywhere near the right ages, will be entered into as a peacemaking ceremony between the two fathers concerned. With a desperate desire to exchange a sister for a sister, the Mundugumor pay little attention to relative ages. A sixteen-year-old sister is regarded as the property of her five-year-old brother. When she chooses a husband, or even when an exchange marriage is arranged for her, his wife must be chosen also—and this wife may be of any age from one year to fourteen or fifteen. If the girl who is given in return is nearing adolescence she is sent almost at once into her betrothed's household, not that she may learn to like living there, or that the transition from one household to another may be easy and gentle, but so that her own kin can shift the responsibility for her elopement if it should occur. They have washed their hands of the whole matter; they have paid for the wife of their son and they can no longer be held responsible. Hastily, unceremoniously, they hand over the pre-adolescent girl to her future parents-in-law.

The girl who has been sent to discharge her brother's debt enters a situation that is well-defined culturally. Her husband is almost always younger than herself, and even if they are nearly of an age he is at least at just the age to be most embarrassed and miserable over having a wife. She has not chosen him; she does not expect to have any use for him. He will avoid her, growl angrily if she is referred to as his wife, and yet watch her every move jealously, continually schooled by his mother in the need for asserting his possessiveness. Since he is too young to possess her sexually, this nervous self-assertion is likely to take the form of spying. Meanwhile the elders are divided. It may be that as the girl develops she catches the eye of the father or of an elder brother of the boy husband. Then a struggle develops within the household, depending primarily upon the strength of the different personalities, and to some extent upon the girl herself. If she prefers one member of the family above another, her choice is often decisive; if she hates the entire family as a group of people who have been forced upon her, she will be pulled about with very little voice in the matter unless she can find a lover who will elope with her. If no older member of the household desires her or considers that it is safe to try to obtain her, the attention of the household will be focused upon chaperoning her, and this chaperonage is more rigid than that afforded her by her blood-kin, because their chances of reclaiming her or getting a return for her will be less. So the affinal group try to get the marriage consummated as quickly as possible. They agree with the Arapesh that precocious sex-indulgence stunts a boy's growth, but far from taking the Arapesh way of stalling off sex-indulgence, they actually force the boy into it. Once married, he may stick to his wife, and she may remain with him rather than eloping; a lot of trouble will be saved. So two sulky, hostile young people are bundled into a mosquito-net. If they quarrel so that one is ejected, no one in the household will shelter the one who has been ejected; he or she must sleep among the mosquitoes. If the boy runs away to some relative and refuses to have anything to do with the girl, he forfeits his right to demand that his kin provide him with a wife. They have fulfilled their obligation and he has refused to accept the wife provided for him. Sometimes he runs away, sometimes she finds herself a lover. The girl, however, is often too young and unformed to be able to do this; most often the two, if near of an age, will remain together, at least for some years. A man now has a first wife to whom he is bound by ties of custom rather than by those of desire. If she becomes pregnant, he will be less annoyed than in the case of the wife of his hot choice. Young, weedy, bewildered, and sulky, he finds himself a father. And the girl once burdened with a child finds her chances of ever escaping less, for Mundugumor men may have affairs with married women but they are not interested in marrying a woman with children. These young wives early attach themselves to their sons, and in middle age seem more like widows than like wives. In fact, I found that in my thoughts I was continually referring to the mothers of adolescent boys as "widows" although they might actually be the first wives of hale and hearty husbands.

This then is the structure of Mundugumor society within which young people grow up, marry, and have children. There is a premium upon virginity, and a vigorous, positively sexed group of young girls who plan their own affairs in spite of a restrictive chaperonage. There is a social standard which prescribes that the sister is used in payment for her brother's wife, and a continuous flouting of this standard by her father, her brother, and the sisterless lover who attempts to abduct her. The marriages that become established are first, the arranged marriages between the very young, which persists because the spouses are too young to escape it, and second, the marriage of choice in which a strong passionate relationship is muted by pregnancy, another wife, and the resulting quarrels and jealousy. Finally, death and the redistribution of the widows creates further confusion, quarrelling between the male heirs, and quarrelling within the polygynous households, especially when a woman brings with her a partly grown daughter or son. While the abduction of a woman is a concern for a whole community, quarrels within the household are frequent and have small effect outside the compound. A man may beat his wife so that she puts on white mourning-paint and sits far from the house, wailing ceremonially so that all passers-by can see her. They may stop in curiosity, but even her own brothers will not participate. It is not a society in which women are regarded as fragile and in need of male assistance. When women are intractable, husband and brothers may band together to keep them in order. Although the trouble which they cause is of a different order from that caused by men and is more confined to the field of personal relations, they are regarded as fully responsible trouble-makers, not as persons in need of protection or guidance. Because the girl is very often more mature than the boy, either because of the conditions of the marriage return or because she has made the first move in a bush liaison, many marriages of young people are dominated by the more aggressive, mature wife. As she ages a little, the husband becomes more conscious of his own powers, and is ready to exercise his initiative in courting younger women if possible. The aggressive wife continues upon her aggressive course, now operating through her son. It is not a society in which anyone retires willingly. Grandmothers who are newly widowed and remarried make a strong bid for their husbands' attention, counting upon the newness of their charms.

The interests of the children are not something upon which the two parents can unite; rather children tend to separate them, or to be used in the conflicts between the parents. The element of fierce, specific sexual antagonism is as strong in a household that contains adolescent children as it is in the marriages of young people. And throughout the battle, the woman is regarded as a fit adversary, who is, it is true, handicapped, but never weak.

13

deviants from the Mundugumor ideal

We have seen how the Mundugumor ideal of character is identical for the two sexes; how both men and women are expected to be violent, competitive, aggressively sexed, jealous, and ready to see and avenge insult, delighting in display, in action, in fighting. The Mundugumor have selected as their ideal the very types of men and women which the Arapesh consider to be so incomprehensible that they hardly allow for their occurrence. Wabe and Temos, Ombomb and Sauwedjo, would have adjusted much more easily to Mundugumor standards than to Arapesh ones. We saw in the discussion of the Arapesh that these more violent personalities were given slight outlet there, and were in fact driven towards a neurotic paranoid response to unintelligible social requirements. What happens in Mundugumor, where this type, so unprovided for among the Arapesh, is given the fullest chance for social development? If the violent, strongly sexed man or women is driven to neurotic conflict with his or her society, does the opposite condition obtain in Mundugumor? What happens to the mild man who would like to shelter his sons as well as his daughters, and the woman who would like to cuddle her baby in her arms? Do they stand out as clearly as misfits as do the Arapesh misfits?

"He was not strong, he had no brothers," say the Mundugumor, in spite of their formulations of mutual hostility and distrust between brothers. And in this often repeated saying, they state the use that Mundugumor society has for its misfits, for the boys whose hands tremble on the massacring knife at their first kill, for the boys who never appoint a rendezvous with a woman in the bush from which they will return proud and bleeding, for the boys who do not try to appropriate all their sisters or, being younger, accept the elder brother's appropriation of them all, for the boys who never defy their fathers, even when their mothers goad them on. They are the ones in whose purposes no brother will co-operate. These become the men who make the continuance of Mundugumor society possible. They can live near other men without continually quarrelling with them or seducing their wives and daughters. They have no ambitions of their own and are content to play a humble part in the fight, to stand back of their aggressive brothers in an intra-hamlet scrap, an inter-hamlet fight, or on a head-hunting raid. They form the constellations about the leaders, living as younger brothers, as sons-in-law, as brothers-in-law, co-operating in house-building, in feast preparations, in raids. Although the Mundugumor ideal is that every man should be a lion, fighting proudly for his share and surrounded by several equally violent lionesses, in actual practice there are a fair number of sheep in the society, men to whom pride, violence, and competitiveness do not appeal. Because of these men a certain number of the rules are kept, and so are passed on to the next generation; some families of sisters are equally divided among brothers, the dead are mourned for, children are fed. When the proud polygynist quarrels with the son whose sister he is about to use in exchange for a wife for himself, the son can take refuge with one of these milder men. The atmosphere of struggle and conflict would become unbearable and actually impossible to maintain if it were not for them, for each man would have only an army of one to put in the field. Instead of complicating the social life by taking up positions that are confusing and unintelligible, as do the misfits among the Arapesh, they actually make possible the violent competitive life that is really so uncongenial to them.

And are such men misfits? If by misfit we mean the individual who makes trouble for his society, they are not. But if we include under the term "misfit" all those who find no congenial outlet for their special talents, who never find throughout life a rôle that is suited to them, then they may be called misfits. Where the ideal of the society is a virgin wife, they must be content with widows, with fought-over women, with women whom other men do not want. Where success is measured in terms of number of wives, number of heads taken, and large displays made, they can only point to one wife, often no heads at all, and certainly no large feasts. They are loyal in a society that counts loyalty to be a stupid disregard of the real facts about the essential enmity which exists between all males; they are parental in a society that is explicit about the lack of reward in parenthood.

Beyond the meek acceptance of this minor, undistinguished rôle, there are two courses open to them, day-dreaming, or the circumvention of the social emphases. The first is the more common. A mild man will keep his sons by him, and talk to them of the days when people kept the rules, when people married correctly and there was none of this irregularity which causes people to "stand up and stare" at each other, when fathers cherished their sons, and sons were careful to observe all the little rituals that preserve their fathers' lives, even forbearing to walk in the path that their fathers had recently trodden. So spoke Kalekúmban, a mild and stupid man who had given shelter at one time or another to some dozen of his young male relatives. And so spoke one-eyed Komeákua, who loved to paint but, not having been born with a cord around his neck, could only do apprentice work beneath the lash of the master craftsman's tongue. Komeákua had always stood by his brothers, and later by his nephews; late in his uneventful life, he had obtained a widow as a wife, and she had borne him two boys whom he paraded about the village in touching disregard of other people's amusement. On his tongue, as on the tongue of Kalekúmban, were the aphorisms that dealt with more peaceful and more organised days. There is a good deal of evidence for the existence in the past of a time when Mundugumor society was less devastated by violence; the kinship organisation bears traces of such a period. But there is no evidence as to whether this was three generations or twenty generations ago. Day-dreamers like Kalekúmban are quite capable of perpetuating and elaborating the legend indefinitely, the legend of the time when everything was "straight," when ropes and patrilineal groups were woven together, when people co-operated with each other and kept the rules. And this day-dreaming is probably a real drawback to the society. It prevents young people from adjusting realistically to the actual conditions and formulating new rules that would deal with them adequately. It keeps the attention of the more law-abiding paralysed with a sterile yearning towards the past, and it gives everyone a sense of guilt. If this former imputed Elysium were ignored, a man might find his erstwhile sister classified as an uncle's wife without tingling with shame and anger. The old residence rules, the old marriage exchanges, being gone for ever, new ones might be worked out. All this the day-dreaming maladjust prevents; too weak, too ineffectual, too unplaced to have very much influence in shaping his present society, he serves to confuse the issues. Whatever gifts he has his society makes slight use of, and the most definite result of his sense of maladjustment is not advantageous.

The other type of maladjusted man is much rarer, and there was only one conspicuous example in the tribe when we were there. This was Ombléan, who was our most gifted informant. He was a slender, delicately made, vivid young man, by temperament committed to none of the Mundugumor ends. He was gentle, co-operative, responsive, easily enlisted in the causes of others. His household was always filled with people for whose care he had no genuine responsibility. Besides his one wife, Ndebáme, whom he had finally obtained by a fluke, and their three little children, he looked after his mother-in-law, Sangofélia, and her two children by her second husband. This husband was one of the most prominent and wealthy men in the community, but he had wearied of Sangofélia and begun to treat her badly. Ombléan had taken her in. Then there was a sister of Ndebáme who had quarrelled with her husband, and with her small baby had taken refuge there. And while we were in the village, Numba, a great gawky immature adolescent who had been forced by his parents to begin sleeping with his gangly young wife, ran away to Ombléan—who was merely a cousin of his—and continued to live in his house. Ombléan thus had on his hands three women, five little children, and a lazy, overgrown boy. None of these people who imposed upon him respected him particularly; he was too slight and too good-natured to beat them with crocodile-skulls or throw fire-sticks at them. As a result, he did a great deal of work himself, growing yams and working sago and hunting to feed his household, where the women often refused to fish. He was indefatigable, resourceful, and too energetic and intelligent to take refuge in day-dreaming. Instead he studied his society, learned every rule and every loop-hole through which intelligence could outmatch brute strength. He was the most intellectual informant we have ever had, so analytical and sophisticated that we found that in order to avoid being repetitious or monotonous he discussed the actual working of the society with Mr. Fortune, and the way theoretically it should work with me. His own alien-ation from all the current motivations had sharpened his already superior intelligence to a point very seldom found within a homogeneous culture. But he was cynical where he would, in another context, have been enthusiastic. He had to spend his splendid intellectual gifts in circumventing a society in which he was spiritually not at home. Two weeks after we left Mundugu-mor, a recruiter's pinnace returned some thirty Mundugumor young men who had been away working in the gold-fields. These men had gone away with rage and anger in their hearts, ritually shaking the dust of the place from their feet, spitting the earth out of their mouths, swearing never to return until the death of the fathers and elder brothers who had robbed them of wives. Now, after two years spent in aggravating each other's vengefulness, they returned, and leapt, knives and tomahawks in hand, upon the group of men who had gathered to witness their return. Ombléan was a government appointee, he had accepted the burden of negotiating between government and the Mundugumor; he thrust himself into the thick of the fray in an effort to stop the slaughter, and was badly wounded.

And who were the maladjusted women in Mundugumor? Kwenda was a good example. Kwenda was plump and soft, where the ideal Mundugumor woman is tall, lithe, and slender. Kwenda loved children. She had refused to throw away her first child, a boy, in spite of her husband Mbunda's request that she do so. While she was suckling the child he had eloped with another woman. Instead of stiffening her back in anger, she had followed him and his new wife. Outraged, he had thrown her out and left her in his maternal village of Biwat, and himself gone off to work for the white man. In Biwat, Kwenda had borne twins; they died. She returned to Kenakatem, and went to live with Yeshimba, a father's brother. Then Gisambut, the reserved sister of Ombléan, bore twin girls, and Kwenda, with no one to help her earn a living, adopted one and soon was able to feed it entirely from her ample breasts. The little twin flourished, grew as tall as the sister who was suckled by her own mother, but on the face of Kwenda's twin there was always a dimpling smile, on the face of the child suckled by her own mother, a harsh set frown. Kwenda's twin was more often about the village, and I was accustomed to greeting it and receiving a happy smile. To encounter Gisambut's twin suddenly and meet the set anxious stare was an experience that had a quality of nightmare about it, which summed up all the difference between the average Mundugumor child's experience and that of Kwenda's little twin, upon whom she lavished a joyous, uninhibited affection. Not only would she work willingly all day for her six-year-old son and the little twin, but she worked also for others. Anyone who wanted a coconut-palm climbed had only to coax Kwenda, and disregarding her plumpness and her heavy breasts, which made climbing more difficult for her than for other women, she would be up it, smiling the while. Not only did she suckle the little twin, but often she took on other women's infants for the day. Her husband returned to the village and took a young, sharp-faced wife, for whom he adopted a child so that she would not have to inconvenience him by bearing one. They went every day into the bush to work sago. He hated the sound of Kwenda's name, and declared he would never take her back. He even tried an experiment that is thoroughly abhorrent to most Mundugumor, but is a standard practice of a neighbouring people; he tried to prostitute her to a boy from another tribe. He did this by pretending that he himself would come to her in the night. The plan failed, and while the community was a little horrified, for prostituting their women is incompatible with Mundugumor pride and possessiveness, there was an undertone of feeling that you couldn't blame a man for being fed up with a wife like Kwenda, a woman who was so consistently, stupidly good-natured, devoted, and maternal. Kwenda, young, warm, and vigorous, would remain a grass widow; no strong man would take her for a wife, no weak one would try because Mbunda, not wanting her himself, would nevertheless demand a high price for her. So in Mundugumor the easy-going, responsive, warmly parental woman, like the easy-going, responsive, warmly parental man, is at a social discount.

On the other hand there are other aberrant personalities who are so violent that even Mundugumor standards have no place for them. A man of this sort becomes too continuously embroiled with his fellows, until he may be finally killed treacherously during an attack on another tribe, or possibly a member of his own tribe may kill him and accept the meagre penalty—a prohibition on wearing head-hunting honours. Or he may flee into the swamps and perish there. A woman of equal violence, who continually tries to attach new lovers and is insatiable in her demands, may in the end be handed over to another community to be communally raped. But the fate of these violent persons is consistent with the Mundugumor ideal, which looks forward to a violent death for women as well as for men. As long as the white man merely raided and burnt Mundugumor hamlets, or killed a few of the Mundugumor on punitive expeditions after some outrage on another tribe or attack on a passing white man, it was impossible to subdue them. To die at the hands of the white man was a little more honourable than to die in a fight with the Andoar men or the men of Kendavi. With pride they relate the story of the Mundugumor who was hung by white men for murder; he had raised his right hand in the air, he had called the names of his ancestors and of his place, and he had died. The only pathetic point was that he had been given a fowl to eat, and as this was his totem, and he had been dying in style—for the Mundugumor are habitually very careless about their totemic taboos—he had refused to eat it and had died hungry. It was not until the fear of prison for the big men was substituted for the fear of a punitive expedition that the Mundugumor came under government control. The leaders were willing to face death, but to face six months in prison wondering who had seduced or stolen their wives—this humiliating inactivity they were not willing to face. So for three years peace had reigned, head-hunting was over, and the cannibal feast was held no longer.

In such a setting, it will be seen that the occasional individual whose greater violence and bad luck resulted in death was not regarded as having had a poor life of it. It was the Ombléans, the Kwendas, who were the real maladjusted persons, whose gifts were spent in a hopeless effort to stem the stream of an uncongenial tradition, where both men and women were expected to be proud, harsh, and violent, and where the tenderer sentiments were felt to be as inappropriate in one sex as in the other.

part three

the lake-dwelling Tchambuli

THE CHOICE OF TCHAMBULI

Study of the Mundugumor people had yielded results similar to those obtained among the Arapesh; both men and women were moulded to the same temperamental pattern, although that pattern itself, in its violence, its individualism, its lust for power and position contrasted sharply with the Arapesh ideal personality, with its gentle, cherishing emphasis. We cast about for a third people, again guided by considerations essentially irrelevant to the relations between the sexes. For counsellor we had the district officer, Mr. Eric Robinson, whose years of service on the Sepik had made him familiar with all parts of his district. He offered two suggestions, the Washkuk mountain people, who lived above the government station at Ambunti and were only barely under control, and the Tchambuli tribe on the Aibom Lake. The Washkuks he described as simple, sturdy, lovable people still untouched by very much contact with the white man. The first recruits from Washkuk had not yet returned to flaunt their pidgin English and their loin-cloths in the old men's faces and introduce a new element into the native life. The Tchambuli had been under control a little longer, about seven years. After having been driven away into the hills by the head-hunters of the middle Sepik, they had been brought back to their original villages under government protection. They were a people with an intricate art, an elaborate culture, with many points in common with the complex culture of the middle Sepik. We determined to inspect the Washkuks first, and made a special expedition to their mountain top. Then we found little bearded men who communicated with us through the medium of two intervening languages and implored us not to come and live with them, because then they would obviously have to stay in their scattered villages to look after us, and they had just completed preparations for a long wandering hunting-trip. There were not many of them and they lived in twos and threes all over the steep mountain side. Because they seemed very much like the Arapesh, because they themselves felt that their lives would be hopelessly upset by our stay, because conditions of transport and of field-work would have been very difficult, we decided to try the Tchambuli instead. And so, knowing only that we went to a group of lake-dwellers with a fine and living art, we came to Tchambuli.

14

the pattern of Tchambuli social life

The Tchambuli people live on a lake that two water-ways connect with the Sepik River, about one hundred and eighty miles from its mouth. This lake lies in fen country, with occasional small abrupt hills along its southern extremity. Its outlines are irregular and its contours are continually changing as the large floating islands of grass are pushed here and there by the shifting winds. Occasionally one of these little islands, which are often large enough to carry several full-grown trees, will lodge permanently against one of the shores of the lake; sometimes it will block the mouth of a water-way and have to be chopped up into segments in order to clear a passage for the native canoes. The condition of the smaller water-ways through the high grass changes with the wind, now offering clear passage, now completely blocked.

The water of the lake is so coloured with dark peat-brown vegetable matter that it looks black on the surface, and when no wind stirs it, resembles black enamel. On this polished surface, in still times the leaves of thousands of pink and white lotuses and a smaller deep-blue water-lily are spread, and among the flowers, in the early morning, the white osprey and the blue heron stand in great numbers, completing the decorative effect, which displays almost too studied a pattern to seem completely real. When the wind blows and ruffles the black surface to a cold blue, the lotus-leaves that lay so inert and thick upon the enamel surface are ruffled, and lifting lightly along their stems, show themselves to be not a green monotone, but a variable rose and silver-green, and of a delicate and pliant thinness. The small sharp hills that edge the lake gather clouds upon their summits which resemble snow and accentuate their steep rise from the fen-land level.

The Tchambuli people are a small tribe; only five hundred in all speak the language, and one division of these speaks it with a different accent and some difference in the vocabulary. They live in three hamlets along the edge of the Tchambuli Mountain, with their ceremonial houses standing on high posts like long-legged birds along the plashy lake-shore. Between the ceremonial houses—there are fifteen in all—runs a road on which men go afoot during low water, and along which they push their narrow dug-out canoes with the forked tips of their grass paddles when the lake has risen and flooded the ground-floors of these houses. This floor is merely of packed clay, with raised platforms along each side where each member of the ceremonial houses has his appointed sitting-place. Fire-places are ranged down the centre, about which stand a few carved stools on which one may sit and let the thick smoke play about one's legs as protection from the mosquitoes. Sometimes long flapping shutters of dark and light green leaves woven into intricate patterns are hung along the sides of the lower story, to protect those within from the eyes of passers-by. When footsteps or voices are heard on the path, these flimsy shutters sway back and forth and the people inside peer out curiously, and shout a formal greeting. This is the men's road, and women and girls only honour it upon festival occasions. The road winds along the irregular lake-shore, and at every second turn one comes upon a new ceremonial house thirty to forty feet long, standing parallel with the lake, with slender high steeples set in each gable-end and a ridge-pole that dips in the centre, giving the roof the profile of a crescent moon. On each thatched and leaf-patterned gable-end there is a huge face, carved in low relief and painted in red and white. When a new house is built, the steeples are first lightly constructed of wattle-work, and wattle-work birds, one male, one female, are set upon the steeple tips. Later, at the leisure of the builders, the steeples are solidly thatched over and the wicker-work birds are discarded for a heavier ornament, a wooden bird whose wings spring from the hollow figure of a man.

From each ceremonial house a path runs a few hundred feet up the steep and rock-strewn hill-side, to the level where the large houses of the women are hidden among the trees. These houses are longer and lower than the men's houses, the ridge-pole is straight and flat; they stand oblong, solid, on firm piles, with well-constructed floors and sturdy ladders leading up to each entrance, strong enough to last a good many years and large enough to house three or four family groups. Pigs root about the ladders, half-woven baskets hang from the ceiling, fishing apparatus stands about. The path to the shore up and down which the women go to their fishing and the men to the gaieties of the ceremonial houses is well worn. The dwelling-houses, which are specifically spoken of as "the houses of the women," are connected by an upper road that runs along the hill-side and upon which women walk from one house to another. Each house shelters from two to four families, and within the roomy walls there is always a group of women, cooking, plaiting, mending their fishing-gear. In their energetic friendly activity there is an air of solidarity, of firm co-operation and group purpose, which is lacking in the gaily decorated ceremonial houses along the shore, where each man sits down daintily in his own place and observes his companions narrowly.

In the early morning, when the first light covers the lake, the people are already astir. The women, with their peaked rain-capes on their heads, come down the hill-sides and wade through the lotuses to their slender canoes, on their way to inspect or to reset their great bell-shaped wicker fish-traps. A few of the men are already in the ceremonial houses, especially in those where one or two small novices, boys of ten or twelve, their bodies smeared with white paint, are crouching in the chill of the early morning. The novices are permitted to sleep in their mothers' houses but must be up and away before day-break, creeping down to the lake-shore cloaked in a rain mat that completely covers them. From one ceremonial house a slit gong may be sounding with the beat peculiar to that house, summoning men from other parts of the settlement to some ceremonial task, to help cut new thatch, or to plait masks for a dance.

On market-days, parties of canoes set off for the distant point in the fens where they meet the sulky intractable people of the bush, to trade fish and shell money for sago and sugar-cane. The currency of the market is green snail-shells, *talibun*.* These shells, which come from the far-away island of Wallis, off the Arapesh coast, have been ground down and ornamented with little scrolls of coiled basketry by the people to the north of the Sepik. The shells come to the Tchambuli each already possessing marked individuality of size, shape, weight, colour, polish, and ornamentation, and the Tchambuli regard each as having sex and personality. Where *talibun* are used, barter at the market becomes not purchase of food for money, but exchange of food for valuables, among which there is wide exercise of choice. It is shopping on both sides, and the possessor of the currency must plead the virtue of his particular coin even more strongly than must the possessor of the food.

As the sun grows hotter women come in from their fishing and climb the hill-side again, and from the tree-hidden houses there comes a continuous sound of women's voices like the twittering of a flock of birds. When people pass each other on the

---

*This is the pidgin-English term and used here because of its wide-spread use in New Guinea.

paths, or in canoes, they greet each other with endless polite phrases: "You come?" "Lo, I come, on my way to pick lotuses." "You go then to pick lotuses." "Yes, I go to pick lotuses to eat." "Go then, and pick lotuses."

The daily life follows the quiet rhythm of women's fishing and weaving, and men's ceremonial occupations. For an event like a feast, or a masked dance, the whole community stops work, the men and children dress in gorgeous holiday attire. The men, with bird-of-paradise or cassowary-feather head-dresses over their carefully arranged curls, the children, with shell-embroidered cowls and heavy shell necklaces and girdles, gather on the dancing-ground, the men moving self-consciously, abashed to eat, among the crowds of smiling, unadorned, efficient women, and the children munching lengths of sugar-cane. An event such as a death, or a scarification of a small boy or girl, necessitates a feast. Fifty or sixty women gather in one house, clustering in cooking groups about the fire-place pots, meticulously brushing off their pottery griddles, and cooking the thin, perfectly symmetrical sago-pancakes that accompany all feasts. At certain points in the proceedings, specially cooked food or shell valuables are carried along the shore-road, from one ceremonial house to another, by small ritually organised parties of men and women. Masked figures often accompany them, clowning and pantomiming their way among the groups of dancing women, who periodically dive between their legs, or break their beautifully etched lime-gourds in a shower of white powder beneath their dancing feet. Almost always there is plenty of food. The people depend not upon an agricultural crop that has to be tended and harvested—although a few of the more energetic and aberrant men occasionally make themselves yam-gardens on the heights or taro-gardens at low water—but upon sago, which is purchased in large quantities and stored in tall earthen pots with grotesque faces in high relief around the neck. There is no need for daily labour; sago is stored, fish is smoked, the market does not come every day, and it is always possible to stop all work for several days and attend whole-heartedly to a ritual or a feast. This is the normal course of life, but occasionally, when there has been much war among the sago-producing bush people, or particularly bad fishing for the Tchambuli, and it is the season when the supplementary taro-gardens are all under water, there is hunger. The people, used to the easy hospitality and bright hard display of abundance, have no code to deal with famine except a pitiless intolerance of theft. The food thief was mercilessly handed over to another of the hamlets, where he or she was executed and his head counted as a trophy to validate the ceremonial house of that group, and a price was paid to the hamlet to which the thief belonged.

Thus head-hunting and the execution of criminals were combined. It was considered necessary that every Tchambuli boy should in childhood kill a victim, and for this purpose live victims, usually infants or young children, were purchased from other tribes. Or a captive in war or a criminal from another Tchambuli hamlet sufficed. The small boy's spear-hand was held by his father, and the child, repelled and horrified, was initiated into the cult of head-hunting. The blood of the victim was splashed on the foot of the upright stones that stand in the little clearing outside the ceremonial house, and if the victim was a child, the body was buried beneath one of the house posts. The head, like the heads of enemies killed in warfare, was built up in clay modelling on the original skull, and painted in fantastic patterns of black and white, with shell eyes, and glued-on curls, and hung up in the ceremonial house as a trophy to boast about. But the Tchambuli were not enthusiastic about warfare or head-hunting; it is true that a ceremonial house must have heads, but they preferred to buy the bastards and orphans and criminals of the bush people and kill them ceremonially in the village, rather than run the risks of battle. The adornment of the heads was a fine art, their possession a point of ritual pride; their acquisition was made as safe and tame as possible.

In this, the Tchambuli contrast sharply with their fierce and warlike neighbours of the middle Sepik, who regarded head-hunting as the most important male occupation. The middle-Sepik people depend upon the Tchambuli for the manufacture of the great plaited mosquito-bags that are regarded as the inevitable and necessary furniture of all native houses in this mosquito-infested region. The Tchambuli also offer a market for the canoes made on the Sepik, as the Sepik natives obtained iron canoe-making tools much earlier and in larger amounts than the Tchambuli. But their Sepik neighbours hold the Tchambuli in great contempt and regard them as good raiding material. About twelve years before, the Tchambuli had finally broken before the continuous raiding, head-taking, and house-burning activities of the middle Sepik, and the inhabitants of the three hamlets fled to their trade-friends, one group going far away to the Kolosomali River, a second into the mountains back of Tchambuli, and a third far to the north. This flight corresponded with the strongest trade-ties and intermarriages that the three hamlets had preserved in previous generations. After the white government entered the Sepik, the Tchambuli came back to their old village sites, persuaded the government officials of their claim to them, ousted the small groups of middle-Sepik invaders, and settled down again in their old homes. The protection of the government meant the virtual abandonment of head-hunting, but the Tchambuli dependence upon head-hunting was slight and ritual and unimportant. They care far more about decorating their ceremonial houses with beautiful carvings, manufacturing the graceful double hooks upon which to hang the highly patterned net bags that they import from the north bank of the Sepik, and plaiting the various masks that belong to the different clans and ceremonial groups. With newly obtained iron tools they now build their own canoes instead of purchasing them at exorbitant rates from the Sepik; with no threat of a raid, the women have time not only for their fishing, but to gather all the delicate varieties of water-lily roots and lotus-seeds and creepers, on which to feast their young male relatives when they come to wheedle *talibun*, and the twentyfold valuable mother-of-pearl crescent, the *kina*, from their

mothers and aunts. Beneath the Pax Britannica Tchambuli culture is undergoing a renaissance, and the lake-shore rings to the
sound of axes hollowing out canoes. Every man's hand is occupied etching a pattern on a lime-gourd, plaiting a bird or a piece
of a mask, brocading a house-blind, or fashioning a cassowary
bone into the semblance of a parrot or a hornbill.

15

the contrasting rôles of Tchambuli men and women

As the Arapesh made growing food and children the greatest adventure of their lives, and the Mundugumor found greatest satisfaction in fighting and competitive acquisition of women, the Tchambuli may be said to live principally for art. Every man is an artist and most men are skilled not in some one art alone, but in many: in dancing, carving, plaiting, painting, and so on. Each man is chiefly concerned with his rôle upon the stage of his society, with the elaboration of his costume, the beauty of the masks that he owns, the skill of his own flute-playing, the finish and *élan* of his ceremonies, and upon other people's recognition and valuation of his performance. The Tchambuli ceremonies are not a by-product of some event in the life of an individual; that is, it cannot be said that in order to initiate young boys the Tchambuli hold a ceremony, but rather that in order to hold a ceremony the Tchambuli initiate young boys. Grief over a death is muffled and practically dissipated by interest in the ceremonial that surrounds it—which flutes are to be played, which masks and clay heads are to decorate the grave; in the etiquette of the groups of formally mourning women, who are given charming little souvenirs of reeds to remember the occasion by. The women's interest in art is confined to sharing in the graceful pattern of social relations, a small amount of painting on their baskets and plaited cowls, and chorus dancing; but to the men, it is the only important matter in life.

The structure of the society is patrilineal. Groups of men all related through male ancestors, and bearing a common name, own strips of territory that stretch from the hill-tops, where occasional gardens are made, down through the wooded mountainside where the women's houses are built, to the lake-shore, where each clan or sometimes two adjacent clans, building together, have their men's club-house. Within this group of related males there are certain taboos. An eldest son is embarrassed and shy in the presence of his father, and his next younger brother observes the same sort of behaviour towards him. The possibility of inheritance is the subject of their embarrassment. The younger sons, far removed from considerations of the succession, are easy with one another. Relationships between a man and his brother's son are also friendly, and these men—whose position is vividly described by the pidgin-English term "small papa"—intervene between small boys and their self-appointed and light-hearted disciplinarians, the bigger boys. The membership in these men's houses varies, and quarrels are frequent. Upon the merest slight—a claim of precedence that is not justified, a failure of the wife of one man to feed the pigs of another, a failure to return a borrowed article—the person who cherishes a sense of hurt will move away, and go to live with some other clan group to which he can claim relationship. Meanwhile there is a strong social feeling that such behaviour is bad, that the men of a clan should sit down together, that in a large number of older men lies the wisdom of the ceremonial house. When illness or misfortune occurs, the shamans explain that the shamanic spirits and the ghosts of the dead that hang about the house-posts are angry because one or more members of the clan have moved away. The solidarity of any of these groups of men is more apparent than real; it is as if all of them sat very lightly, very impermanently, on the edges of their appointed sitting-shelves, ready to be off at a look, a touch, a word of hostility.

Each clan possesses certain privileges: long lists of names that it is privileged to give to the children of all women of the clan; clan songs, and a mass of ceremonial possessions, masks, dances, songs, flutes, slit drums, special calls; and a set of supernaturals of its own, *marsalais* of the lake, sometimes one of the shamanic spirits, and other minor supernaturals whose voices are heard through flute and the drum and the bull-roarer. The men's house of one clan insists that masked dancers who pass that way must stand for a moment beside the standing stones that are set up outside; other ceremonial houses have the privilege of swinging the bull-roarers for high water.

In addition to the clan organisation there are various other formal ways in which the society is organised. There is a dual organisation; all the members of one clan usually belong either to the Sun or to the Mother people, but occasionally a clan is split in half and one half belongs to each. Marriage should be across the dividing-line of the dual organisation, but is not always so. These two divisions also have many ceremonial rights and possessions, the latter usually being kept in one of the men's houses. Each man also belongs to several other groups, in which he plays a special part in initiatory ceremonies and in feasts of other kinds. Although his clan membership is perhaps the most fixed of his allegiances, he can also think of himself as proud of and ennobled by the ceremonial display of any one of these other cross-cutting associations. He may also have his feelings hurt as a member of any of these groups, and by proclaiming his partisanship in one kind of ceremonial dispute become involved in coldness and disgruntlement with his associates in some other activity. Each man has a high feeling of the importance and the value of each one of these allegiances. He is like an actor who plays many parts, and can, for the duration of any play, identify himself with the rest of the company. One day as a member of the Sun moiety he objects because the members of the Mother moiety have got out their flutes for a funeral when it was not their turn; a week later all of this is forgotten in a furore over the way the other initiatory group behaved at a small initiation-feast. Each of these passing and incompatible loyalties serves to confuse the others; the same man is his ally one day, his opponent the next, an indifferent, carefully nonchalant bystander on the third. All that remains to the individual Tchambuli man, with his delicately arranged curls, his handsome pubic covering of a flying-fox skin highly ornamented with shells, his mincing step and self-conscious mien, is the sense of himself as an actor, playing a series of charming parts—this and his relationship to the women.

His relations to all other males are delicate and difficult, as he sits down a little lightly even in his own clansmen's house, and is so nervous and sensitive that he will barely eat in the houses of other clans, but his relations to women are the one solid and reliable aspect of his life. As a small child, he was held lightly in the arms of a laughing casual mother, a mother who nursed him generously but nonchalantly, while her fingers were busy plaiting reeds into sleeping-baskets or rain-capes. When he tumbled down, his mother picked him up and tucked him under her arm as she went on with her conversation. He was never left alone; there were always some eight or ten women about, working, laughing, attending to his needs, willingly enough, but unobsessively. If his father's other wife failed to feed him as generously as his mother, his mother needed only to make the light reproach: "Are children plentiful that you should neglect them?" His childhood days were spent tumbling about the floor of the great dwelling house, where his antics were privileged, where he could tickle and wrestle with the other children. His mouth was never empty. Women weaned their children as carelessly and casually as they nursed them, stuffing their mouths with delicacies to stop their crying. Afterwards the women fed them bountifully with food, lotus-stems, lily-stems, lotus-seed, Malay apples, pieces of sugar-cane, and a little boy could sit and munch in the great roomy house filled with other children of his kin and with groups of working, kindly women. Sometimes there was a ceremony, and his mother took him with her when she went to spend the day cooking in another house. There, in a larger crowd of women, with more children rolling about on the floor, he also munched. His mother took plenty of dainties along in her basket, to give him whenever he cried for them.

By the time a boy is seven or eight, he is beginning to hang about the edges of the men's ceremonial life. If he goes too close to the men's house during a ceremony, he will be chased away, although on ordinary occasions he can slip in and hide behind a small papa's protection. The older boys will haze him lightly, send him on errands, throw sticks at him, or beat him if he disobeys. Back he runs, scurrying up the hillside to his mother's house, whither the big boys will not pursue him. The next time that he and those big boys are in a woman's house together, he will take advantage of the older boy's embarrassment; he will tease and plague him, caricature his walk and manner—with impunity; the older boy will not attack him.

At some point when he is between eight and twelve, a period that is not determined by his age so much as by his father's ceremonial ambitions, he will be scarified. He will be held squirming on a rock while a distantly related maternal "uncle" and an expert scarifier cut patterns on his back. He can howl as much as he likes. No one will comfort him, no one will attempt to stop his howls. Nor will anyone take any delight in them. Casually, efficiently, performing as relatives their ritual duty, for which they will receive graceful recognition, or performing their duty as artists, they cut patterns on the little boy's back. They paint him with oil and turmeric. All about him is an elaborate ceremonial pattern that he does not share. His father gives presents to his mother's brother. His mother's brother's wives are given beautiful new grass skirts, new rain-capes, new carrying-baskets. His scarification is the occasion for all this display, but no one pays any attention to him.

There follows a long period of seclusion. At night he is

allowed to go home to sleep, but in the chill morning, before dawn, he must creep away from the women's house, wrapped from head to foot in a great coarse rain cape. His body is smeared with white clay. All day he must stay inside the men's house. Every fourth day he washes and assumes a new coat of paint. It is all very uncomfortable. Sometimes two men of the same clan combine to scarify their sons, but as often a boy is initiated alone. There is no suggestion that this is done for his welfare. Nor is there any suggestion that the adults are interested in the discomfort of his position or the pain of his scarifications. All about him goes on the discussion of ceremonial policy, and if his father can make a more effective ceremony by waiting for three months to wash him, he waits. The child is not considered. Or in a great pet over some slight or indignity put upon him by those who should assist him in the ceremony, the father incontinently washes the child within a week or so after his scarification. The washing is ritual, and ends the period of seclusion. The boy's mother's brother presents him with an elaborately woven belt, shell ornaments, a beautiful incised bamboo lime gourd with a lovely filigree spatula. He may now walk about with these under his arm, accompanying parties of people who take food or *talibun* and *kinas* to other people in his name. After this he is supposed to spend more time in the men's house, but he still takes refuge among the women whenever possible. He grows gradually into young manhood; his father and elder brothers watching jealously his attitude towards their younger wives and suspecting him if he walks about upon the women's roads.

The women remain, however, a solid group upon whom he depends for support, for food, for affection. There is no split between the women of his blood-group and the wife whom he marries, for he marries a daughter of one of his mother's half-brothers or cousins. He calls her by the name by which he calls his own mother, *aiyai*. All of the little girls of his mother's clan, to all of whom he looks hopefully, he addresses as *aiyai*. One of his "mothers" will some day be his wife. The gifts that his father gave in his name when he was very small, the gifts which he is now being taught to take himself to his mother's brothers, these are the earnest of his claim upon a woman of his mother's clan. In this way, one clan is linked with another from generation to generation, the men of one clan having a lien upon the women of the other.* Women are therefore divided for him into the group upon which he depends; these are all considered as of the order of mothers and include his mother, his mother's sisters, his father's brothers' wives, his mother's brothers' wives, and the daughters of his mother's brothers. Towards his father's sister and his father's sister's daughter his behaviour is more formal, for these can never be either mother, wife, or mother-in-law, the three relationships that Tchambuli feeling groups together. For the actual marriage, in addition to the presents that have been sent on ceremonial occasions the bride must be paid for in many *kinas* and *talibun*, and for this payment the young man is dependent upon his immediate male kin. An orphan, if he is allowed to live, has small hope of obtaining a bride while he is a young man. He is no one's child; how, indeed, can he hope to have a wife?

As the young man's attitude towards the women is single-hearted, rather than complicated with different conflicting attitudes appropriate to mother, sister, wife, and mother-in-law, so also the women in the house in which he has been brought up are a solid unit. When a girl marries, she goes not into the house of strangers but into the house of her father's sister, who now becomes her mother-in-law. If a man has two wives they usually, although not always, come from the same clan, and are sisters as well as cowives. To have been cowives, even although separated by death of the husband and subsequent remarriage, is regarded as a great tie between women. The prototype of Tchambuli polygyny is a pair of sisters entering as brides a house into which

---

*For a discussion of this lien system see Dr. Fortune, "A Note on Cross-Cousin Marriage," *Oceania*, 1933.

one or more of their father's sisters have married before them; in
which the old woman who sits by the fire, and occasionally utters
a few carping comments, is a woman of their own clan also, and
so will not deal harshly with them. And this unusual picture of
great amity and solidarity within the two feminine relationships
that are often most trying, that of cowives and that of mother-
in-law and daughter-in-law, pervades the interrelations of all
women. Tchambuli women work in blocks, a dozen of them
together, plaiting the great mosquito-bags from the sale of which
most of the *talibun* and *kina* are obtained. They cook together for
a feast, their clay fireplaces (circular pots with terraced tops,
which can be moved from place to place) set side by side. Each
dwelling-house contains some dozen to two dozen fire-places, so
that no woman need cook in a corner alone. The whole emphasis
is upon comradeship, efficient, happy work enlivened by continuous brisk banter and chatter. But in a group of men, there is
always strain, watchfulness, a catty remark here, a *double entendre*
there: "What did he mean by sitting down on the opposite side of
the men's house when he saw you upon this side?" "Did you see
Koshalan go by with a flower in his hair? What do you suppose he
is up to?"

As a boy grows up he sees the world into which he will enter
as a network of conflicting courses, each one adorned with airy
graces. He will learn to play the flute beautifully, to play the flute
that sounds like a cassowary, the flute that barks like a dog, the
flutes that cry like birds, the set of flutes that are blown together
to produce an organ-like effect. If he is politic, if he is well liked,
he may have two wives, or even three, like Walinakwon. Walinakwon was beautiful, a graceful dancer, a fluent speaker, proud,
imperious, but withal soft-spoken, and resourceful. In addition
to his first wife, who had been given him as a child by his
mother's clan, two other women had chosen him as a husband.
He was a fortunate man. All three of his wives could plait mosquito-bags, and Walinakwon was therefore in a fair way to
become a rich man.

For although Tchambuli is patrilineal in organisation, although there is polygyny and a man pays for his wife—two institutions that have been popularly supposed to degrade women—it is the women in Tchambuli who have the real position of power in the society. The patrilineal system includes houses and land, residence land and gardening-land, but only an occasional particularly energetic man gardens. For food, the people depend upon the fishing of the women. Men never fish unless a sudden school of fish appears in the lake, when they may leap into canoes in a frolicsome spirit, and spear a few fish. Or in high water when the shore-road is become a water way, they may do a little torch-light fishing for sport. But the real business of fishing is controlled entirely by the women. For traded fish they obtain sago, taro, and areca-nut. And the most important manufacture, the mosquito-bags, two of which will purchase an ordinary canoe, are made entirely by women. The people of the middle Sepik purchase these mosquito-bags, in fact they are so much in demand that purchasers take options on them long before they are finished. And the women control the proceeds in *kinas* and *talibun*. It is true that they permit the men to do the shopping, both for food at the market and in trading the mosquito-bags. The men make a gala occasion of these latter shopping-trips; when a man has the final negotiations for one of his wives' mosquito-bags in hand, he goes off resplendent in feathers and shell ornaments to spend a delightful few days over the transaction. He will hesitate and equivocate, advance here, draw back there, accept this *talibun*, reject that one, demand to see a more slender *kina* or one that is better cut, insist on changing half of the purchasing items after they have been spread out, have a very orgy of choice such as a modern woman with a well-filled purse looks forward to in a shopping-trip to a big city. But only with his wife's approval can he spend the *talibun* and *kina* and the strings of *conus* rings that he brings back from his holiday. He has wheedled a good price from the purchaser; he has still to wheedle the items of the price from his wife. From boyhood up, this is the

men's attitude towards property. Real property, which one actually owns, one receives from women, in return for languishing
looks and soft words. Once one has obtained it, it becomes a
counter in the games that men play; it is no longer concerned
with the underlying economics of life, but rather with showing
one's appreciation of one's brother-in-law, soothing someone's
wounded feelings, behaving very handsomely when a sister's son
falls down in one's presence. The minor war-and-peace that goes
on all the time among the men, the feelings that are hurt and
must be assuaged, are supported by the labour and contributions
of the women. When a woman lies dying, her thought is for the
young boys whom she has been helping, her son, her sister's son,
her husband's sister's son; how will this one, who, it is true, is an
orphan also and has no one to help him, fare when she is dead?
And if there is time, she will send for this handsome stripling or
accomplished youth, and give him a *kina* or so, or some *talibun*.
Such a handsome one is sure to arouse jealousy, to get into
scrapes; he must be provided with the means by which to bribe
his way back into favour.

The women's attitude towards the men is one of kindly tolerance and appreciation. They enjoy the games that the men play,
they particularly enjoy the theatricals that the men put on for
their benefit. A big masked show is the occasion for much pleasure. When a *mwai* dance is made, for instance, it means that a
group of women dance about each of the sets of masked dancers.
These masked figures wear wooden masks balanced in the midst
of a head-dress of leaves and flowers in which dozens of slender
little carvings are thrust on sticks. They have great paunches
made up of a long row of the crescent-shaped *kina* shells, which
extend below their waists rather like elephants' tusks. They wear
bustles in which grimacing carved faces are stuck. Their legs are
concealed with straw leggings, and they descend from a platform,
which has been specially built with a back-drop resembling the
distant mountains. The two male masks carry spears, the two
female masks carry brooms; trumpeting and singing esoteric

songs through little bamboo megaphones, they parade up and down a long cleared way that is lined with watching women and children. The masks are clan-owned, and when their own masks appear, the women of that clan and other women also go out and dance about them, making a gay chorus, and picking up any feathers or ornaments that fall from them. There are no men upon the dancing-ground except the four men hidden within the mask—older men in the male masks, young and frivolous ones within the female masks. These young men take a strange inverted pleasure in thus entering, in semi-disguise—not wholly in disguise, for most of them have whispered the details of their leggings to at least one woman—into the women's group. Here masked they can take part in the rough homosexual play that characterises a group of women on any festive occasion. When there are no masks on the dancing-ground, the women play among themselves, jocosely going through pantomimes of inter-course. When the masked figures appear, the women include the female masks in their play, but not the male masks. The women treat these latter with gentle, careful gravity, lest their feelings be hurt. To the female masks the women give very definite atten-tion, poking them with bundles of leaves that they carry in their hands, bumping against them in definitely provocative positions, tickling and teasing them. The *double entendre* of the situation, the spectacle of women courting males disguised as females, expresses better than any other ritual act that I witnessed the complexities of the sex-situation in Tchambuli, where men are nominally the owners of their homes, the heads of their families, even the owners of their wives, but in which the actual initiative and power is in the hands of the women. To the male mask the women give lip-service, and some of them, usually the older and graver women, dance with it; they pick up its ornaments when they fall. With the female masks they display aggressive sexual desire, and flaunt their right to initiative. After all, the young men can only whisper to the women in which masks they plan to dance and how their legs may be distinguished. Then, imprisoned in the clumsy, unstable, top-heavy masks and partially chaperoned by the older men who are dancing in the male masks, they can only parade blindly up and down the dancing-ground, waiting for a whisper and a blow to advise them that particular women have pressed against them. These ceremonies usually break up in a far shorter number of days than the original plan provides for, as rumors of liaisons flutter about to frighten the older men, who decide that they have lured their wives out on the dancing-ground for no good purpose. For even if no new alliance has sprung up under cover of the dancing, the dance of the women is itself designed to produce a high degree of sexual excitation, which may become an explosive in the days to come. It is the young wives of old men who enjoy these ceremonies most.

These festivals are a break in the vigorous workaday life of the women. Swift-footed, skilful-fingered, efficient, they pass back and forth from their fish-traps to their basket-plaiting, from their cooking to their fish-traps, brisk, good-natured, impersonal. Jolly comradeship, rough, very broad jesting and comment, are the order of the day. To each household is added once in so often a child-bride, a girl who at ten or eleven is sent to marry her cousin, one of the sons of the household. The bride is not difficult for the women to assimilate. She is their brother's child, they have known her always; they welcome her, teach her more skills, give her a fire-place at which to cook. And whereas the lives of the men are one mass of petty bickering, misunderstanding, reconciliation, avowals, disclaimers, and protestations accompanied by gifts, the lives of the women are singularly unclouded with personalities or with quarreling. For fifty quarrels among the men, there is hardly one among the women. Solid, preoccupied, powerful, with shaven unadorned heads, they sit in groups and laugh together, or occasionally stage a night dance at which, without a man present, each woman dances vigorously all by herself the dance-step that she has found to be most exciting. Here again the solidarity of women, the inessentialness of men, is demonstrated. Of this relationship the Tchambuli dwelling-house is the symbol.

It presents the curious picture of the entire centre firmly occupied by well-entrenched women, while the men sit about the edges, near the door, one foot on the house-ladder almost, unwanted, on sufferance, ready to flee away to their men's houses, where they do their own cooking, gather their own firewood, and generally live a near-bachelor life in a state of mutual discomfort and suspicion.

Tchambuli young men develop their attitudes towards one another in the highly charged atmosphere of courtship, in which no one knows upon whom a woman's choice will fall, each youth holds his breath and hopes, and no young man is willing to trust another. Such courtship arises from the presence of widows or dissatisfied wives. The dissatisfied wives are created by the same fidelity to a pattern without regard for practical considerations that occurs in the exchanges in Mundugumor. If among the "mothers" of his generation, one of whom he has a right to marry, there is no girl a little younger than a boy, his mother's clan will give him a girl who is a little older. While he is still adolescent, insecure, frightened of sex, she matures, and becomes involved in a liaison either with one of his brothers or possibly with an older relative. His mother's brothers will try to prevent this; they will publicly deride the boy who does not enter his betrothed wife's sleeping-bag, and threaten him that trouble will result and she may be lost to another clan. The boy, shamed and prickly with misery, becomes more tongue-tied, more recalcitrant than ever to his wife's advances. Then some rearrangement, her marriage to another man of the same clan, is likely to follow. With a young widow also, it is the girl's choice that is decisive, for men will not be foolish enough to pay for a girl who has not indicated her choice of a husband by sleeping with him. It will be, as they say, money thrown away. A young widow is a tremendous liability to a community. No one expects her to remain quiet until her remarriage has been arranged. Has she not a vulva? they ask. This is the comment that is continually made in Tchambuli: Are women passive sexless creatures who can be expected to wait upon the dilly-dallying of formal considerations of bride-price? Men, not so urgently sexed, may be expected to submit themselves to the discipline of a due order and precedence.

Yet the course of true love runs no smoother here where women dominate than it does in societies dominated by men. There is sometimes a tendency in describing marriage arrangements to consider that one of the inevitable effects of the dominance of women is the woman's freedom to marry whom she will, but this is no more a necessary aspect of women's power than the right of a young man to choose his wife is an inevitable result of patriliny. The social ambitions of a mother may ruin her son's marriage under the most patriarchal form of society, and in Tchambuli neither men nor women are minded to give young people any more rein than they can help. The ideal is to marry pairs of cousins as children and thus settle at least part of the difficulty. The opportunities that polygyny offers wait, then, upon the ripening of the boy's charms. The older men see with jaundiced eyes the beauty and grace of their younger brothers and later of their sons, a beauty and grace that will soon displace them in the eyes of women, especially of their young wives, whose favour they had perhaps caught in the last flutter of powerful middle age. The young men say bitterly that the old men use every bit of power and strategy which they possess to cut out their young rivals, to shame and disgrace them before the women.

The method of discrediting a young rival that the men find readiest to their jealous hands is the accusation of being an orphan. If a boy's father is alive, he will contribute perhaps 10, perhaps 20, per cent of the bride price, seldom more, and the other men of the clan contribute the rest. The principal contribution is made by the man or men whose marriages were mainly financed by the bridegroom's father. The state of being an orphan, then, does not mean that the boy is actually unable to pay a bride price, but merely that he is in an exposed state of which the other men can take advantage. And cruelly the old lascivious man, nearing his grave, will use this power to interfere

between an orphan boy of his clan and the young widow who
expressed a preference for that boy. One of these dramas was
played out in detail while we were in Tchambuli. Tchuikumban
was an orphan; his father and mother having both been killed
in head-hunting raids, he belonged to a vanishing clan. But he
was tall and straight and charming, although more arrogant and
masterful that Tchambuli men usually are. Yepiwali was his
"mother," a girl of his mother's clan, but she had been married as
a child in a distant part of the settlement, and Tchuikumban has
seen little of her. Then, just about the time we arrived in Tchambuli, the two potential mates, Yepiwali, now a widow for many
moons, Tchuikumban, an orphan of a poor clan and with no
betrothed wife, found themselves seeing each other daily, Yepiwali, suffering from a bad framboesia sore, was visiting her own
parents, and Tchuikumban was helping work on the new men's
house of Monbukimbit, a service that all uterine nephews owe to
their mother's brothers. Yepiwali saw him and he found favour in
her eyes. She told an older woman that Tchuikumban had given
her two bead armlets. This was not true, but was a boast that she
intended to capture his favour. Then she sent the head of a fish to
Tchuikumban through his brother-in-law. Tchuikumban ate the
head of the fish, but did nothing in reply to her overtures. A few
days later, Tchuikumban was given a pair of snake-birds. Yepiwali heard of it and she sent word to him: "If you have any bones,
send me some of that snake-bird in return for my fish." So
Tchuikumban sent her half the breast of a snake-bird. The next
day he made a journey to Kilimbit hamlet, and passed Yepiwali
on the road. He did not speak to her, nor she to him, but she
noted the new white belt that he was wearing.* That night she
sent word to him that if he had any bones, he would send her that
belt, and some soap and matches.* This he did.

About this time, the father of Yepiwali decided that the need

---

*Traded from our house-boys.

to remarry her was urgent. Rumours of her liaisons were rife, and it was not safe to leave her so long unmarried. He could not discuss her marriage with her himself, but he sent for a male cousin, Tchengenbonga, whom she called "brother," to do so. Tchengenbonga asked her which of her "sons" she wished to marry, and she said that Tavalavban had tried to win her affection, he had passed her on a path and held her breasts, but she didn't like him. She showed Tchengenbonga the gifts that she had elicited from Tchuikumban and said that she would like to marry him. Tchengenbonga asked her for the belt, and she gave it to him. Tchuikumban saw the belt on Tchengenbonga but said nothing. Soon after this there were offers for Yepiwali's hand from a man from another tribe, but after prolonged negotiations these were refused—not, however, before her choice of Tchuikumban had been published. The question of paying for her came up among Tchuikumban's relatives, and they refused to pay for her, because she did not know how to make mosquito-baskets. They were not going to have one of their boys marrying a woman who would not be a good provider. His foster-father was merciless: "You are an orphan. How can you expect to marry a wife of your own choice? This girl is no good. She is worn out with loose living. She cannot weave. How will it profit for you to marry her?" He reduced Tchuikumban to sulking misery. Soon after this Tchuikumban encountered Yepiwali on a deserted path; she paused and smiled at him, but he fled, too ashamed of his miserable status as an orphan to stay and make love to her. Yepiwali lost her patience. She had chosen this man, and why did he hesitate? She sent a message to the men of the next hamlet, together with two baskets of food, saying that since the men of her own hamlet had no bones, one of them might come and carry her off. Her relatives became alarmed. She was watched more closely. Then in the midst of the ceremony and confusion of a house of mourning, word got about that Yepiwali had been meeting someone clandestinely, and this someone turned out to be Akerman, an older man of the clan who had the right to marry her. Still longing for Tchuikumban, although in a fine rage with him and with all of the young men, she was led away to marry Akerman, followed by the consoling words of an older woman: "The other wife of Akerman is your father's sister. She will be kind to you and not scold you because you do not know how to make baskets." The other wife of Akerman made good baskets, Akerman was old and rich, and it was no one's concern if he took a young wife. So the love-affair was defeated because his relatives shamed Tchuikumban in terms of his orphanhood and because Yepiwali was not able to provide for a young husband.

So the conflict over women, outlawed in Arapesh because of the emphasis upon finding wives for sons and so important a part of the struggle and clash of life in Mundugumor, exists too in Tchambuli, where young men and old struggle stealthily for the possession of women's favours—but the struggle is for the most part an underground one. It is not a fight but a secret competition, in which young men and young women are both likely to lose to the will of their elders.

Relevant also to the position of the sexes are the secrets of the men's cults and the sanctity of the men's houses. These men's houses, which combine the functions of club and green-room, places where men can keep themselves out of the women's way and prepare their own food, workshops and dressing-rooms for ceremonies, are not kept inviolate from a woman's entrance on certain ceremonial occasions. For the scarification of a child, the woman who carries the child enters the men's house in state, and sits there proudly upon a stool. If there is a quarrel, the women gather on the hill-side and shout advice and directions into the very centre of the house where the debate is going on. They come armed with thick staves, to take part in the battle if need be. The elaborate ceremonies, the beating of water-drums, the blowing of flutes, are no secrets from the women. As they stood, an appreciative audience, listening solemnly to the voice of the crocodile, I asked them: "Do you know what makes that noise?" "Of course, it is a water-drum, but we don't say we know for fear the men would be ashamed." And the young men answer, when asked if the women know their secrets: "Yes, they know them, but they are good and pretend not to, for fear we become ashamed. Also— we might become so ashamed that we would beat them."

"We might become so ashamed that we would beat them." In that sentence lies the contradiction at the root of Tchambuli society, in which men are theoretically, legally dominant, but in which they play an emotionally subservient rôle, dependent upon the security given them by women, and even in sex-activity looking to women to give the leads. Their love magic consists in charms made of stolen stones that the women use for auto-erotic practices: this the men deeply resent, feeling that they should benefit by the greater sexual specificity and drive of the women. What the women will think, what the women will say, what the women will do, lies at the back of each man's mind as he weaves his tenuous and uncertain web of insubstantial relations with other men. Each man stands alone, playing his multiplicity of parts, sometimes allied with one man, sometimes with another; but the women are a solid group, confused by no rivalries, brisk, patronising, and jovial. They feed their male children, their young male relatives, on lotus-seeds and lily-roots, their husbands and lovers upon doled-out pellets of love. And yet the men are after all stronger, and a man can beat his wife, and this possibility serves to confuse the whole issue of female dominance and masculine charming, graceful, coquettish dancing attention.

16

the unplaced Tchambuli man and woman

The Tchambuli ideal man and woman contrast sharply with the ideals of both the Mundugumor and the Arapesh, and have in fact very little in common with either. With the Arapesh and the Mundugumor men and women ideally possess the same social personality, while in Tchambuli their personalities ideally oppose and complement each other. In addition both the Arapesh and the Mundugumor are primarily concerned with human relations for their own sakes, while the Tchambuli, in theory, devote themselves to impersonal artistic ends. Although the Mundugumor seek to exalt the self, to bend other human beings to the service of the self, to exploit the weak ruthlessly and sweep aside the opposing strong, and the Arapesh seek rather to depress the self, their ideal man or woman being the individual who finds fulfillment in devotion to the ends of others, nevertheless the Arapesh and the Mundugumor are ultimately personal in their emphases. The structure of their societies is constantly bent or broken to serve personal needs and ambitions, and there is no feeling that that structure is so valid and beautiful that the individual should be subordinated to its perpetuation and elaboration, that the dance and not the dancer is valuable.

But the Tchambuli value primarily their intricate, delicately patterned social life, their endless cycles of ceremonies and dances, the shining surface of their interrelations. Neither men nor women are ideally concerned with personal ends in any way; the woman co-operates with a large kin-group, the man is a member of several companies whose aims and ends he is supposed to reconcile. For delight in this pattern, the women fish and again set their traps, row out upon the lake in the chill early dawn, and climb back to their houses to sit all day plaiting mosquito-bags that will bring more *kina* and *talibun* into circulation, and it is by the presence of *kina* and *talibun* that the ceremonial life is kept moving, each dance, each ceremony necessitating the expenditure of food and valuables. To these services the women bring an impersonal, vigorous efficiency; they work not for a husband or a son, primarily, but so that the dance can go on in splendid style.

As the women's task is to pay for the dance, the men's duty is to dance, to perfect the steps and notes that will make the performance a success. The women's contribution is general; the money and the food that make the dance possible. The men's, on the other hand, is specific and delicately adjusted, a matter of detailed training in perfection. Prestige that comes from individual exploit has practically been eliminated, and bought victims who are sacrificed on the ceremonial ground have taken the place of victims killed in war by personal prowess. Marriage is supposed to be arranged along completely formal lines, on the basis of long-established emotional ties and blood-ties, a secure background for the conduct of life.

The description of this ideal of an impersonal artistic Utopia may ring strangely in the readers' ears after the material presented in the last chapter, outlining the amount of bickering, hurt feelings, and intrigue that characterises the life of the men. And it is meant to do so, for the Tchambuli, like the Mundugumor and the Arapesh, have selected as the decreed path for all humanity one that is too special to be congenial to all temperaments. And they have further complicated the issue by decreeing that men shall feel and act in one way, women feel and act in quite a different way. This immediately introduces a new educational problem. If boys and girls are to be adequately adjusted to such contrasting attitudes towards life, it might be expected that their early education would present contrasting features. Yet until the Tchambuli boy and girl reach the age of six or seven the two are treated exactly alike, and at this age, while the girl is rapidly trained in handicrafts and absorbed into the sober, responsible life of the women, the boy is given no such adequate training for his future rôle. He is left about upon the edges of his society, a little too old for the women, and a little too young for the men. He is not old enough to be trusted inside the men's houses while secret preparations are in progress. His untutored tongue might slip. He is not old enough to learn faultless execution on the big flutes; he cannot be trusted with the elaborate secret clan songs that he will learn to trumpet through a megaphone when he is older. If the emphasis were all upon skill, upon the acquisition of a smooth and perfect technique, these small boys as soon as they leave their mother's sides might be trained as diminutive performers. The secrecy of the green room, the Tchambuli heritage from the *tamberan* cults of New Guinea, prevents such a possibility. This secrecy, which is so meaningless, so functionless, such a heavy weight upon the interests of the Tchambuli tribe—interests that are always artistic and never religious—is also their undoing. It makes it impossible for them to bind the growing boy into an impersonal devotion. The arrangement of people at a big ceremony shows in sharp relief the position of the eight-year-old boy. In the green-room, behind the screens of palm-leaf mats, are the old men, the young men, and the just initiated boys, bobbing about on small errands. On the dancing-ground are groups of women and girls, some of them dancing with a set of masks, others sitting about in happy chatting groups. Some of the little girls are dancing, others are sitting with the women, holding the babies, peeling sugar cane for the younger children to eat, thoroughly, solidly identified with their own sex. Only the little boys are excluded. They belong nowhere, they are in everybody's way. In sullen, disconsolate clusters, they sit about on logs. Occasionally they accept food that is offered them, only to go off to eat it sulkily and perhaps quarrel over it with another similarly placed small boy. It is everybody's party but theirs.

This period of three, sometimes four, years in the lives of the boys sets up habits that prevail throughout their lives. A sense of neglect, of exclusion, settles upon them. When the men or big boys ask them to run an errand, they feel they are being used, they who are wanted at no other time. The big boys chase them home at nightfall, and in the houses of the women, where they are still pampered with an even-handed impersonal generosity that does not serve to soothe their hurt feelings, they sit and listen to the flutes. Even the women, they know, are on the inside of the secrets, and their little sisters, who, being oftener with the women, have picked up more of the women's talk, hush their giggling remarks on a ceremony when an uninitiated boy approaches them. No one suggests that it is for their own sakes that this delay occurs, the explanation that is given small Arapesh boys. No, it is for the convenience of the older men. So the smaller boys glower in a resentment that never entirely lifts, and grow up to be typical Tchambuli men, overquick to feel hurt or slight and to burst into hysterical vituperation. One by one, as the years pass, they are admitted to the secrets, with no sense that at last beautiful, awe-inspiring things are being shown to them, for the Tchambuli have no such religious feeling. The beautiful, the almost awe-inspiring spectacle is the finished production that the little boys have seen since childhood. The secrets of the green-room turn out to be the assemblage of little bits of odds and ends, half-masks, unpainted standards, pieces of ratan, from which the spectacle is built up. When they are initiated they enter a group that is already characterised by rivalries and jealousies, many of them the kind of rivalries that are prevalent in a ballet company, where the subordination of all to the pattern is always coming in conflict with individual ambition and vanity. The piecemeal admission to the secrets, and the way in which as initiates they are made mere pawns with no rôle of their own, complete the mischief, and perfect devotion to the dance, on which the Tchambuli ideal counts, is never attained.

Nevertheless, this slight flaw in the unanimity and harmoniousness of the actors would not seriously mar the surface of Tchambuli life. The play goes on, new masks with the slanting eyes that suggest the face of a werewolf, new flutes with graceful little birds adorning the ends, are made, and as the sun sinks over the smooth, unreal lake, the music of flute-playing rises from the men's houses. If the actors are more interested in their own steps than in the whole dance, still their dancing is perfect. It is true that a slight unreality pervades the whole life. Realistic emotions are so muffled by ceremonial observance that all feeling becomes a little unreal, until the expression of anger and of fear becomes also only a figure in the dance. So from the plashy edge of the lake where the young men are bathing come screams of agony, shouts for help, and the rattling sounds of death. This is no one drowning, although such drowning does occur—did occur last week in fact, when the child of Kalingmale waded out of his depth and was entangled by the weeds. But these shrieks are only the young men playing, playing at death. On a hill-side not so far away Kalingmale sits with his eye on an ax that the women are keeping away from him. His wife has accused him of being responsible for the child's straying in the water; he wants that ax to kill the mother of the child who was with his dead child, but who was not drowned. Twice he has assaulted her, and now the watching women never leave him. But down on the lake-shore the young men laugh hysterically as the death-rattle is realistically imitated, now by one young voice, then by another.

Or news may come that a woman has been stolen by another tribe. She has been set upon as she was fishing and carried off to be the wife of an enemy. The young men sit in the men's house, drawing patterns on new line gourds, and making a *bon mot* with each twist of the carving tool. "Are you angry," one asks them, "over the abduction of your sister?" "We do not know yet," they answer. "The old men have not told us."

But underneath this type of gay disassociation, which is implicit in the formal patterning of life away from primary emotions in the interest of a graceful form, there is a more serious cultural cause of maladjustment. It will be remembered that there is contradiction in Tchambuli society, that underneath patriarchal forms women dominate the scene. With a social personality far more dominating and definite than is usually developed in women even under matriliny, the women are theoretically subject to the men; they have indeed been bought and paid for, and this fact is frequently mentioned. So the Tchambuli boy grows up within two sets of conflicting ideas; he hears that his father bought his mother, he hears how much his father paid for his mother and how much his father will now collect to pay for his son's young wife. He hears remarks like the one I quoted at the end of the last chapter: "We might become so ashamed that we would beat them." He sees young girls who are inappropriately wedded become involved in intrigue, become pregnant, and harried by both men and women, dash madly down house-ladders and up and down rocky paths, until they miscarry. And he sees them in the end consulted about their choices after all. At the same time he leads a life that is attuned to the voices of the women, where ceremonies are given for the sake of the women, where the women have the first and the last voice in the economic arrangements. All that he hears of sex stresses the woman's right to initiative. The boy who is chosen will receive a gift and a dare from the girl who has chosen him; men may possess desire but it profits them little unless their wives are actively interested; their wives indeed may prefer auto-eroticism. Here is a conflict at the very root of his psycho-sexual adjustment; his society tells him that he rules women, his experience shows him at every turn that women expect to rule him, as they rule his father and his brother.

But the actual dominance of the women is far more real than the structural position of the men, and the majority of Tchambuli young men adjust themselves to it, become accustomed to wait upon the words and the desires of women. In the top of their men's houses, shut away by blinds from the eyes of passers-by, is the wooden figure of a woman with an enormously exaggerated vulva, painted scarlet. She is the symbol that controls their emotions. But while the majority adjust, here, as in the other two societies we have examined, there are some individuals who are unable to adjust to the phrasing of life upon which their culture insists. Among the Tchambuli the unadjusted men are men of the same temperament as those who were unadjusted among the Arapesh, the more viriloid youths, violent, possessive, and actively sexed, intolerant of any control, any activity that they have not themselves initiated. But in Arapesh such young men had the whole weight of their society against them, only rags and tags of folk-lore, bits of obsolete garden magic, gave them any objective material upon which to hang their distrust and suspicions. If they wooed their wives more fiercely than Arapesh feeling dictated, at least their wives did not regard this as an invasion of their feminine prerogatives. In Tchambuli, however, the conditions are more difficult. The violent young man with a will to initiate and to dictate finds a wealth of formal justification for his ambitions. Along the sides of his men's house hang rows of heads, theoretically taken from the enemy. He has dreamt of head-hunting expeditions for years before he realises that these are the spoils of traffic in treachery, not of a battle. He sees payments being made for his wife. Some day she will be his and he will do what he likes with her; has she not been paid for? It is all quite enough to confuse him. And such young men are definitely maladjusted among the Tchambuli, more maladjusted than any similar group that I have studied. Táukumbank was covered with tinea; during a short period away from his village he forgot his own language and had to speak to his father in the trade-jargon of the middle Sepik. (His confusion was further intensified by an irregular marriage between his father and his mother, which made him a member of conflicting social groups and completely blurred his understanding of the working of his society.) Tchuikumban was hysterically deaf, hearing no command that was addressed to him. Yangítimi had a series of boils, and grew lamer and lamer, and more recessive. Kavíwon, a fine muscular youth, the son of the government-appointed Luluai, tried to realise through his father's position his desire to rule. But his father only shook his curls and side-stepped. Kavíwon, seated on his house-floor, was seized by an ungovernable desire to thrust a spear into the group of chattering women, his two wives and their sisters, who sat beneath his house. He said simply that he could bear their laughter no longer. The spear, pushed compulsively through a crack in the floor, pierced his wife's cheek, and for a while it was feared that she would die. Neurotic symptoms, unaccountable acts of rage and violence, characterise these young men whose society tells them they are masters in their homes, even after any such behaviour has become thoroughly obsolete.

The wives of these unadjusted young men suffer also, not only erratic spears through their cheeks, but because they find it necessary to make their dominance so much clearer. So it was with Tchubukéima, the wife of Yangítimi, a fine tall girl with a prima-donna temperament. During her pregnancy Yangítimi took little interest; he sulked and his boils grew worse. She retaliated by continual fainting-fits, in the most public and conspicuous circumstances. These fits made ritual observances, fuss, commotion necessary. Yangítimi would temporarily take up an appropriately solicitous attitude. When her birth-pains began, Yangítimi soon wearied of his position of helpless and worried spectator, sitting at the far end of the house while his wife was closeted with the midwife and her father's sisters, between whose knees a woman in labour must kneel. Yangítimi began to laugh and jest with the magician who had been called in to put a spell on the proceedings. His wife heard his light-hearted laugh and rage rose within her. She stalked out into the centre of the house, where she was not supposed to go. She groaned and moaned. His light-hearted talk stopped. She retired. Again to her ears came the sound of typical irresponsible male conversation. She abruptly ceased her rhythmic moaning, which had increased to a periodicity of every five seconds, and went to sleep. Worry descended upon the house. If she lost her strength, she and the baby would die. The women tried to wake her up. The men's light-hearted conversation was hushed. She woke up. The moans began again, and again Yangítimi's impatience of his rôle asserted itself. And again Tchubukéima paraded, exhibited her sufferings, and finally again relapsed into a doze. This procedure, begun early in the morning, went on and on. By noon the men were a little frightened. They canvassed the magical possibilities, the possibilities for sorcery. One by one these were divined about and rejected. The women said grimly, unimpressed, that Tchubukéima had not carried enough firewood during her pregnancy. By mid-afternoon, desperate measures were resorted to. It was decided that the spirits of the house were inimical and that the wife of Yangítimi should be moved to a house at the far end of the village. This, said the people, often induced the woman to put forth the proper effort and brought the child. So away we went, clambering over a rough and slippery path to a house a mile and a half away, the woman in labour, consumed with fury, in advance, the rest of the attending women following after her. I myself, just over an attack of fever, brought up the rear. Arrived in the chosen house, a new enclosure was made, and again Tchubukéima knelt between her father's sister's knees. But now a new complication ensued; the woman also had lost patience. Her aunt sat with her head turned towards another woman, chattering briskly away, about the palm-boards that the people of Indéngai hamlet were cutting, about a recent reconciliation in Wómpun, about the state of Kavíwon's wife's face, and what she thought of men who put spears through their wives' faces. At intervals she turned to the furious kneeling girl to remark: "Have your baby!" Tchubukéima again lay down in a sulk and went to sleep. It was not until two o'clock in the morning, when the now genuinely worried Yangítimi had paid a *kina* to the earthly representative of one of the shamanic spirits, that Tchubukéima settled down to the business of delivering her child. The dominating wife of an aberrant man, she had been forced to unusual lengths to demonstrate her position.

The discussion of the position of the deviant in Mundugumor showed how the maladjustment of the mild person in a position that his culture dictated should be handled violently and aggressively is less pronounced than the maladjustment of the violent individual condemned, but not disciplined, to play a mild and responsive rôle. Tchambuli conditions confirm this conclusion. The men are the conspicuous maladjusts, subject to neurasthenia, hysteria, and maniacal outbursts. The quiet, undominating woman as a rule slips along within the comfortable confines of the large women's group, overshadowed by a younger wife, directed by a mother-in-law. Her maladjustment is in no way conspicuous; if she does not play as conspicuous a rôle as her sex entitles her to, she does not greatly rebel over her position.

If she be particularly intelligent she may, like Ombléan of Mundugumor, outwit her culture. Such a woman was Tchengokwále, the mother of nine children, the elder wife of Tanum, a violent, overbearing, thoroughly maladjusted man, who was our nearest neighbour. Tchengokwále adjusted to his violence, and by her acquiescence in it no doubt had accentuated it. At the same time, she was a little remote from the highly sexed, aggressive younger women, his other wife and his son's betrothed wife. And she had made a career for herself as a midwife, an occupation that was regarded almost as a little soft and sentimental by the Tchambuli. And when a group of men were gathered together to consult over some complication, the only woman among them, the one woman who felt herself more in rapport with the anxious, harassed men than with the dominant, self-confident women, was Tchengokwále, the midwife.

part four

the implication of these results

17

the standardisation of sex-temperament

We have now considered in detail the approved personalities of each sex among three primitive peoples. We found the Arapesh—both men and women—displaying a personality that, out of our historically limited preoccupations, we would call maternal in its parental aspects, and feminine in its sexual aspects. We found men, as well as women, trained to be co-operative, unaggressive, responsive to the needs and demands of others. We found no idea that sex was a powerful driving force either for men or for women. In marked contrast to these attitudes, we found among the Mundugumor that both men and women developed as ruthless, aggressive, positively sexed individuals, with the maternal cherishing aspects of personality at a minimum. Both men and women approximated to a personality type that we in our culture would find only in an undisciplined and very violent male. Neither the Arapesh nor the Mundugumor profit by a contrast between the sexes; the Arapesh ideal is the mild, responsive man married to the mild, responsive woman; the Mundugumor ideal is the violent, aggressive man married to the violent, aggressive woman. In the third tribe, the Tchambuli, we found a genuine reversal of the sex-attitudes of our own culture, with the woman the dominant, impersonal, managing partner, the man the less responsible and the emotionally dependent person. These three situations suggest, then, a very definite conclusion. If those temperamental attitudes which we have traditionally regarded as feminine—such as passivity, responsiveness, and a willingness to cherish children—can so easily be set up as the masculine pattern in one tribe, and in another be outlawed for the majority of women as well as for the majority of men, we no longer have any basis for regarding such aspects of behaviour as sex-linked. And this conclusion becomes even stronger when we consider the actual reversal in Tchambuli of the position of dominance of the two sexes, in spite of the existence of formal patrilineal institutions.

The material suggests that we may say that many, if not all, of the personality traits which we have called masculine or feminine are as lightly linked to sex as are the clothing, the manners, and the form of head-dress that a society at a given period assigns to either sex. When we consider the behaviour of the typical Arapesh man or woman as contrasted with the behaviour of the typical Mundugumor man or woman, the evidence is overwhelmingly in favour of the strength of social conditioning. In no other way can we account for the almost complete uniformity with which Arapesh children develop into contented, passive, secure persons, while Mundugumor children develop as characteristically into violent, aggressive, insecure persons. Only to the impact of the whole of the integrated culture upon the growing child can we lay the formation of the contrasting types. There is no other explanation of race, or diet, or selection that can be adduced to explain them. We are forced to conclude that human nature is almost unbelievably malleable, responding accurately and contrastingly to contrasting cultural conditions. The differences between individuals who are members of different cultures, like the differences between individuals within a culture, are almost entirely to be laid to differences in conditioning, especially during early childhood, and the form of this conditioning is culturally determined. Standardised personality differences between the sexes are of this order, cultural creations to which each generation, male and female, is trained to conform. There remains, however, the problem of the origin of these socially standardised differences.

While the basic importance of social conditioning is still imperfectly recognised—not only in lay thought, but even by the scientist specifically concerned with such matters—to go beyond it and consider the possible influence of variations in hereditary equipment is a hazardous matter. The following pages will read very differently to one who has made a part of his thinking a recognition of the whole amazing mechanism of cultural conditioning—who has really accepted the fact that the same infant could be developed into a full participant in any one of these three cultures—than they will read to one who still believes that the minutiae of cultural behaviour are carried in the individual germ-plasm. If it is said, therefore, that when we have grasped the full significance of the malleability of the human organism and the preponderant importance of cultural conditioning, there are still further problems to solve, it must be remembered that these problems come *after* such a comprehension of the force of conditioning; they cannot precede it. The forces that make children born among the Arapesh grow up into typical Arapesh personalities are entirely social, and any discussion of the variations which do occur must be looked at against this social background.

With this warning firmly in mind, we can ask a further question. Granting the malleability of human nature, whence arise the differences between the standardised personalities that different cultures decree for all of their members, or which one culture decrees for the members of one sex as contrasted with the members of the opposite sex? If such differences are culturally created, as this material would most strongly suggest that they are, if the new-born child can be shaped with equal ease into an unaggressive Arapesh or an aggressive Mundugumor, why do these striking contrasts occur at all? If the clues to the different personalities decreed for men and women in Tchambuli do not lie in the physical constitution of the two sexes—an assumption that we must reject both for the Tchambuli and for our own society—where can we find the clues upon which the Tchambuli, the Arapesh, the Mundugumor, have built? Cultures are manmade, they are built of human materials; they are diverse but comparable structures within which human beings can attain full human stature. Upon what have they built their diversities?

We recognise that a homogeneous culture committed in all of its gravest institutions and slightest usages to a co-operative, unaggressive course can bend every child to that emphasis, some to a perfect accord with it, the majority to an easy acceptance, while only a few deviants fail to receive the cultural imprint. To consider such traits as aggressiveness or passivity to be sex-linked is not possible in the light of the facts. Have such traits, then, as aggressiveness or passivity, pride or humility, objectivity or a preoccupation with personal relationships, an easy response to the needs of the young and the weak or a hostility to the young and the weak, a tendency to initiate sex relations or merely to respond to the dictates of a situation or another person's advances—have these traits any basis in temperament at all? Are they potentialities of all human temperaments that can be developed by different kinds of social conditioning and which will not appear if the necessary conditioning is absent?

When we ask this question we shift our emphasis. If we ask why an Arapesh man or an Arapesh woman shows the kind of personality that we have considered in the first section of this book, the answer is: Because of the Arapesh culture, because of the intricate, elaborate, and unfailing fashion in which a culture is able to shape each new-born child to the cultural image. And if we ask the same question about a Mundugumor man or woman, or about a Tchambuli man as compared with a Tchambuli woman, the answer is of the same kind. They display the personalities that are peculiar to the cultures in which they were born and educated. Our attention has been on the differences between Arapesh men and women as a group and Mundugumor men and women as a group. It is as if we had represented the Arapesh personality by a soft yellow, the Mundugumor by a deep red, while the Tchambuli female personality was deep orange, and that of the Tchambuli male, pale green. But if we now ask whence came the original direction in each culture, so that one now shows yellow, another red, the third orange and green by sex, then we must peer more closely. And leaning closer to the picture, it is as if behind the bright consistent yellow of the Arapesh, and the deep equally consistent red of the Mundugumor, behind the orange and green that are Tchambuli, we found in each case the delicate, just discernible outlines of the whole spectrum, differently overlaid in each case by the monotone which covers it. This spectrum is the range of individual differences which lie back of the so much more conspicuous cultural emphases, and it is to this that we must turn to find the explanation of cultural inspiration, of the source from which each culture has drawn.

There appears to be about the same range of basic temperamental variation among the Arapesh and among the Mundugumor, although the violent man is a misfit in the first society and a leader in the second. If human nature were completely homogeneous raw material, lacking specific drives and characterised by no important constitutional differences between individuals, then individuals who display personality traits so antithetical to the social pressure should not reappear in societies of such differing emphases. If the variations between individuals were to be set down to accidents in the genetic process, the same accidents should not be repeated with similar frequency in strikingly different cultures, with strongly contrasting methods of education.

But because this same relative distribution of individual differences does appear in culture after culture, in spite of the divergence between the cultures, it seems pertinent to offer a hypothesis to explain upon what basis the personalities of men and women have been differently standardised so often in the history of the human race. This hypothesis is an extension of that advanced by Ruth Benedict in her *Patterns of Culture*. Let us assume that there are definite temperamental differences between human beings which if not entirely hereditary at least are established on a hereditary base very soon after birth. (Further than this we cannot at present narrow the matter.) These differences finally embodied in the character structure of adults, then, are the clues from which culture works, selecting one temperament, or a combination of related and congruent types, as desirable, and embodying this choice in every thread of the social fabric—in the care of the young child, the games the children play, the songs the people sing, the structure of political organisation, the religious observance, the art and the philosophy.

Some primitive societies have had the time and the robustness to revamp all of their institutions to fit one extreme type, and to develop educational techniques which will ensure that the majority of each generation will show a personality congruent with this extreme emphasis. Other societies have pursued a less definitive course, selecting their models not from the most extreme, most highly differentiated individuals, but from the less marked types. In such societies the approved personality is less pronounced, and the culture often contains the types of inconsistencies that many human beings display also; one institution may be adjusted to the uses of pride, another to a casual humility that is congruent neither with pride nor with inverted pride. Such societies, which have taken the more usual and less sharply defined types as models, often show also a less definitely patterned social structure. The culture of such societies may be likened to a house the decoration of which has been informed by no definite and precise taste, no exclusive emphasis upon dignity or comfort or pretentiousness or beauty, but in which a little of each effect has been included.

Alternatively, a culture may take its clues not from one temperament, but from several temperaments. But instead of mixing together into an inconsistent hotchpotch the choices and emphases of different temperaments, or blending them together into a smooth but not particularly distinguished whole, it may isolate each type by making it the basis for the approved social personality for an age-group, a sex-group, a caste-group, or an occupational group. In this way society becomes not a monotone with a few discrepant patches of an intrusive colour, but a mosaic, with different groups displaying different personality traits. Such specialisations as these may be based upon any facet of human endowment—different intellectual abilities, different artistic abilities, different emotional traits. So the Samoans decree that all young people must show the personality trait of unaggressiveness and punish with opprobrium the aggressive child who displays traits regarded as appropriate only in titled middle-aged men. In societies based upon elaborate ideas of rank, members of the aristocracy will be permitted, even compelled, to display a pride, a sensitivity to insult, that would be deprecated as inappropriate in members of the plebeian class. So also in professional groups or in religious sects some temperamental traits are selected and institutionalised, and taught to each new member who enters the profession or sect. Thus the physician learns the bed-side manner, which is the natural behaviour of some temperaments and the standard behaviour of the general practitioner in the medical profession; the Quaker learns at least the outward behaviour and the rudiments of meditation, the capacity for which is not necessarily an innate characteristic of many of the members of the Society of Friends.

So it is with the social personalities of the two sexes. The traits that occur in some members of each sex are specially assigned to one sex, and disallowed in the other. The history of the social definition of sex-differences is filled with such arbitrary arrangements in the intellectual and artistic field, but because of the assumed congruence between physiological sex and emotional endowment we have been less able to recognise that a similar arbitrary selection is being made among emotional traits also. We have assumed that because it is convenient for a mother to wish to care for her child, this is a trait with which women have been more generously endowed by a carefully teleological process of evolution. We have assumed that because men have hunted, an activity requiring enterprise, bravery, and initiative, they have been endowed with these useful attitudes as part of their sex temperament.

Societies have made these assumptions both overtly and implicitly. If a society insists that warfare is the major occupation for the male sex, it is therefore insisting that all male children display bravery and pugnacity. Even if the insistence upon the differential bravery of men and women is not made articulate, the difference in occupation makes this point implicitly. When, however, a society goes further and defines men as brave and women as timorous, when men are forbidden to show fear and women are indulged in the most flagrant display of fear, a more explicit element enters in. Bravery, hatred of any weakness, of flinching before pain or danger—this attitude which is so strong a component of *some human* temperaments has been selected as the key to masculine behaviour. The easy unashamed display of fear or suffering that is congenial to a different temperament has been made the key to feminine behaviour.

Originally two variations of human temperament, a hatred of fear or willingness to display fear, they have been socially translated into inalienable aspects of the personalities of the two sexes. And to that defined sex-personality every child will be educated, if a boy, to suppress fear, if a girl, to show it. If there has been no social selection in regard to this trait, the proud temperament that is repelled by any betrayal of feeling will display itself, regardless of sex, by keeping a stiff upper lip. Without an express prohibition of such behaviour the expressive unashamed man or woman will weep, or comment upon fear or suffering. Such attitudes, strongly marked in certain temperaments, may by social selection be standardised for everyone, or outlawed for everyone, or ignored by society, or made the exclusive and approved behaviour of one sex only.

Neither the Arapesh nor the Mundugumor have made any attitude specific for one sex. All of the energies of the culture have gone towards the creation of a single human type, regardless of class, age, or sex. There is no division into age-classes for which different motives or different moral attitudes are regarded as suitable. There is no class of seers or mediums who stand apart drawing inspiration from psychological sources not available to the majority of the people. The Mundugumor have, it is true, made one arbitrary selection, in that they recognise artistic ability only among individuals born with the cord about their necks, and firmly deny the happy exercise of artistic ability to those less unusually born. The Arapesh boy with a tinea infection has been socially selected to be a disgruntled, antisocial individual, and the society forces upon sunny co-operative children cursed with this affliction a final approximation to the behaviour appropriate to a pariah. With these two exceptions no emotional rôle is forced upon an individual because of birth or accident. As there is no idea of rank which declares that some are of high estate and some of low, so there is no idea of sex-difference which declares that one sex must feel differently from the other. One possible imaginative social construct, the attribution of different personalities to different members of the community classified into sex-, age-, or caste-groups, is lacking.

When we turn however to the Tchambuli, we find a situation that while bizarre in one respect, seems nevertheless more intelligible in another. The Tchambuli have at least made the point of sex-difference; they have used the obvious fact of sex as an organising point for the formation of social personality, even though they seem to us to have reversed the normal picture. While there is reason to believe that not every Tchambuli woman is born with a dominating, organising, administrative temperament, actively sexed and willing to initiate sex-relations, possessive, definite, robust, practical and impersonal in outlook, still most Tchambuli girls grow up to display these traits. And while there is definite evidence to show that all Tchambuli men are not, by native endowment, the delicate responsive actors of a play staged for the women's benefit, still most Tchambuli boys manifest this coquettish play-acting personality most of the time. Because the Tchambuli formulation of sex-attitudes contradicts our usual premises, we can see clearly that Tchambuli culture has arbitrarily permitted certain human traits to women, and allotted others, equally arbitrarily, to men.

If we then accept this evidence drawn from these simple societies which through centuries of isolation from the main stream of human history have been able to develop more extreme, more striking cultures than is possible under historical conditions of great intercommunication between peoples and the resulting heterogeneity, what are the implications of these results? What conclusions can we draw from a study of the way in which a culture can select a few traits from the wide gamut of human endowment and specialise these traits, either for one sex or for the entire community? What relevance have these results to social thinking? Before we consider this question it will be necessary to discuss in more detail the position of the deviant, the individual whose innate disposition is too alien to the social personality required by his culture for his age, or sex, or caste ever to wear perfectly the garment of personality that his society has fashioned for him.

18

the deviant

What are the implications for an understanding of the social deviant of the point of view outlined in the last chapter? Under the term "deviant" I include any individual who because of innate disposition or accident of early training, or through the contradictory influences of a heterogeneous cultural situation, has been culturally disenfranchised, the individual to whom the major emphases of his society seem nonsensical, unreal, untenable, or downright wrong. The average man in any society looks into his heart and finds there a reflection of the world about him. The delicate educational process that has made him into an adult has assured him this spiritual membership in his own society. But this is not true of the individual for whose temperamental gifts his society has no use, nor even tolerance. The most cursory survey of our history is enough to demonstrate that gifts honoured in one century are disallowed in the next. Men who would have been saints in the Middle Ages are without vocation in modern England and America. When we take into account primitive societies that have selected far more extreme and contrasting attitudes than did our own ancestral cultures, the matter becomes even clearer. To the extent that a culture is integrated and definite in its goals, uncompromising in its moral and spiritual preferences, to that very extent it condemns some of its members—members by birth only—to live alien to it, in perplexity at the best, at the worst in a rebellion that may turn to madness.

It has become the fashion to group together all of those by whom the cultural norm is not accepted as neurotics, individuals who have turned from "reality" (that is, the present-day solutions of their own society) to the comfort or inspiration of fantasy situations, taking refuge in some transcendental philosophy, in art, in political radicalism, or merely in sexual inversion or some other elaborated idiosyncrasy of behaviour—vegetarianism or the wearing of a hair shirt. The neurotic is furthermore regarded as immature; he has not grown up sufficiently to understand the obviously realistic and commendable motivations of his own society.

In this blanket definition two quite different concepts have become blurred and confused, each one rendering the other nugatory. Among the deviants in any society, it is possible to distinguish those who are physiologically inadequate. They may have weak intellects or defective glands; any one of a number of possible organic weaknesses may predetermine them to failure in any but the simplest tasks. They may—very, very rarely such an individual is found—have practically all of the physiological equipment of the opposite sex. None of these individuals are suffering from any discrepancy between a purely temperamental bent and social emphasis; they are merely the weak and the defective, or they are abnormal in the sense that they are in a group which deviates too far from human cultural standards—not particular cultural standards—for effective functioning. For such individuals any society must provide a softer, a more limited, or a more special environment than that which it provides for the majority of its members.

But there is another type of neurotic that is continually being confused with these physiologically handicapped individuals, and this is the cultural deviant, the individual who is at variance with the values of his society. Modern psychiatric thought tends to attribute all of his maladjustment to early conditioning and so places him in the invidious category of the psychically maimed. A study of primitive conditions does not bear out such a simple explanation. It does not account for the fact that it is always those individuals who show marked temperamental proclivities in opposition to the cultural emphases who are in each society the maladjusted persons; or for the fact that it is a different type of individual which is maladjusted among the Mundugumor from the type which is maladjusted among the Arapesh. It does not explain why materialistic, bustling America and a materialistic, bustling tribe in the Admiralty Islands both produce hoboes, or why it is the individual endowed with a capacity to feel strongly who is maladjusted in Zuñi and Samoa. Such material suggests that there is another type of unadjusted person, whose failure to adjust should be referred not to his own weakness and defect, not to accident or to disease, but to a fundamental discrepancy between his innate disposition and his society's standards.

When society is unstratified and the social personalities of both sexes are fundamentally alike, these deviants are drawn indiscriminately from both sexes. Among the Arapesh the violent man and the violent woman, among the Mundugumor the trustful, co-operative man and the trustful, co-operative woman are the deviants. Too much positive self-feeling predetermines one to maladjustment among the Arapesh, too much negative self-feeling is an equal liability among the Mundugumor. In earlier chapters we have discussed the personalities of some of these deviating individuals, and shown how the very gifts that Mundugumor society would have honoured were disallowed among the Arapesh, how Wabe and Temos and Amitoa would have found Mundugumor life intelligible, and Ombléan and Kwenda would have been well placed among the Arapesh. But the alienness of both these groups in their own cultures, although it impaired their social functioning, reducing the uses to which their gifts might have been put, nevertheless left their psycho-sexual functioning unimpaired. Amitoa's positive drive made her behave not like a man, but like a woman of the Plains. Ombléan's love for children and willingness to work strenuously in order to care for a number of dependents did not make him suspect that he was like a woman, nor did it provoke in his associates an accusation of effeminacy. In loving children and peace and order, he might be behaving like some white men or some tribe they had never seen, but certainly no more like a Mundugumor woman than like a Mundugumor man. There was no homosexuality among either the Arapesh or the Mundugumor.

But any society that specialises its personality types by sex, which insists that any trait—love for children, interest in art, bravery in the face of danger, garrulity, lack of interest in personal relations, passiveness in sex relations; there are hundreds of traits of very different kinds that have been so specialised—is inalienably bound up with sex, paves the way for a kind of maladjustment of a worse order. Where there is no such dichotomy, a man may stare sadly at his world and find it essentially meaningless but still marry and rear children, finding perhaps a definite mitigation of his misery in this one whole-hearted participation in a recognised social form. A woman may day-dream all her life of a world where there is dignity and pride instead of the mean shopkeeping morality that she finds all about her, and yet greet her husband with an easy smile and nurse her children through the croup. The deviant may translate his sense of remoteness into painting or music or revolutionary activity and yet remain in his personal life, in his relations to members of his own and the opposite sex, essentially unconfused. Not so, however, in a society which, like that of the Tchambuli or that of historical Europe and America, defines some temperamental traits as masculine, some as feminine. In addition to, or aside from, the pain of being born into a culture whose acknowledged ends he can never make his own, many a man has now the added misery of being disturbed in his psycho-sexual life. He not only has the wrong feelings but, far worse and more confusing, he has the feelings of a woman. The significant point is not whether this malorientation, which makes the defined goals of women in his society intelligible to him and the goals of the man alien and distasteful, results in inversion or not. In extreme cases in which a man's temperament conforms very closely to the approved feminine personality, and if there is in existence a social form behind which he can shelter himself, a man may turn to avowed inversion and transvesticism. Among the Plains Indians, the individual who preferred the placid activities of the women to the dangerous, nerve-racking activities of the men could phrase his preference in sex terms; he could assume women's dress and occupations, and proclaim that he really was more a woman than a man. In Mundugumor, where there is no such pattern, a man may engage in feminine activities, such as fishing, without its occurring to him to symbolise his behaviour in female attire. Without any contrast between the sexes and without any tradition of transvesticism, a variation in temperamental preference does not result in either homosexuality or transvesticism. As it is unevenly distributed over the world, it seems clear that transvesticism is not only a variation that occurs when there are different personalities decreed for men and women, but that it need not occur even there. It is in fact a social invention that has become stabilised among the American Indians and in Siberia, but not in Oceania.

I observed in some detail the behaviour of an American Indian youth who was in all probability a congenital invert, during the period when he was just making his transvesticism explicit. This man had, as a small boy, showed such marked feminine physical traits that a group of women had once captured him and undressed him to discover whether he was really a boy at all. As he grew older he began to specialise in women's occupations and to wear female underclothing, although he still affected the outer costume of a male. He carried in his pockets, however, a variety of rings and bangles such as were worn only by women. At dances in which the sexes danced separately, he would begin the evening dressed as a man and dancing with the men, and then, as if acting under some irresistible compulsion, he would begin to move closer and closer to the women, as he did so putting on one piece of jewelry after another. Finally a shawl would appear, and at the end of the evening he would be dressed as a *berdache*, a transvestite. The people were just beginning to speak of him as "she." I have cited his case in this connexion to make clear that this is the type of maladjusted individual with which this discussion is not concerned. His aberrancy appeared to have a specific physiological origin; it was not a mere temperamental variation that his society had decided to define as feminine.

This discussion is concerned neither with the congenital invert nor with overt behaviour of the practising homosexual. There are, it is true, ways in which the different types of maladjustment intersect and reinforce each other, and the congenital invert may be found among those who have found shelter in transvesticism. But the deviants with whom we are concerned here are those individuals whose adjustment to life is conditioned by their temperamental affinity for a type of behaviour that is regarded as unnatural for their own sex and natural for the opposite sex. To produce this type of maladjustment, not only is it necessary to have a definite approved social personality, but also this personality must be rigidly limited to one of the two sexes. The coercion to behave like a member of one's own sex becomes one of the strongest implements with which the society attempts to mould the growing child into accepted forms. A society without a rigid sex-dichotomy merely says to the child who shows aberrant behaviour traits: "Don't behave like that." "People don't do that." "If you behave like that, people won't like you." "If you behave like that, you will never get married." "If you behave like that, people will sorcerise you"—and so on. It invokes—as against the child's natural inclination to laugh or cry or sulk in the wrong places, to see insult where there is none, or fail to see insult that is intended—considerations of human conduct as socially defined, not of sex-determined conduct. The burden of the disciplinary song is: "You will not be a real human being unless you suppress these tendencies which are incompatible with our definition of humanity." But it does not occur to either the Arapesh or the Mundugumor to add: "You aren't behaving like a boy at all. You are behaving like a girl"—even when actually this may be the case. It will be remembered that among the Arapesh, boys, owing to their slightly different parental care, do cry more than girls and have temper tantrums until a later age. Yet because the idea of sex-difference in emotional behaviour is lacking, this real difference was never invoked. In societies without a sex-dichotomy of temperament, one aspect, one very basic aspect, of the child's sense of its position in the universe is left unchallenged—the genuineness of its membership in its own sex. It can continue to watch the mating behaviour of its elders and pattern its hopes and expectations upon it. It is not forced to identify with a parent of opposite sex by being told that its own sex is very much in question. Some slight imitation of a father by a daughter, or of a mother by a son, is not seized upon and converted into a reproach, or a prophecy that the girl will grow up to be a tomboy or the boy a sissy. The Arapesh and Mundugumor children are spared this form of confusion.

Consider in contrast the way in which children in our culture are pressed into conformity: "Don't act like a girl." "Little girls don't do that." The threat of failing to behave like a member of one's own sex is used to enforce a thousand details of nursery routine and cleanliness, ways of sitting or relaxing, ideas of sportsmanship and fair play, patterns of expressing emotions, and a multitude of other points in which we recognise socially defined sex differences, such as limits of personal vanity, interest in clothes, or interest in current events. Back and forth weaves the shuttle of comment: "Girls don't do that." "Don't you want to grow up to be a real man like Daddy?"—tangling the child's emotions in a confusion that, if the child is unfortunate enough to possess even in some slight degree the temperament approved for the opposite sex, may well prevent the establishment of any adequate adjustment to its world. Every time the point of sex-conformity is made, every time the child's sex is invoked as the reason why it should prefer trousers to petticoats, baseball-bats to dolls, fisticuffs to tears, there is planted in the child's mind a fear that indeed, in spite of anatomical evidence to the contrary, it may not really belong to its own sex at all.

How little weight the anatomical evidence of own sex has, as over against the social conditioning, was vividly dramatised recently in a case in a Middle Western city, where a boy was found who had lived twelve years as a girl, under the name of Maggie, doing a girl's tasks and wearing a girl's clothes. He had discovered several years before that his anatomy was that of a boy, but that did not suggest to him the possibility of being classified as a boy socially. Yet when social workers discovered the case and effected the change of his classification, he did not show any traits of inversion; he was merely a boy who had been mistakenly classified as a girl, and whose parents, for some reasons that were not discovered, refused to recognise and rectify their error. This bizarre case reveals the strength of social classification as over against merely anatomical membership in a sex, and it is this social classification which makes it possible for society to plant in children's minds doubts and confusions about their sex position.

Such social pressure exerts itself in a number of ways. There is first the threat of sex-disenfranchisement against the child who shows aberrant tendencies, the boy who dislikes rough-and-tumble play or weeps when he is rebuked, the girl who is only interested in adventures, or prefers battering her playmates to dissolving in tears. Second, there is the attribution of the emotions defined as feminine to the boy who shows the mildest preference for one of the superficial sex-limited occupations or avocations. A small boy's interest in knitting may arise from a delight in his own ability to manipulate a needle; his interest in cooking may derive from a type of interest that might later make him a first-class chemist; his interest in dolls may spring from no tender cherishing feelings but from a desire to dramatise some incident. Similarly, a girl's overwhelming interest in horseback-riding may come from a delight in her own physical co-ordination on horseback, her interest in her brother's wireless set may come from pride in her proficiency in handling the Morse code. Some physical or intellectual or artistic potentiality may accidentally express itself in an activity deemed appropriate to the opposite sex. This has two results: The child is reproached for his choice and accused of having the emotions of the opposite sex, and also, because the occupational choice or hobby throws him more with the opposite sex, he may come in time to take on much of the socially sex-limited behaviour of that opposite sex.

A third way in which our dichotomy of social personality by sex affects the growing child is the basis it provides for a cross-sex identification with the parents. The invocation of a boy's identification with his mother to explain his subsequent assumption of a passive rôle towards members of his own sex is familiar enough in modern psychiatric theory. It is assumed that through a distortion of the normal course of personality development the boy fails to identify with his father and so loses the clue to normal "masculine" behaviour. Now there is no doubt that the developing child searching for clues to his social rôle in life usually finds his most important models in those who stand in a parental relationship to him during his early years. But I would suggest that we have still to explain why these identifications occur, and that the cause lies not in any basic femininity in the small boy's temperament, but in the existence of a dichotomy between the standardised behaviour of the sexes. We have to discover why a given child identifies with a parent of opposite sex rather than with the parent of its own sex. The most conspicuous social categories in our society—in most societies—are the two sexes. Clothes, occupation, vocabulary, all serve to concentrate the child's attention upon its similarity with the parent of the same sex. Nevertheless some children, in defiance of all this pressure, choose the parents of opposite sex, not to love best, but as the persons with whose motives and purposes they feel most at one, whose choices they feel they can make their own when they are grown.

Before considering this question further, let me restate my

hypothesis. I have suggested that certain human traits have been socially specialised as the appropriate attitudes and behaviour of only one sex, while other human traits have been specialised for the opposite sex. This social specialisation is then rationalised into a theory that the socially decreed behaviour is natural for one sex and unnatural for the other, and that the deviant is a deviant because of glandular defect, or developmental accident. Let us take a hypothetical case. Attitudes towards physical intimacy vary enormously among individuals and have been very differently standardised in different societies. We find primitive societies, such as those of the Dobu and the Manus, where casual physical contact is so interdicted for both sexes, so hedged about with rules and categories, that only the insane will touch another person lightly and casually. Other societies, such as that of the Arapesh, permit a great deal of easy physical intimacy between individuals of different ages and both sexes. Now let us consider a society that has specialised to one sex this particular temperamental trait. To men has been assigned the behaviour characteristic of the individual who finds casual physical contact intolerable, to women, as their "natural" behaviour, that of individuals who accept it easily. To men, the hand on the arm or across the shoulder, sleeping in the same room with another man, having to hold another man on the lap in a crowded automobile—every contact of this kind would be, by definition, repellent, possibly even, if the social conditioning were strong enough, disgusting or frightening. To women in this given society, however, physical contact that was easy and unstylised would be, by definition, welcome. They would embrace each other, caress each other's hair, arrange each other's clothes, sleep in the same bed, comfortably and without embarrassment. Now let us take a marriage between a well-brought-up man in this society, who would be intolerant of any physical casualness, and a well-brought-up woman, who would consider it as natural when displayed by women and never expect it among boys or men. To this couple is born a girl who displays from birth a *noli me tangere* attitude that nothing her mother can do will dispel. The little girl slips off her mother's lap, wriggles away when her mother tries to kiss her. She turns with relief to her father, who will not embarrass her with demonstrations of affection, who does not even insist upon holding her hand when he takes her for a walk. From such a simple clue as this, a preference that in the child is temperamental, in the father is socially stabilised male behaviour, the little girl may build up an identification with her father, and a theory that she is more like a boy than like a girl. She may come in time to be actually better adjusted in many other ways to the behaviour of the opposite sex. The psychiatrist who finds her later in life wearing mannish attire, following a male occupation, and unable to find happiness in marriage may say that identification with the opposite sex was the cause of her failure to adjust as a woman. But this explanation does not reveal the fact that the identification would not have occurred in these terms if there had been no dichotomy of sex-attitudes in the society. The Arapesh child who is more like a reserved father than like a demonstrative mother may feel that it resembles its father more than its mother, but this has no further effects on its personality in a society in which it is not possible to "feel like a man" or "feel like a woman." The accident of a differentiation of sex-attitudes makes these chance identifications dynamic in the adjustment of the child.

This example is admittedly hypothetical and simple. The actual conditions in a modern society are infinitely more complicated. To list merely some of the kinds of confusions that occur should be sufficient to focus attention upon the problem. One of the child's parents may be aberrant, and therefore be a false guide to the child in its attempt to find its rôle. Both the children's parents may deviate from the norm in opposite ways, the mother showing more pronounced temperamental traits usually specialised as male, the father showing the opposite traits. This condition is very likely to occur in modern society, in which, because it is believed marriage must be based upon contrasting personalities, deviant men often choose deviant women. So the child, groping for clues, may make a false identification because its own temperament is like that decreed for the opposite sex, or a false identification because, while it is itself fitted for easy adjustment, the parent of its own sex is maladjusted.

I have discussed first identification along temperamental lines, but the identification may also be made in other terms. The original identification may be through intelligence or specific artistic gifts, the gifted child identifying with the more gifted parent, regardless of sex. Then, if the double standard of personality exists, this simple identification on the basis of ability or interest will be translated into sex terms, and the mother will lament: "Mary is always working with Will's drafting instruments. She hasn't any more normal girl's interests at all. Will says it's a pity she wasn't born a boy." From this comment, it is very easy for Mary to come to the same conclusion.

Worth mentioning here is the way in which the boy's plight differs from the girl's in almost every known society. Whatever the arrangements in regard to descent or ownership of property, and even if these formal outward arrangements are reflected in the temperamental relationships between the two sexes, the prestige values always attach to the occupations of men, if not entirely at the expense of the women's occupations, at least to a great extent. It almost always follows, therefore, that the girl "who should have been a boy" has at least the possibility of a partial participation in activities that are surrounded by the aura of masculine prestige. For the boy "who should have been a girl" there is no such possibility open. His participation in women's activities is almost always a matter for double reproach: he has shown himself unworthy to be categorised as a man, and has thereby condemned himself to activities with a low prestige value.

Furthermore, it is seldom that the particular attitudes and interests which have been classified as feminine in any society have been given any very rich expression in art or in literature. The girl who finds the defined masculine interests closer to her

own can find for herself forms of vicarious expression; the boy
who might have found similar outlets if there were a comparable
feminine art and literature is denied such satisfactory escape.
Kenneth Grahame has immortalised the perplexity of all small
boys before the special and limited interests of girls in his famous
chapter, "What They Talked About":

> "She's off with those Vicarage girls again," said Edward,
> regarding Selina's long black legs twinkling down the path.
> "She goes out with them every day now; and as soon as ever
> they start, all their heads go together and they chatter, chatter,
> chatter, the whole blessed time! I can't make out what they
> find to talk about. . . ."
>
> "P'raps they talk about birds'-eggs," I suggested sleep-
> ily . . . "and about ships, and buffaloes, and desert islands; and
> why rabbits have white tails; and whether they'd sooner have a
> schooner or a cutter; and what they'll be when they're men—
> at least, I mean there's lots of things to talk about, if you *want*
> to talk."
>
> "Yes; but they don't talk about those sort of things at all,"
> Edward persisted. "How *can* they? They don't *know* anything;
> they can't *do* anything—except play the piano, and nobody
> would want to talk about *that*; and they don't care about any-
> thing—anything sensible, I mean. So what *do* they talk
> about? . . . But it's these girls I can't make out. If they've any-
> thing really sensible to talk about, how is it nobody knows
> what it is? And if they haven't—and we know they *can't* have,
> naturally—why don't they shut up their jaw? This old rabbit
> here—*he* doesn't want to talk. . . ."
>
> "O but rabbits *do* talk!" interposed Harold. "I've watched
> them often in their hutch. They put their heads together and
> their noses go up and down, just like Selina's and the Vicarage
> girls'!" . . .
>
> "Well, if they do," said Edward unwillingly, "I'll bet they

don't talk such rot as those girls do!" Which was ungenerous, as well as unfair; for it has not yet transpired—nor has it to this day—*what* Selina and her friends talked about.*

This perplexity is likely to remain throughout life. The woman who either by temperament or accident of training has become more identified with the interests of men, if she cannot adjust to the current sex standards, loses out in her essentially feminine rôle of child-bearing. The man who has been disenfranchised from his own sex's interests suffers a subtler disenfranchisement, since a great part of the artistic symbolism of his society is rendered unavailable and there is no substitute to which he can turn. He remains a confused and bewildered person, unable to feel as men "naturally" feel in his society, and equally unable to find any satisfaction in rôles that have been defined by women, although their social personality is more akin to his temperament.

And so, in a thousand ways, the fact that it is necessary to feel not only like a member of a given society in a given period, but like a member of one sex and not like a member of the other, conditions the development of the child, and produces individuals who are unplaced in their society. Many students of personality lay these multiple, imponderable maladjustments to "latent homosexuality." But such a judgment is fathered by our two-sex standard; it is *post hoc* diagnosis of a result, not diagnosis of a cause. It is a judgment that is applied not only to the invert but to the infinitely more numerous individuals who deviate from the social definition of appropriate behaviour for their sex.

If these contradictory traits of temperament which different societies have regarded as sex-linked are not sex-linked, but are merely human potentialities specialised as the behaviour of one

---

*From *The Golden Age*, by Kenneth Grahame. Copyright 1895, 1922, by Dodd, Mead and Company, Inc.

sex, the presence of the deviant, who need no longer be branded as a latent homosexual, is inevitable in every society that insists upon artificial connexions between sex and bravery, or between sex and positive self-feeling, or between sex and a preference for personal relations. Furthermore, the lack of correspondence between the actual temperamental constitution of members of each sex and the rôle that a culture has assigned to them has its reverberations in the lives of those individuals who were born with the expected and correct temperament. It is often assumed that in a society which designates men as aggressive and dominating, women as responsive and submissive, the maladjusted individuals will be the dominant, aggressive woman and the responsive, submissive man. Theirs is, indubitably, the most difficult position. Human contacts of all sorts, and especially courtship and marriage, may present insoluble problems to them. But consider also the position of the boy naturally endowed with an aggressive, dominating temperament and reared to believe that it is his masculine rôle to dominate submissive females. He is trained to respond to responsive and submissive behaviour in others by a display of his self-conscious aggressiveness. And then he encounters not only submissive females, but also submissive males. The stimulus to dominating behaviour, to an insistence upon unquestioning loyalty and reiterated statements of his importance, is presented to him in one-sex groups, and a "latent homosexual" situation is created. Similarly, such a man has been taught that his ability to dominate is the measure of his manhood, so that submissiveness in his associates continually reassures him. When he encounters a woman who is as naturally dominating as he is himself, or even a woman who, although not dominating temperamentally, is able to outdistance him in some special skill or type of work, a doubt of his own manhood is set up in his mind. This is one of the reasons why men who conform most closely to the accepted temperament for males in their society are most suspicious and hostile towards deviating women who, in spite of a contrary training, show the same temperamental traits.

Their hold upon their conviction of their own sex-membership rests upon the non-occurrence of similar personalities in the opposite sex.

And the submissive, responsive woman may find herself in an equally anomalous position, even though her culture has defined her temperament as the proper one for women. Trained from childhood to yield to the authority of a dominant voice, to bend all of her energies to please the more vulnerable egotism of dominant persons, she may often encounter the same authoritative note in a feminine voice and thus she, who is by temperament the ideal woman in her society, may find women so engrossing that marriage adjustments never enter the picture. Her involvement in devotion to members of her own sex may in turn set up in her doubts and questions as to her essential femininity.

Thus the existence in a given society of a dichotomy of social personality, of a sex-determined, sex-limited personality, penalises in greater or less degree every individual born within it. Those whose temperaments are indubitably aberrant fail to adjust to the accepted standards, and by their very presence, by the anomalousness of their responses, confuse those whose temperaments are the expected ones for their sex. So in practically every mind a seed of doubt, of anxiety, is planted, which interferes with the normal course of life.

But the tale of confusions is not ended here. The Tchambuli, and in a milder degree parts of modern America, represent a further difficulty that a culture which defines personality in terms of sex can invent for its members. It will be remembered that while Tchambuli theory is patrilineal, Tchambuli practice gives the dominant position to women, so that the position of the man with aberrant—that is, dominating—temperament is rendered doubly difficult by the cultural forms. The cultural formulation that a man has paid for his wife and can therefore control her continually misleads these aberrant individuals into fresh attempts at such control, and brings them into conflict with all their childhood training to obey and respect women, and their wives' training to expect such respect. Tchambuli institutions and the emphases of their society are, to a certain extent, at odds with one another. Native history attributes a high development of dominating temperaments to various neighbouring tribes, whose women have for many generations run away and married the Tchambuli. In explanation of its own inconsistencies, it invokes the situation that was just frequent enough among the Arapesh to confuse the adjustments of men and women there. These inconsistencies in Tchambuli culture were probably increased by a diminished interest in war and head-hunting and a greater interest in the delicate arts of peace. The importance of the women's economic activities may also have increased without any corresponding enhancement of the men's economic rôle. Whatever the historical causes, and they are undoubtedly multiple and complex, Tchambuli today presents a striking confusion between institutions and cultural emphases. And it also contains a larger number of neurotic males than I have seen in any other primitive culture. To have one's aberrancy, one's temperamental inability to conform to the prescribed rôle of responsive dancing attendance upon women, apparently confirmed by institutions—this is too much, even for members of a primitive society living under conditions far simpler than our own.

Modern cultures that are in the throes of adjusting to women's changing economic position present comparable difficulties. Men find that one of the props of their dominance, a prop which they have often come to think of as synonymous with that dominance itself—the ability to be the sole support of their families—has been pulled from beneath them. Women trained to believe that the possession of earned income gave the right to dictate, a doctrine which worked well enough as long as women had no incomes, find themselves more and more often in a confused state between their real position in the household and the one to which they have been trained. Men who have been trained to believe that their sex is always a little in question and who believe that their earning power is a proof of their manhood are plunged into a double uncertainty by unemployment; and this is further complicated by the fact that their wives have been able to secure employment.

All such conditions are aggravated in America also by the large number of different patterns of decreed behaviour for each sex that obtain in different national and regional groups, and by the supreme importance of the pattern of intersex behaviour that children encounter within the closed four walls of their homes. Each small part of our complex and stratified culture has its own set of rules by which the power and complementary balance between the sexes is maintained. But these rules differ, and are sometimes even contradictory, as between different national groups or economic classes. So, because there is no tradition which insists that individuals should marry in the group within which they were reared, men and women are continually marrying whose pictures of the interrelationships between the sexes are entirely different. Their confusions are in turn transmitted to their children. The result is a society in which hardly anyone doubts the existence of a different "natural" behaviour for the sexes, but no one is very sure what that "natural" behaviour is. Within the conflicting definitions of appropriate behaviour for each sex, almost every type of individual is left room to doubt the completeness of his or her possession of a really masculine or a really feminine nature. We have kept the emphasis, the sense of the importance of the adjustment, and at the same time we have lost the ability to enforce the adjustment.

conclusion

The knowledge that the personalities of the two sexes are socially produced is congenial to every programme that looks forward towards a planned order of society. It is a two-edged sword that can be used to hew a more flexible, more varied society than the human race has ever built, or merely to cut a narrow path down which one sex or both sexes will be forced to march, regimented, looking neither to the right nor to the left. It makes possible a Fascist programme of education in which women are forced back into a mould that modern Europe had fatuously believed to be broken forever. It makes possible a Communist programme in which the two sexes are treated as nearly alike as their different physiological functions permit. Because it is social conditioning that is determinative, it has been possible for America, without conscious plan but none the less surely, partially to reverse the European tradition of male dominance, and to breed a generation of women who model their lives on the pattern of their school-teachers and their aggressive, directive mothers. Their brothers stumble about in a vain attempt to preserve the myth of male dominance in a society in which the girls have come to consider dominance their natural right. As one fourteen-year-old girl said in commenting on the meaning of the term "tomboy," "Yes, it's true that it used to mean a girl who tried to act like a boy, dress like a boy, and things like that. But that belonged to the hoop-skirt era. Nowadays all girls have to do is to act exactly like boys, quite quietly." The tradition in this country has been changing so rapidly that the term "sissy," which ten years ago meant a boy who showed personality traits regarded as feminine, can now be applied with scathing emphasis by one girl to another, or can be defined by a small girl as "the kind of boy who always wears a baseball glove and goes about shouting, 'Put her there! Put her there!' and when you throw him a soft one he can't catch it." These penetrating comments are sharply indicative of a trend that lacks the concerted planning behind Fascist or Communist programmes, but which has nevertheless gained in acceleration in the last three decades. Plans that regiment women as home-makers, or which cease to differentiate the training of the two sexes, have at least the virtue of being clear and unambiguous. The present development in this country has all the insidious ambiguity of the situation that we found illustrated among the Tchambuli head-hunters, where the man is still defined as the head of the house, although the woman is trained to a greater celerity and sureness in taking that position. The result is an increasing number of American men who feel they must shout in order to maintain their vulnerable positions, and an increasing number of American women who clutch unhappily at a dominance that their society has granted them— but without giving them a charter of rules and regulations by which they can achieve it without damage to themselves, their husbands, and their children.

There are at least three courses open to a society that has realised the extent to which male and female personality are socially produced. Two of these courses have been tried before, over and over again, at different times in the long, irregular, repetitious history of the race. The first is to standardise the personality of men and women as clearly contrasting, complementary, and antithetical, and to make every institution in the society congruent with this standardisation. If the society declared that woman's sole function was motherhood and the teaching and care of young children, it could so arrange matters that every woman who was not physiologically debarred should become a mother and be supported in the exercise of this function. It could abolish the discrepancy between the doctrine that women's place is the home and the number of homes that were offered to them. It could abolish the discrepancy between training women for marriage and then forcing them to become the spinster supports of their parents.

Such a system would be wasteful of the gifts of many women who could exercise other functions far better than their ability to bear children in an already overpopulated world. It would be wasteful of the gifts of many men who could exercise their special personality gifts far better in the home than in the market-place. It would be wasteful, but it would be clear. It could attempt to guarantee to each individual the rôle for which society insisted upon training him or her, and such a system would penalise only those individuals who, in spite of all the training, did not display the approved personalities. There are millions of persons who would gladly return to such a standardised method of treating the relationship between the sexes, and we must bear in mind the possibility that the greater opportunities open in the twentieth century to women may be quite withdrawn, and that we may return to a strict regimentation of women.

The waste, if this occurs, will be not only of many women, but also of as many men, because regimentation of one sex carries with it, to greater or less degree, the regimentation of the other also. Every parental behest that defines a way of sitting, a response to a rebuke or a threat, a game, or an attempt to draw or sing or dance or paint, as feminine, is moulding the personality of each little girl's brother as well as moulding the personality of the sister. There can be no society which insists that women follow one special personality-pattern, defined as feminine, which does not do violence also to the individuality of many men.

Alternatively, society can take the course that has become especially associated with the plans of most radical groups: admit that men and women are capable of being moulded to a single pattern as easily as to a diverse one, and cease to make any distinction in the approved personality of both sexes. Girls can be trained exactly as boys are trained, taught the same code, the same forms of expression, the same occupations. This course might seem to be the logic which follows from the conviction that the potentialities which different societies label as either masculine or feminine are really potentialities of some members of each sex, and not sex-linked at all. If this is accepted, is it not reasonable to abandon the kind of artificial standardisations of sex-differences that have been so long characteristic of European society, and admit that they are social fictions for which we have no longer any use? In the world today, contraceptives make it possible for women not to bear children against their will. The most conspicuous actual difference between the sexes, the difference in strength, is progressively less significant. Just as the difference in height between males is no longer a realistic issue, now that lawsuits have been substituted for hand-to-hand encounters, so the difference in strength between men and women is no longer worth elaboration in cultural institutions.

In evaluating such a programme as this, however, it is necessary to keep in mind the nature of the gains that society has achieved in its most complex forms. A sacrifice of distinctions in sex-personality may mean a sacrifice in complexity. The Arapesh recognise a minimum of distinction in personality between old and young, between men and women, and they lack categories of rank or status. We have seen that such a society at the best condemns to personal frustration, and at the worst to maladjustment, all of those men and women who do not conform to its simple emphases. The violent person among the Arapesh cannot find, either in the literature, or in the art, or in the ceremonial, or in the history of his people, any expression of the internal drives that are shattering his peace of mind. Nor is the loser only the individual whose own type of personality is nowhere recognised in his society. The imaginative, highly intelligent person who is essentially in tune with the values of his society may also suffer by the lack of range and depth characteristic of too great simplicity. The active mind and intensity of one Arapesh boy whom I knew well was unsatisfied by the laissez-faire solutions, the lack of drama in his culture. Searching for some material upon which to exercise his imagination, his longing for a life in which stronger emotions would be possible, he could find nothing with which to feed his imagination but tales of the passionate outbursts of the maladjusted, outbursts characterised by a violent hostility to others that he himself lacked.

Nor is it the individual alone who suffers. Society is equally the loser, and we have seen such an attenuation in the dramatic representations of the Mundugumor. By phrasing the exclusion of women as a protective measure congenial to both sexes, the Arapesh kept their *tamberan* cult, with the necessary audiences of women. But the Mundugumor developed a kind of personality for both men and women to which exclusion from any part of life was interpreted as a deadly insult. And as more and more Mundugumor women have demanded and been given the right of initiation, it is not surprising that the Mundugumor ceremonial life has dwindled, the actors have lost their audience, and one vivid artistic element in the life of the Mundugumor community is vanishing. The sacrifice of sex-differences has meant a loss in complexity to the society.

So in our own society. To insist that there are no sex-differences in a society that has always believed in them and depended upon them may be as subtle a form of standardising personality as to insist that there are many sex-differences. This is particularly so in a changing tradition, when a group in control is attempting to develop a new social personality, as in the case today in many European countries. Take, for instance, the current assumption that women are more opposed to war than men, that any outspoken approval of war is more horrible, more revolting, in women than in men. Behind this assumption women can work for peace without encountering social criticism in communities that would immediately criticise their brothers or husbands if they took a similarly active part in peace propaganda. This belief that women are naturally more interested in peace is undoubtedly artificial, part of the whole mythology that considers women to be gentler than men. But in contrast let us consider the possibility of a powerful minority that wished to turn a whole society whole-heartedly towards war. One way of doing this would be to insist that women's motives, women's interests, were identical with men's, that women should take as bloodthirsty a delight in preparing for war as even men do. The insistence upon the opposite point of view, that the woman as a mother prevails over the woman as a citizen at least puts a slight drag upon agitation for war, prevents a blanket enthusiasm for war from being thrust upon the entire younger generation. The same kind of result follows if the clergy are professionally committed to a belief in peace. The relative bellicosity of different individual clerics may be either offended or gratified by the prescribed pacific rôle, but a certain protest, a certain dissenting note, will be sounded in society. The dangerous standardisation of attitudes that disallows every type of deviation is greatly reinforced if neither age nor sex nor religious belief is regarded as automatically predisposing certain individuals to hold minority attitudes. The removal of all legal and economic barriers against women's participating in the world on an equal footing with men may be in itself a standardising move towards the wholesale stamping-out of the diversity of attitudes that is such a dearly bought product of civilisation.

Such a standardised society, in which men, women, children, priests, and soldiers were all trained to an undifferentiated and coherent set of values, must of necessity create the kind of deviant that we found among the Arapesh and the Mundugumor, the individual who, regardless of sex or occupation, rebels because he is temperamentally unable to accept the one-sided emphasis of his culture. The individuals who were specifically unadjusted in terms of their psycho-sexual rôle would, it is true, vanish, but with them would vanish the knowledge that there is more than one set of possible values.

To the extent that abolishing the differences in the approved personalities of men and women means abolishing any expression of the type of personality once called exclusively feminine, or once called exclusively masculine, such a course involves a social loss. Just as a festive occasion is the gayer and more charming if the two sexes are dressed differently, so it is in less material matters. If the clothing is in itself a symbol, and a woman's shawl corresponds to a recognised softness in her character, the whole plot of personal relations is made more elaborate, and in many ways more rewarding. The poet of such a society will praise virtues, albeit feminine virtues, which might never have any part in a social Utopia that allowed no differences between the personalities of men and women.

To the extent that a society insists upon different kinds of personality so that one age-group or class or sex-group may follow purposes disallowed or neglected in another, each individual participant in that society is the richer. The arbitrary assignment of set clothing, set manners, set social responses, to individuals born in a certain class, of a certain sex, or of a certain colour, to those born on a certain day of the week, to those born with a certain complexion, does violence to the individual endowment of individuals, but permits the building of a rich culture. The most extreme development of a society that has attained great complexity at the expense of the individual is historical India, based, as it was, upon the uncompromising association of a thousand attributes of behaviour, attitude, and occupation with an accident of birth. To each individual there was given the security, although it might be the security of despair, of a set rôle, and the reward of being born into a highly complex society.

Furthermore, when we consider the position of the deviant individual in historical cultures, those who are born into a complex society in the wrong sex or class for their personalities to have full sway are in a better position than those who are born into a simple society which does not use in any way their special temperamental gifts. The violent woman in a society that permits violence to men only, the strongly emotional member of an aristocracy in a culture that permits downright emotional expression only in the peasantry, the ritualistically inclined individual who is bred a Protestant in a country which has also Catholic institutions—each one of these can find expressed in some other group in the society the emotions that he or she is forbidden to manifest. He is given a certain kind of support by the mere existence of these values, values so congenial to him and so inaccessible because of an accident of birth. For those who are content with a vicarious spectator-rôle, or with materials upon which to feast the creative imagination, this may be almost enough. They may be content to experience from the sidewalks during a parade, from the audience of a theatre or from the nave of a church, those emotions the direct expression of which is denied to them. The crude compensations offered by the moving pictures to those whose lives are emotionally starved are offered in subtler forms by the art and literature of a complex society to the individual who is out of place in his sex or his class or his occupational group.

Sex-adjustments, however, are not a matter of spectatorship, but a situation in which the most passive individual must play some part if he or she is to participate fully in life. And while we may recognise the virtues of complexity, the interesting and charming plots that cultures can evolve upon the basis of accidents of birth, we may well ask: Is not the price too high? Could not the beauty that lies in contrast and complexity be obtained in some other way? If the social insistence upon different personalities for the two sexes results in so much confusion, so many unhappy deviants, so much disorientation, can we imagine a society that abandons these distinctions without abandoning the values that are at present dependent upon them?

Let us suppose that, instead of the classification laid down on the "natural" bases of sex and race, a society had classified personality on the basis of eye-colour. It had decreed that all blue-eyed people were gentle, submissive, and responsive to the needs of others, and all brown-eyed people were arrogant, dominating, self-centered, and purposive. In this case two complementary social themes would be woven together—the culture, in its art, its religion, its formal personal relations, would have two threads instead of one. There would be blue-eyed men, and blue-eyed women, which would mean that there were gentle, "maternal" women, and gentle, "maternal" men. A blue-eyed man might marry a woman who had been bred to the same personality as himself, or a brown-eyed woman who had been bred to the contrasting personality. One of the strong tendencies that makes for homosexuality, the tendency to love the similar rather than the antithetical person, would be eliminated. Hostility between the two sexes as groups would be minimised, since the individual interests of members of each sex could be woven together in different ways, and marriages of similarity and friendships of contrast need carry no necessary handicap of possible psycho-sexual maladjustment. The individual would still suffer a mutilation of his temperamental preferences, for it would be the unrelated fact of eye-colour that would determine the attitudes which he was educated to show. Every blue-eyed person would be forced into submissiveness and declared maladjusted if he or she showed any traits that it had been decided were only appropriate to the brown-eyed. The greatest social loss, however, in the classification of personality on the basis of sex would not be present in this society which based its classification on eye-colour. Human relations, and especially those which involve sex, would not be artificially distorted.

But such a course, the substitution of eye-colour for sex as a basis upon which to educate children into groups showing contrasting personalities, while it would be a definite advance upon a classification by sex, remains a parody of all the attempts that society has made through history to define an individual's rôle in terms of sex, or colour, or date of birth, or shape of head.

However, the only solution of the problem does not lie between an acceptance of standardisation of sex-differences with the resulting cost in individual happiness and adjustment, and the abolition of these differences with the consequent loss in social values. A civilisation might take it cues not from such categories as age or sex, race or hereditary position in a family line, but instead of specialising personality along such simple lines recognise, train, and make a place for many and divergent temperamental endowments. It might build upon the different potentialities that it now attempts to extirpate artificially in some children and create artificially in others.

Historically the lessening of rigidity in the classification of the sexes has come about at different times, either by the creation of a new artificial category, or by the recognition of real individual differences. Sometimes the idea of social position has transcended sex-categories. In a society that recognises gradations in wealth or rank, women of rank or women of wealth have been permitted an arrogance which was denied to both sexes among the lowly or the poor. Such a shift as this has been, it is true, a step towards the emancipation of women, but it has never been a step towards the greater freedom of the individual. A few women have shared the upper-class personality, but to balance this a great many men as well as women have been condemned to a personality characterised by subservience and fear. Such shifts as these mean only the substitution of one arbitrary standard for another. A society is equally unrealistic whether it insists that only men can be brave, or that only individuals of rank can be brave.

To break down one line of division, that between the sexes, and substitute another, that between classes, is no real advance. It merely shifts the irrelevancy to a different point. And meanwhile, individuals born in the upper classes are shaped inexorably to one type of personality, to an arrogance that is again uncongenial to at least some of them, while the arrogant among the poor fret and fume beneath their training for submissiveness. At one end of the scale is the mild, unaggressive young son of wealthy parents who is forced to lead, at the other the aggressive, enterprising child of the slums who is condemned to a place in the ranks. If our aim is greater expression for each individual temperament, rather than any partisan interest in one sex or its fate, we must see these historical developments which have aided in freeing some women as nevertheless a kind of development that also involved major social losses.

The second way in which categories of sex-differences have become less rigid is through a recognition of genuine individual gifts as they occurred in either sex. Here a real distinction has been substituted for an artificial one, and the gains are tremendous for society and for the individual. Where writing is accepted as a profession that may be pursued by either sex with perfect suitability, individuals who have the ability to write need not be debarred from it by their sex, nor need they, if they do write, doubt their essential masculinity or femininity. An occupation that has no basis in sex-determined gifts can now recruit its ranks from twice as many potential artists. And it is here that we can find a ground-plan for building a society that would substitute real differences for arbitrary ones. We must recognise that beneath the superficial classifications of sex and race the same potentialities exist, recurring generation after generation, only to perish because society has no place for them. Just as society now permits the practice of an art to members of either sex, so it might also permit the development of many contrasting temperamental gifts in each sex. It might abandon its various attempts to make boys fight and to make girls remain passive, or to make all children fight, and instead shape our educational institutions to develop to the full the boy who shows a capacity for maternal behaviour, the girl who shows an opposite capacity that is stimulated by fighting against obstacles. No skill, no special aptitude, no vividness of imagination or precision of thinking would go unrecognised because the child who possessed it was of one sex rather than the other. No child would be relentlessly shaped to one pattern of behaviour, but instead there should be many patterns, in a world that had learned to allow to each individual the pattern which was most congenial to his gifts.

Such a civilisation would not sacrifice the gains of thousands of years during which society has built up standards of diversity. The social gains would be conserved, and each child would be encouraged on the basis of his actual temperament. Where we now have patterns of behaviour for women and patterns of behaviour for men, we would then have patterns of behaviour that expressed the interests of individuals with many kinds of endowment. There would be ethical codes and social symbolisms, an art and a way of life, congenial to each endowment.

Historically our own culture has relied for the creation of rich and contrasting values upon many artificial distinctions, the most striking of which is sex. It will not be by the mere abolition of these distinctions that society will develop patterns in which individual gifts are given place instead of being forced into an ill-fitting mould. If we are to achieve a richer culture, rich in contrasting values, we must recognise the whole gamut of human potentialities, and so weave a less arbitrary social fabric, one in which each diverse human gift will find a fitting place.

index and glossary*

Abelam, 11
Aberrant. *See* Deviant
Abduction, 13, 102, 116–17, 118, 127, 144, 251–52
abüllü (a yam harvest ceremony), 73
Abuting (a long yam masks used in initiation), 93
Aden, 79
Adolescence, 115; inhibitions, 136; sons of Mundugumor, 163, 202
Adoption, 16, 180, 181, 217
Admiralty Islands, 273
Adultery, 119, 122, 123
Affinal Relations, 16, 17, 19, 26, 45, 77, 78, 79, 80, 99, 117, 118, 127, 165, 174, 193, 235
Age: age class, 269; age contrast, 129; as betrothed, 85, 200; emphasis, 128; group, 55, 74; in behaviour, 43; in marriage, 111; responsibility, 72, 172
Agehu (central place of village), 7, 32, 61, 65, 75, 88, 89, 107, 113

Agilapwe, 146–47, 148
Ahalesmihi, 123
Aibom Lake, 220, 221
Airape, 79
Aiyai (mother), 234
Akerman, 245
Akikiyu, xxxii
Alinpinagle, 16
Alis, 95, 96, 97
Alitoa, x, 5, 65, 89, 95, 103, 110, 112, 137, 140, 143, 146, 148, 188
Aliwhiwas (plant used in magic), leaves, 88
Ambunti, 220
America, 132, 189, 273, 286, 287
Amitoa, 138–41, 144, 145, 148, 149, 273, 274
Amus, 141
Ancestors, 7, 15, 16, 169, 230
Andoar, 158, 162
Anointing, 33
Anyuai, 83, 84

*Pronounce all vowels as in Italian.

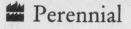 Perennial

Books by Margaret Mead:

COMING OF AGE IN SAMOA
A Psychological Study of Primitive Youth for Western Civilisation
ISBN 0-688-05033-6 (A Perennial Classic)

Margaret Mead's psychological study of youth in a primitive society is today recognized as a scientific classic, detailing her historic solo field work in American Samoa. Focusing on adolescent girls, the book presented to the public for the first time the idea that the psychological experience of developmental stages could be shaped by cultural demands and expectations.

GROWING UP IN NEW GUINEA
A Comparative Study of Primitive Education
ISBN 0-688-17811-1 (A Perennial Classic)

On Manus Island in New Guinea, Mead studied the play and imaginations of younger children and how they were shaped by adult society. Her enlightening and perceptive analysis of Manus family life—attitudes toward sex, marriage, the raising of children, and the supernatural—is not only fascinating in itself, but is made doubly so by the intriguing parallels Mead draws with modern life.

SEX AND TEMPERAMENT
In Three Primitive Societies
ISBN 0-06-093495-6

Mead's sociological study of gender in three New Guinea tribes—the gentle, mountain-dwelling Arapesh, the fierce, cannibalistic Mundugumor, and the graceful headhunters of Tchambuli—advances the theory that many so-called masculine and feminine characteristics are not based on fundamental sex differences, but reflect the cultural conditioning of different societies.

MALE AND FEMALE
ISBN 0-06-093496-4

The classic gender study by renowned anthropologist Margaret Mead, first published in 1949. Drawing on her anthropological research in seven Pacific island cultures, Mead examines the inherent meaning of "maleness" and "femaleness" and defines basic gender differences that recur around the world. She then delves into the fascinating and complex sexual patterns that drive American society.